Contents

INTRODUCTION

I have been involved in the website construction and web design industry since 2007. At that time, the industry was still not popular and coding skills were considered gold. Not everyone is proficient in digital languages such as PHP, Html, C ++, and Java. If you do not know to code, then you have to pay tens of thousands for the construction of a website.

Today anyone can build a website with WordPress as the most popular free-source CMS. Anyone can become a blogger, content creator, and web designer without the need for an IT background.

In this book, I will show one by one how we can build a website for free. Yes, it means free domain and web hosting. This book is suitable for beginners who want to tame in this industry. I will teach you from the initial phase of website construction to the phase of how to become an email admin up to the payment gateway phase.

On this occasion, I would like to thank the support author, A. Ayiez Zarqali for inspiring and allowing me to publish this book. I believe this book will be of great benefit to you who are just starting out or for those of you who are new to online marketing.

My objective in publishing this book is to teach beginners out there who are just about to start building their website without any capital. If you already know the basics, then you can create it using paid and trusted domains such as domain hostwinds, 000webhost, and Godaddy.

If you already have basic knowledge, then this book is not suitable for you, because I will use a free domain and hosting. Usually, if the name is a free domain, then your website is impossible to get top ranking in Google search. So, SEO strategies are unfounded and unusable in this guide. If your goal is to make money from the website you build, I recommend getting a domain that ends with .com or .my or .net.

Any questions, you can directly contact the author of this book at the link below:

A. Nabil Rosli

REGISTER A DOMAIN

Surely you are wondering, what is a domain? If you are new to the world of websites and hosting. Basically, a domain or domain name is a physical address. For example, if you want to go somewhere you do not know, whether it is to the office or to a relative's home, you need a navigation to the address of the place you are going to, such as street name and zip code, for the 'Google Maps / Waze' system. can provide correct directions. This is similar to a web browser that requires a domain name to direct visitors to the website.

Examples are, Facebook.com, Twitter.com, Lazada.com. 'Facebook' is the name of the website while '.com' is the domain extension. There are various domain names available and can be used out there such as .ml, .ga, .my, .info, .net, .org and many more.

In this ebook, I will show you how to create your website with domain extension either .ml, .tk, .ga, .cf or .gq. You can choose any one to your liking. It is all Free of Charge.

1. Open Google Chrome/Firefox web browser, make sure you are not open 'new window' in Ignito mode.
2. Go to <u>FreeNom</u> < Click this link here

3. In search bar **'Check Availability'** , enter the name of the website you want to create then click the **'Check Availability'** button . For example, if you are a shoe dealer, you can enter the name of **orishoes** or **originalshoe** or any other name you like. Or you can use your own brand.

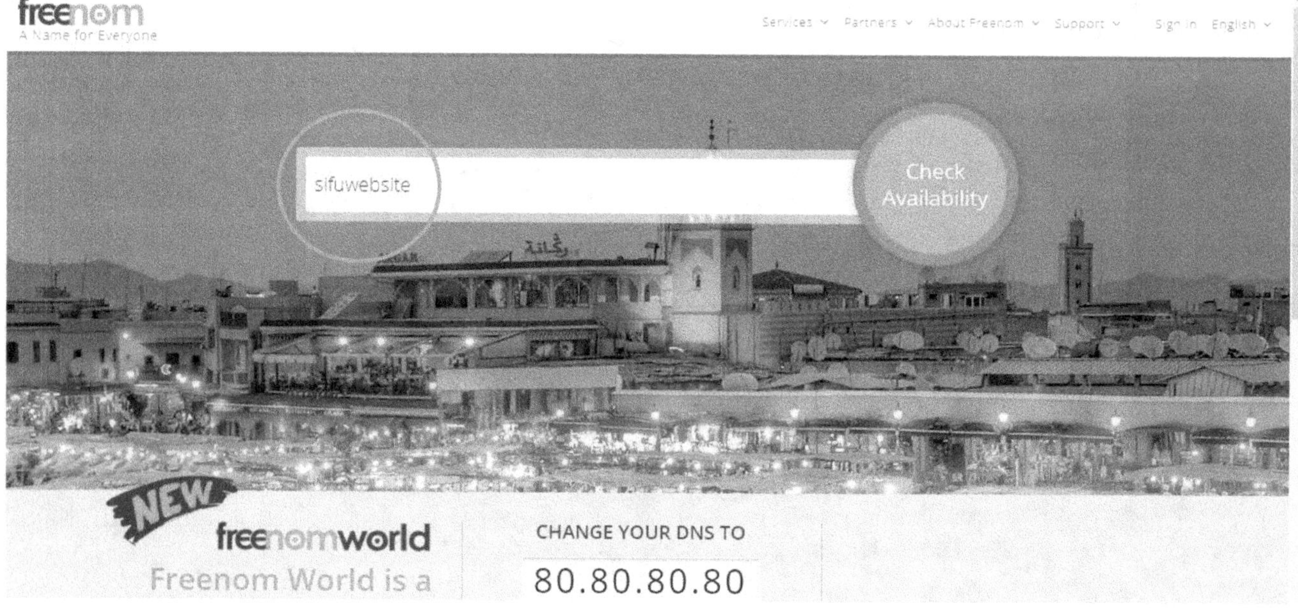

4. Next, you will see a list of free and paid domains. Click on any free domain extension you like.

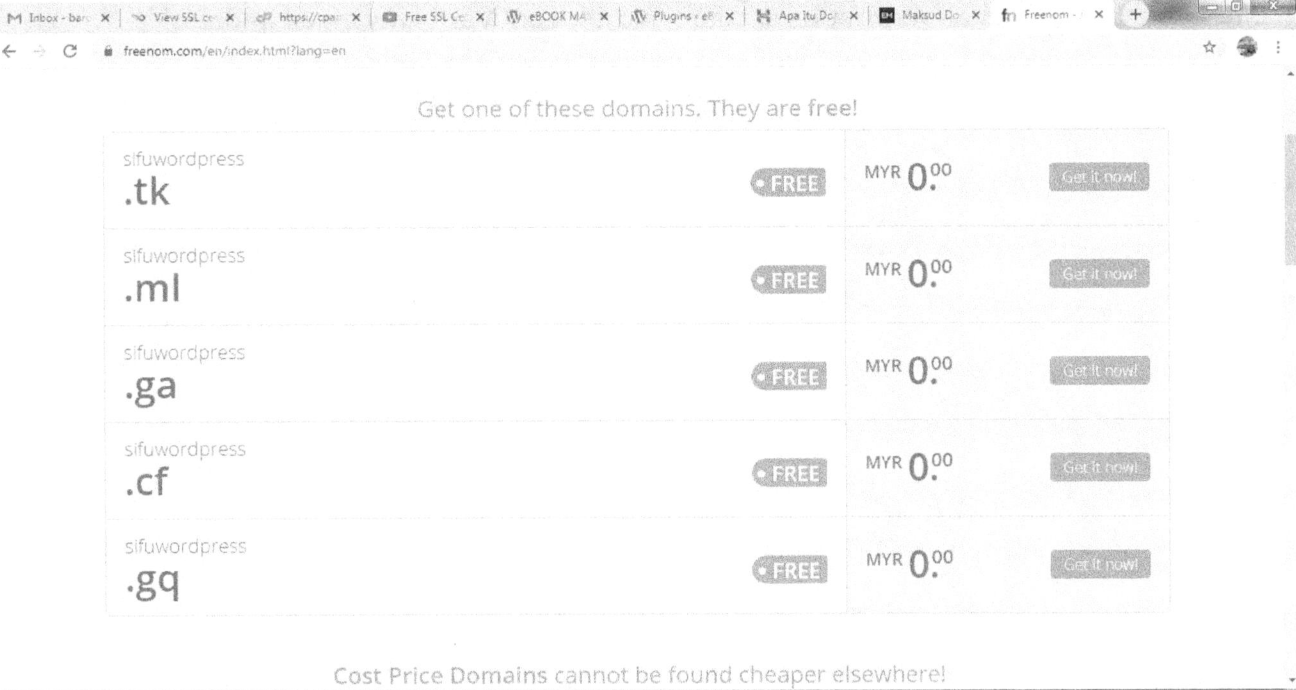

5. Click on 'Get it now'

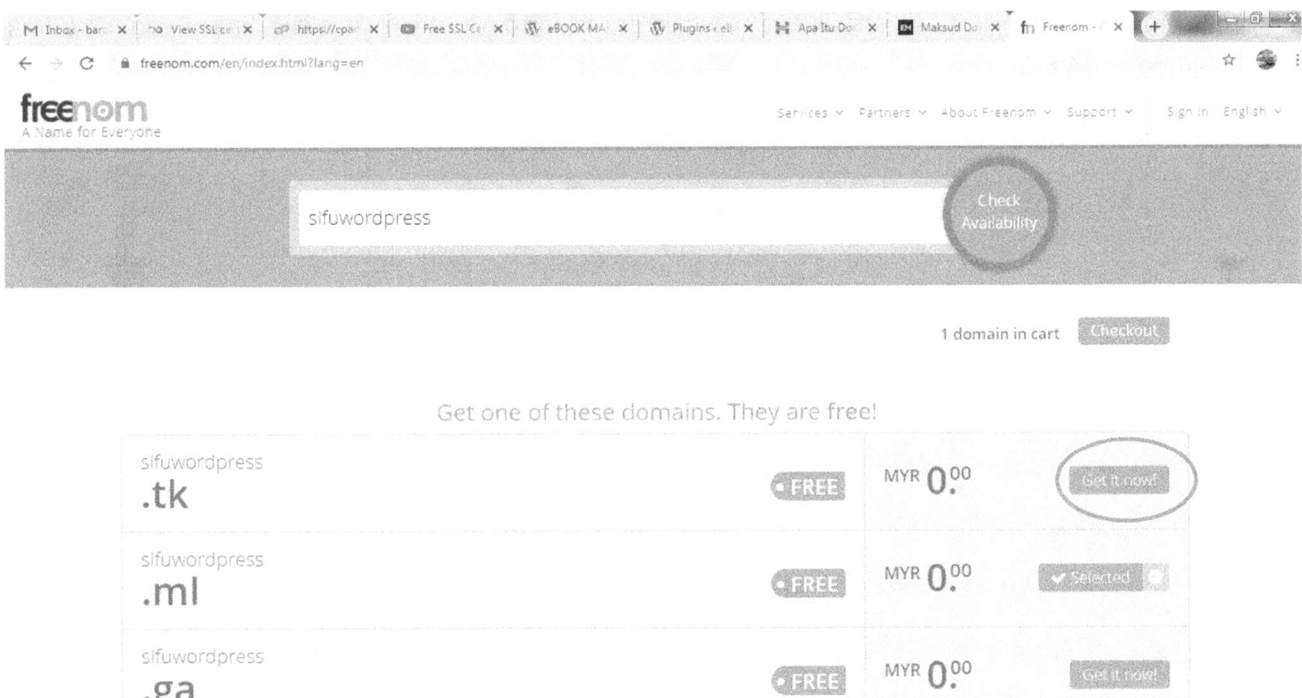

6. Click on **'Checkout'**
7. Go to **Period** > choose **'12 months @ FREE'** (This domain will be free for 1 year. The next you can renew it for free). What a deal !!
8. Next, click on **'Continue'**

9. Enter your email in email verification section, and click on **'Verify my email address'**

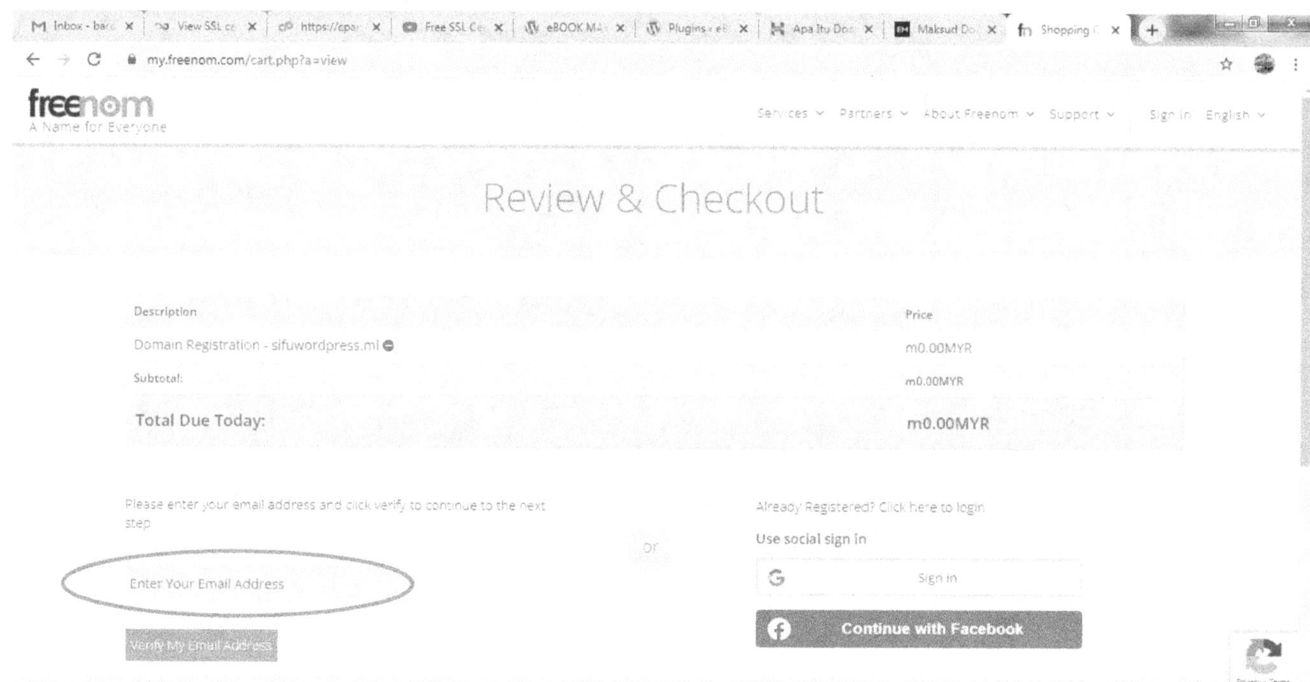

10. Verification link sent to your email. Go to your email inbox and click on the link given. The link only valid for 24 hours.

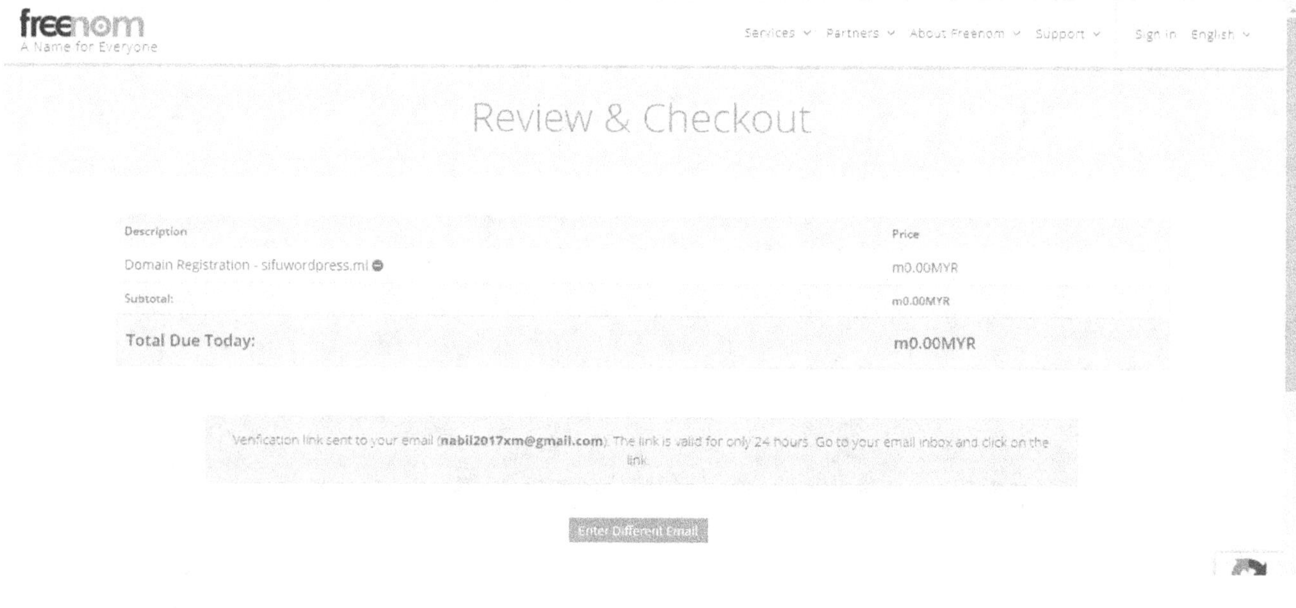

11. Fill up your details

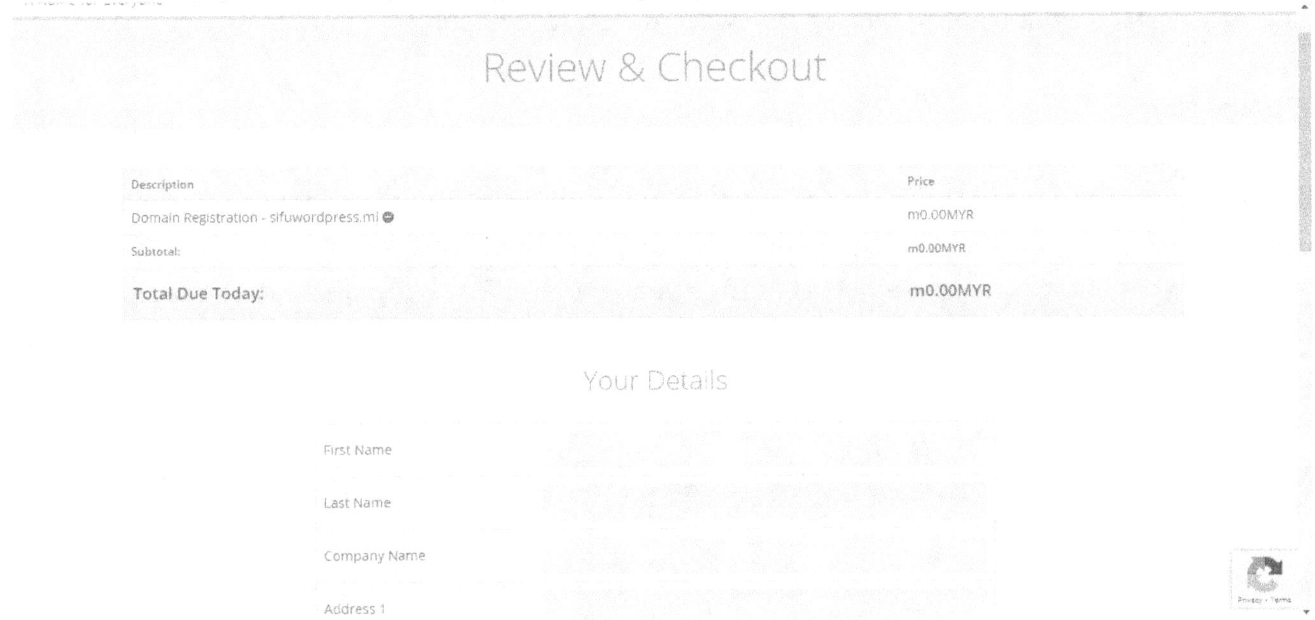

12. **Cilck on** 'I have read and agree to the Terms & Conditions' after you are done > Click on '**Complete order**'

13. You will be given your order number after confirmation.

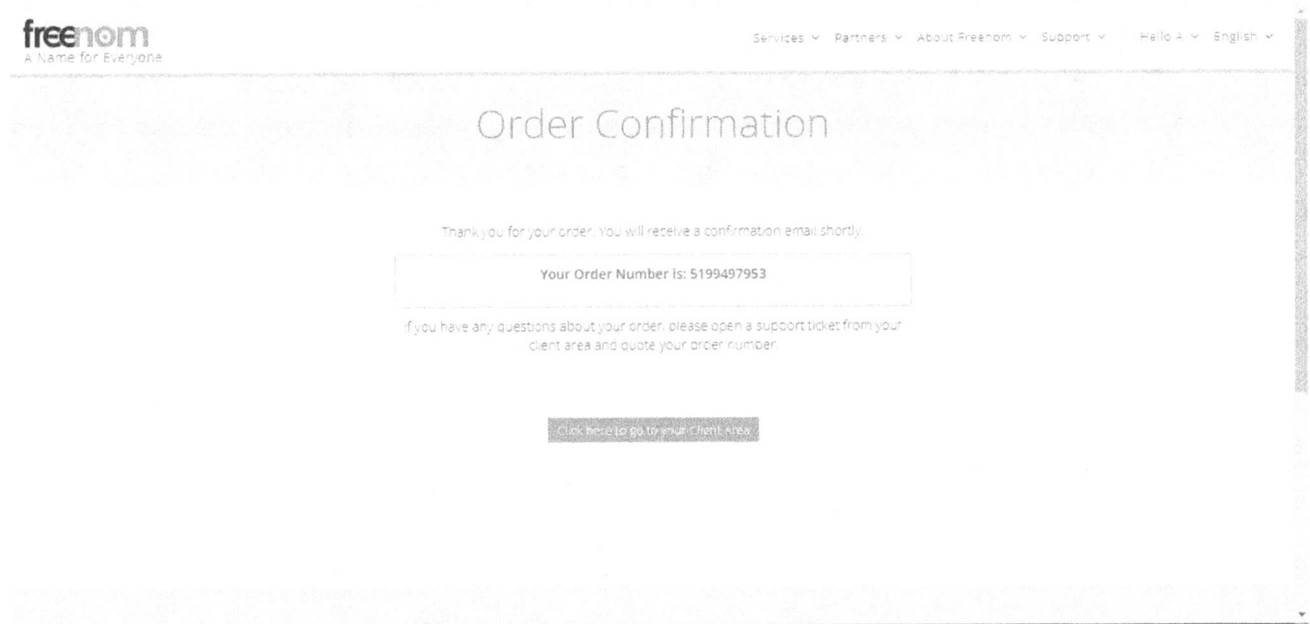

14. Go to 'Client Area' and Log in to your account.

15. After Log in, you will see a task bar menu. Go to **Services** > Click on **My Domains**
16. **Congratulations !! you have obtained your own website domain.... It is all free.**
17. After getting your website domain, we will create a web hosting.

Additional Note :

**If you want a domain other than .tk, .ml, .ga, .cf, or .gq, you can buy paid domains such as .com, .net and others according to the package provided. You can choose the duration of the time package according to your choice. There are packages for a year and also for two years. You can see for yourself. For example, if the package is for a year, and after duration has ended, you need to 'renew' again with that price. For example:

Cost Price Domains cannot be found cheaper elsewhere!

Domain		Cost Price
sifuwordpress	.com	MYR 34.19
sifuwordpress	.net	MYR 27.37
sifuwordpress	.org	MYR 39.08
sifuwordpress	.biz	MYR 53.68
sifuwordpress	.info	MYR 35.45
sifuwordpress	.eu	MYR 21.73
sifuwordpress	.nl	MYR 18.69
sifuwordpress	.tv	MYR 103.42
sifuwordpress	.cc	MYR 83.02
sifuwordpress	.me	MYR 52.04

The price in the box is the package price for a year. For example, sifuwordpress.com is less than 1 dollar per month to be paid. If you want to get a **.com** or **.net** domain, just follow the same steps as I showed before. Click Select> Check out> Continue. You can pay by bank transfer, pay pal or credit card. Then, Click Complete Order.

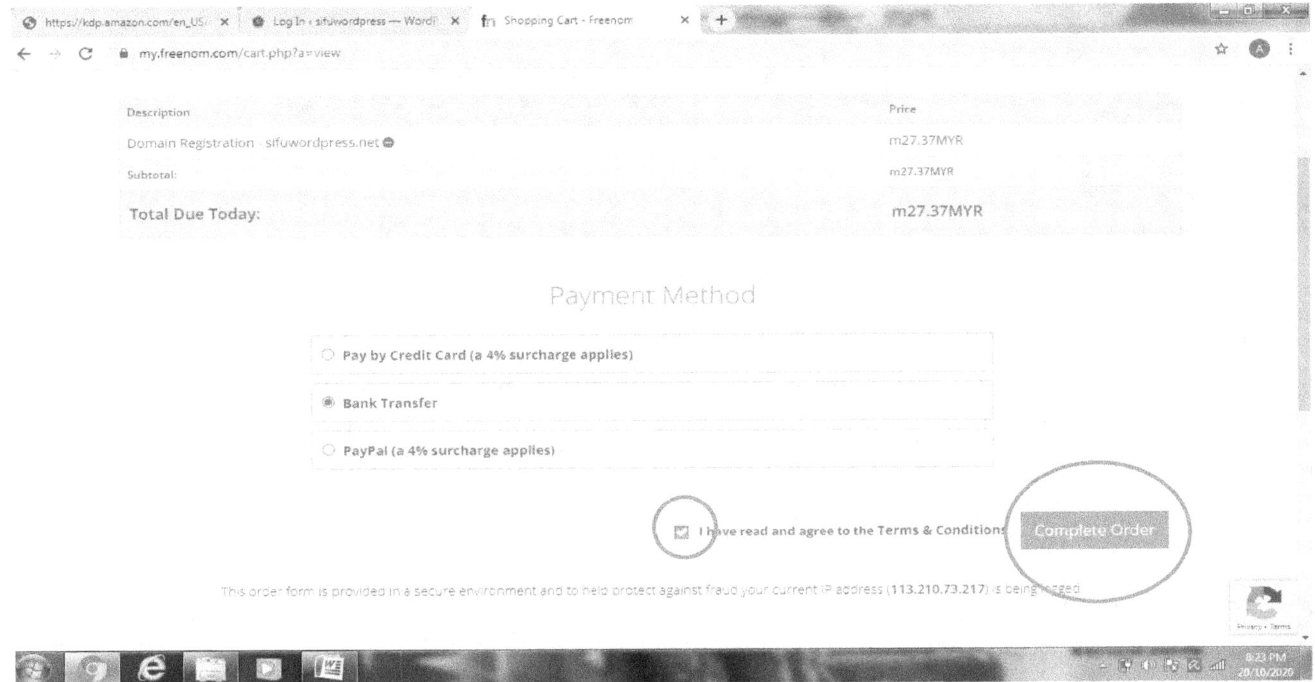

These are all free themes. No hidden fees. It can be used to create simple blogs, landing pages, and websites. If you do E-commerce, I recommend a blank theme as your theme. You need to build your website from scratch. My objective in publishing this book is to teach beginners out there who are just about to start building their website without any capital. If you already know the basics, then you can create it using paid and trusted domains such as domain hostwinds, 000webhost, and Godaddy.

If you already have basic knowledge, then this book is not suitable for you, because I will use a free domain and hosting. Usually, if the name is a free domain, then your website is impossible to get top ranking in Google search. So, SEO strategies are unfounded and unusable. If your goal is to make money from the website you build, I recommend getting a domain that ends with .com or .my or .net.

OPEN A WEB HOSTING

If the domain is your home address, then hosting is your house. In your house, you will definitely want to decorate with furniture and finishes to look beautiful. Especially if guests or visitors come to your house. You will definitely be happy if they praise how amazing your house are. There are many web hosting on the internet but I chose infinityfree.net because they provide unlimited disk-space size, no forced ads, SSL certificate provided and most importantly it is free.

1. Go to www.infinityfree.net
2. Click on **'Sign Up Now' button** and register your account.

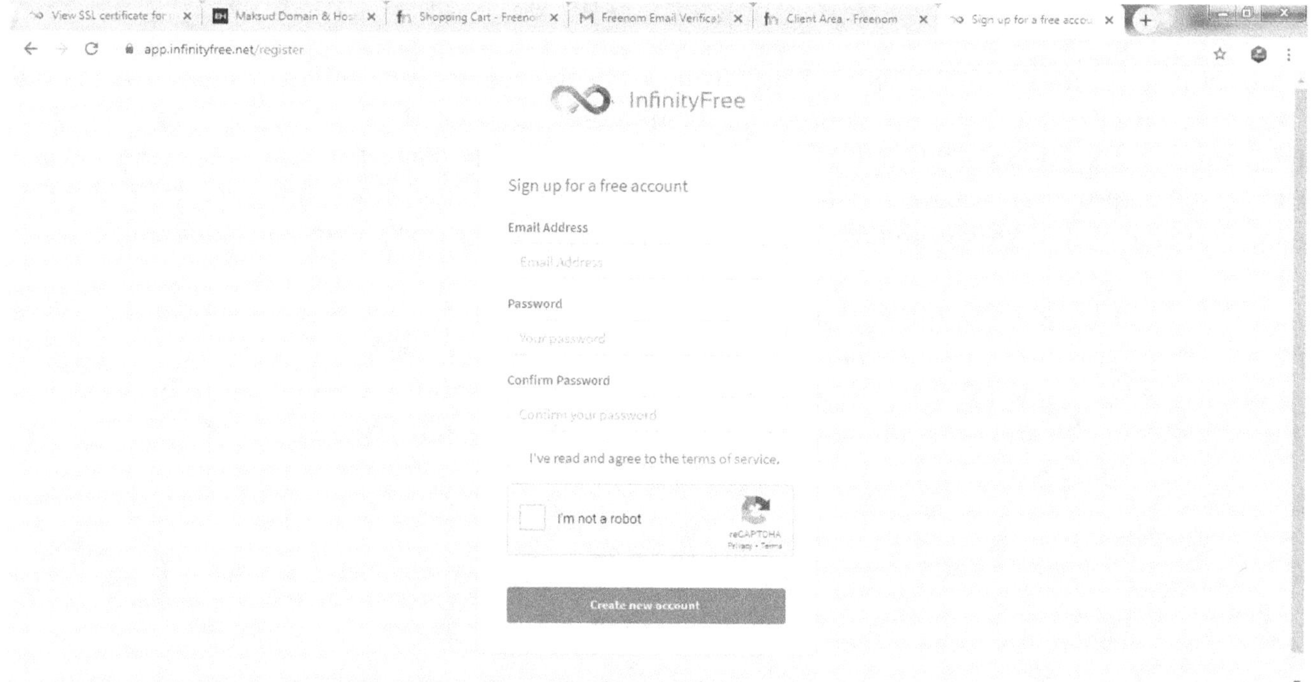

3. After finished, Click on **'Create new account'** button
4. Next, 'verification link' sent to your email inbox. Open your email inbox and click on that link.

5. Then, **Log In** to your account. After **Log in** > Click on '**Accounts**' in menu

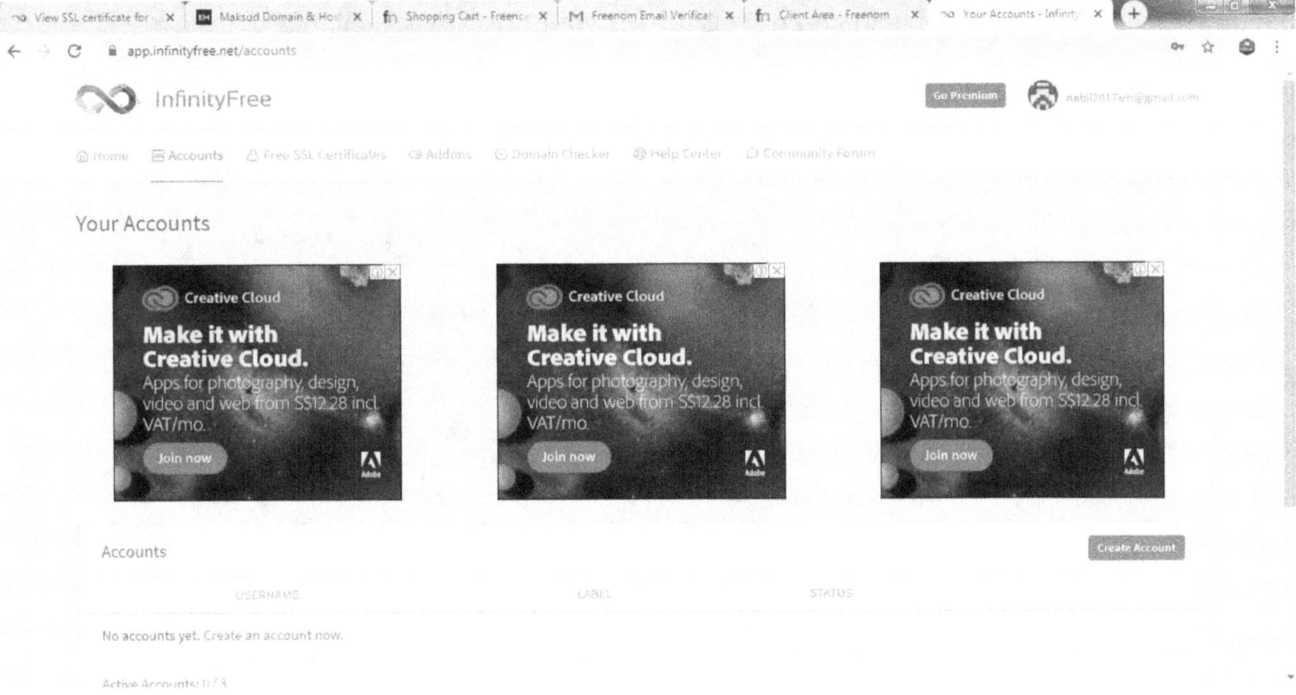

6. Click on '**Create Account**' button
7. Scroll down and you will see tittle 'Create a Hosting Account'
8. Click on '**Custom Domain**'

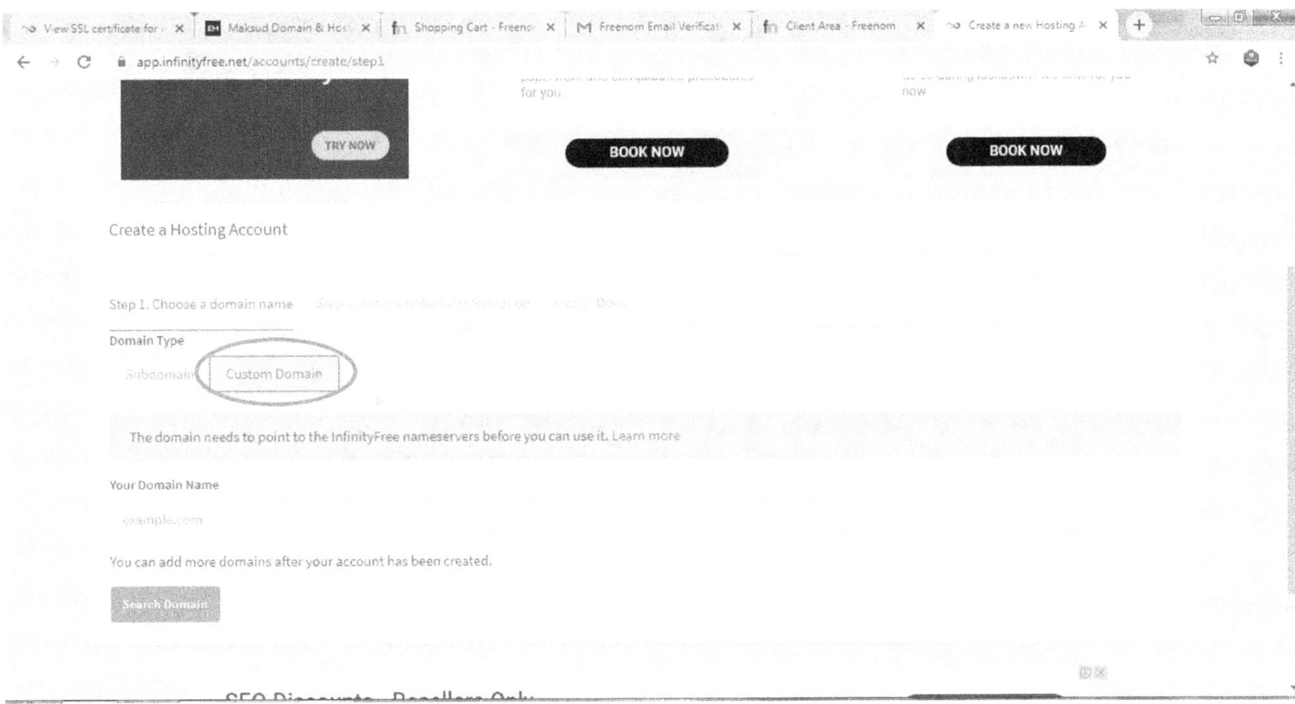

9. Under **Your Domain Name** > Enter the name of your website domain (from Chapter 1). For me, I will enter my website domain : sifuwordpress.ml

10. You will see success message in green. This means your domain is available.

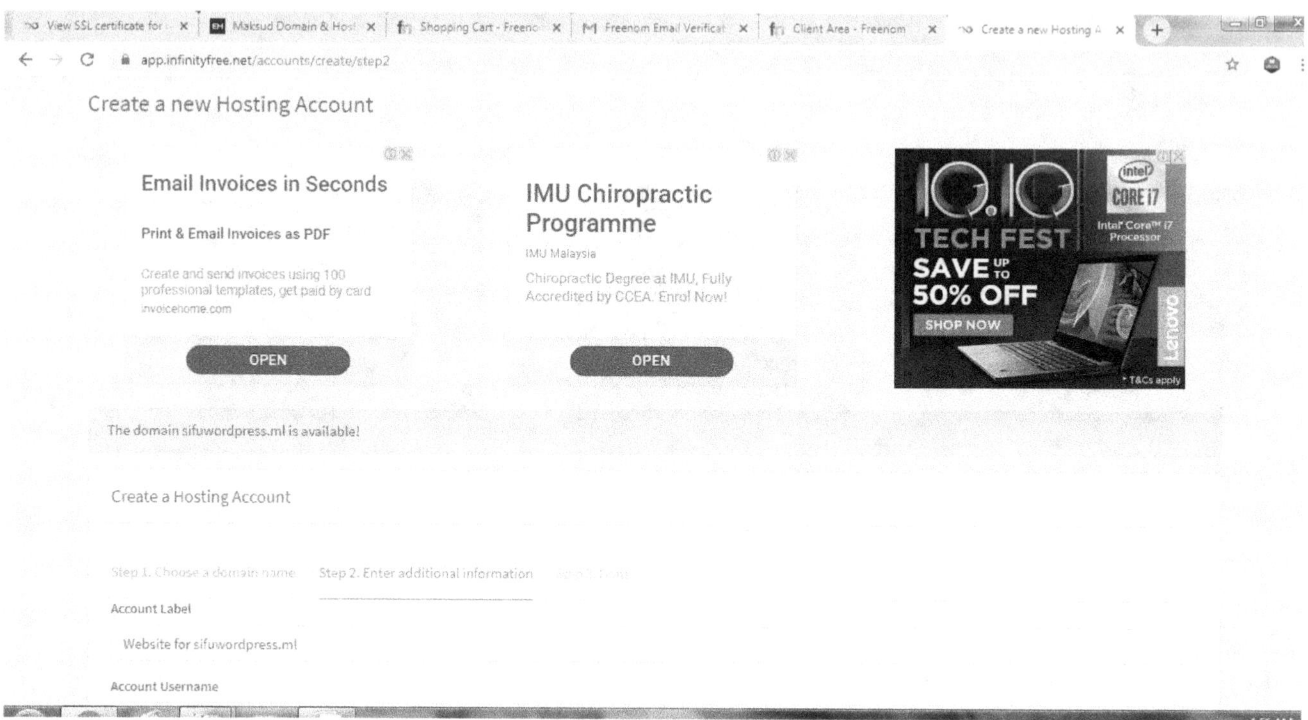

11. Next, go to (Freenom) and Log in to your account > Go to Services > Click on My Domains > Click on '**Manage Domain**'

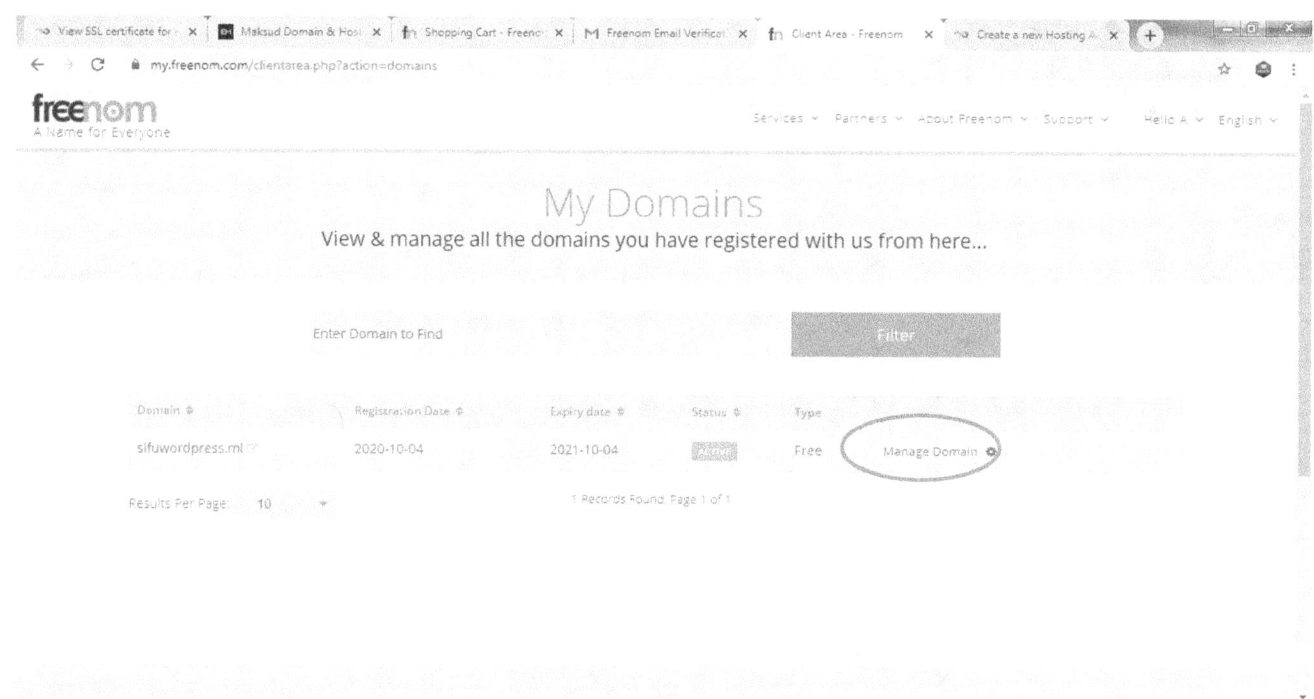

12. Click on Management Tools > Nameservers > Use Custom nameservers

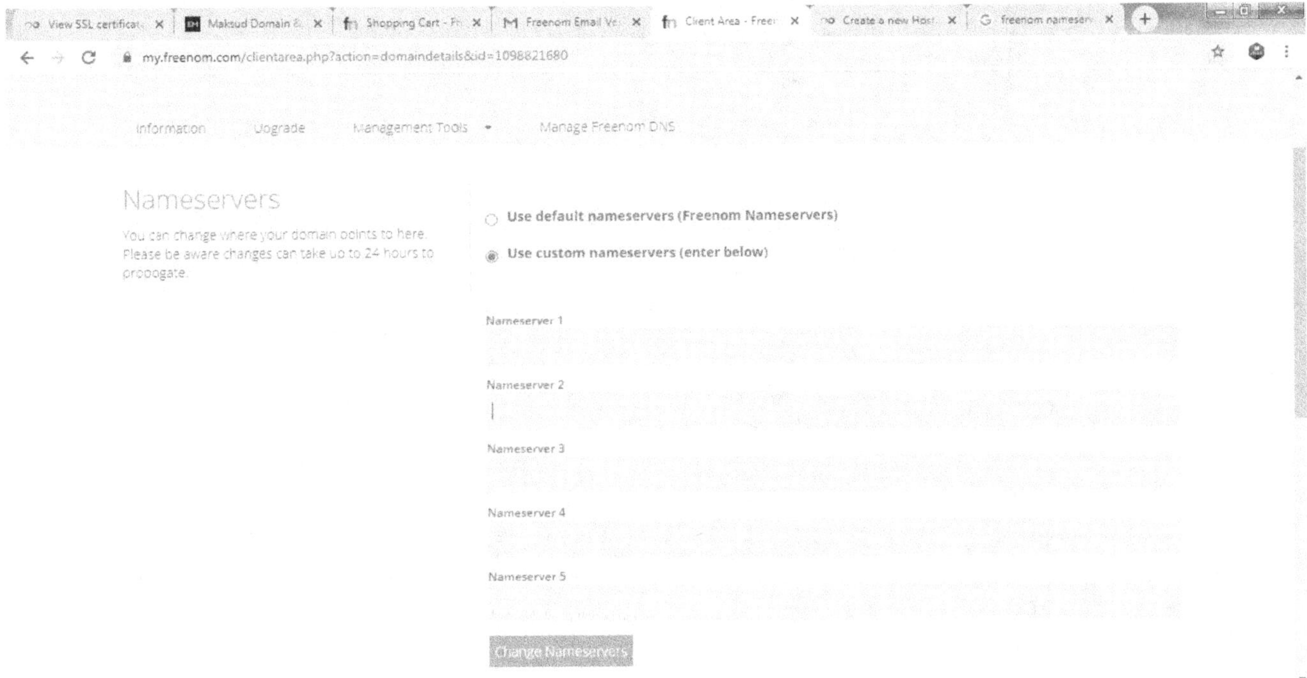

13. You will see 5 task bar to be fill named Nameserver 1, Nameserver 2, Nameserver 3, Nameserver 4 and Nameserver 5.
14. Type ns1.epizy.com in Nameserver 1 and ns2.epizy.com in Nameserver 2 > Then, Click on **'Change Nameservers'**
15. These are the server name that infinityfree provided.

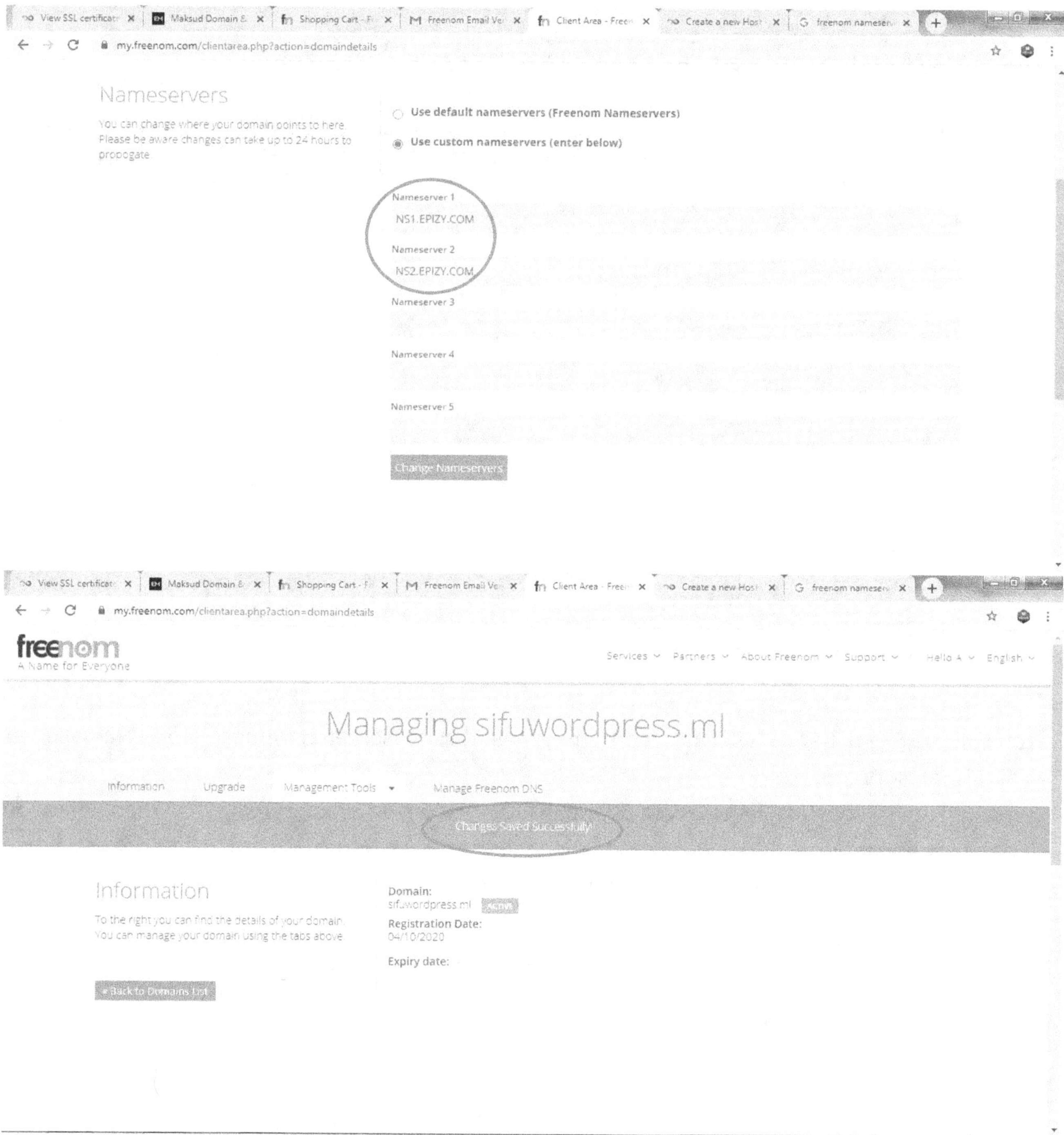

16. After that, go to your infinity account > Enter password > Click on '**Create Account**'
17. You will see your username stated in success message.

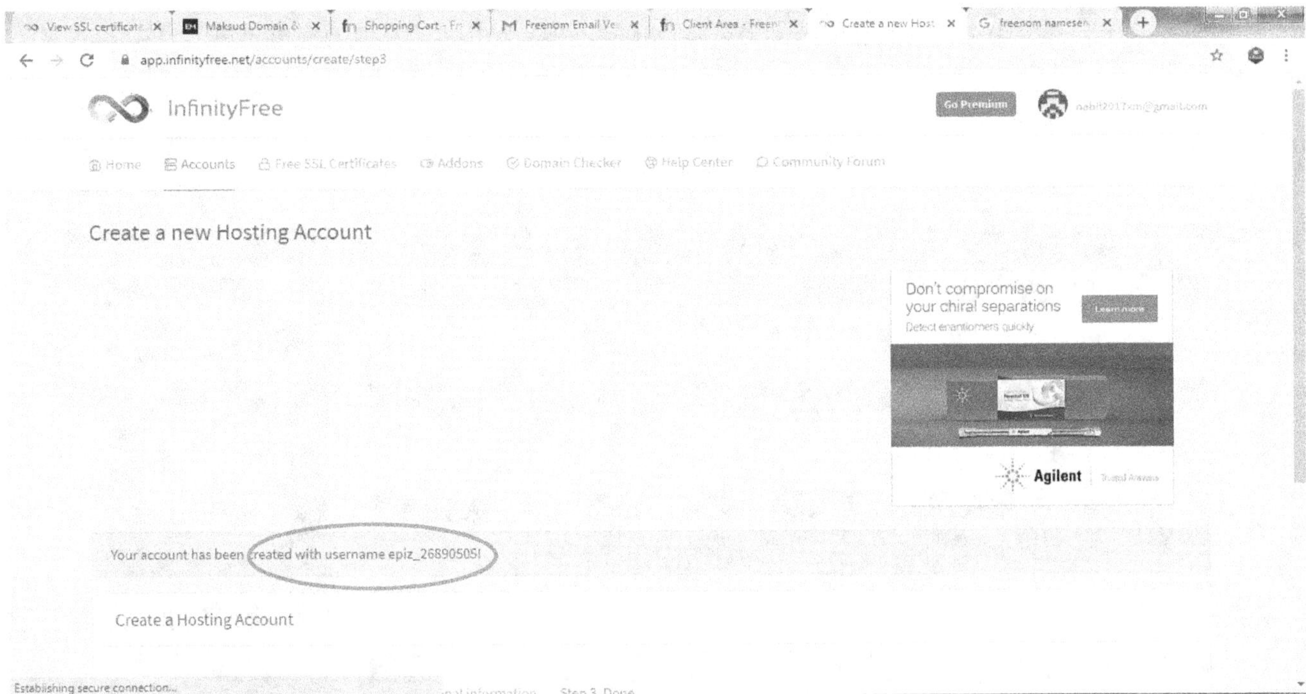

18. Then Click on '**Open Client Area**'. You will see the details of your account such as FTP and SQL.

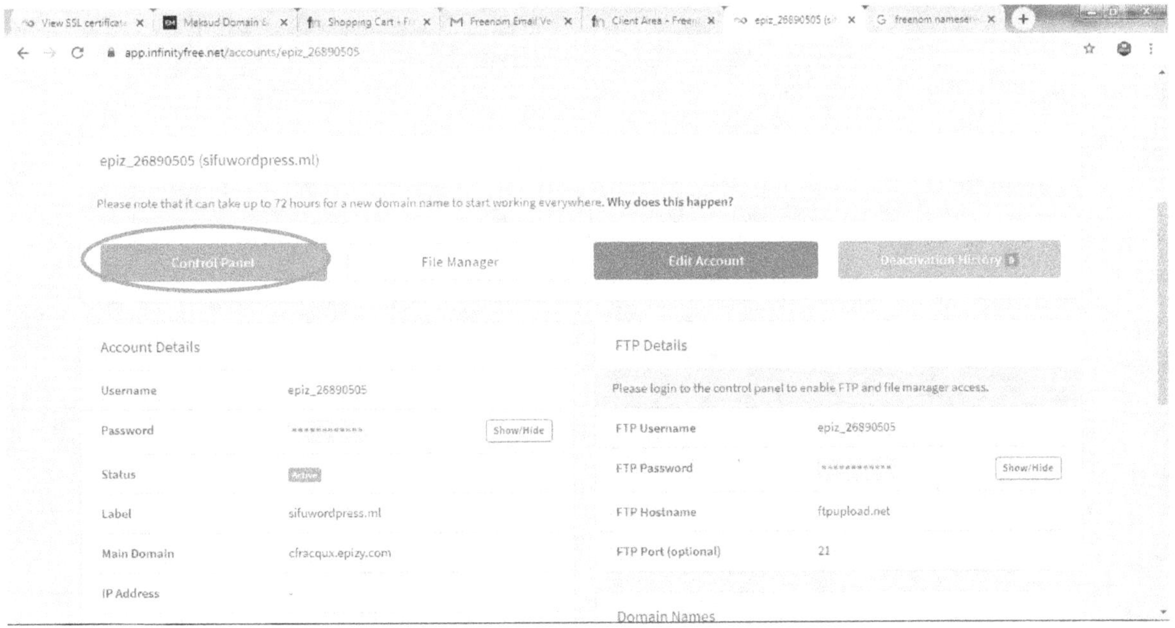

19. Click on '**Control Panel**'. You will be directed to PDPA notice, you can choose either Approve or Dissapprove.

20. You will see control panel page. Here is a place for you to control all the hosting on your website.

SSL CERTIFICATE (SECURITY)

We will start by installing a SSL certificate. The purpose of an SSL Certificate is to make your website secure. So, your website is safe from attackers. All money transactions in the website are safe. For ecommerce site, visitors who come to your website who want to make a payment will feel safe.

This is because nowadays, many scammer problem reports are made. Before this, most people who have been scammed do not know if the website they are visiting is safe or not. And now, many people are aware of the security of such a website, so there is speculation telling you should not buy anything from that website if there is no key logo in their browser search bar.

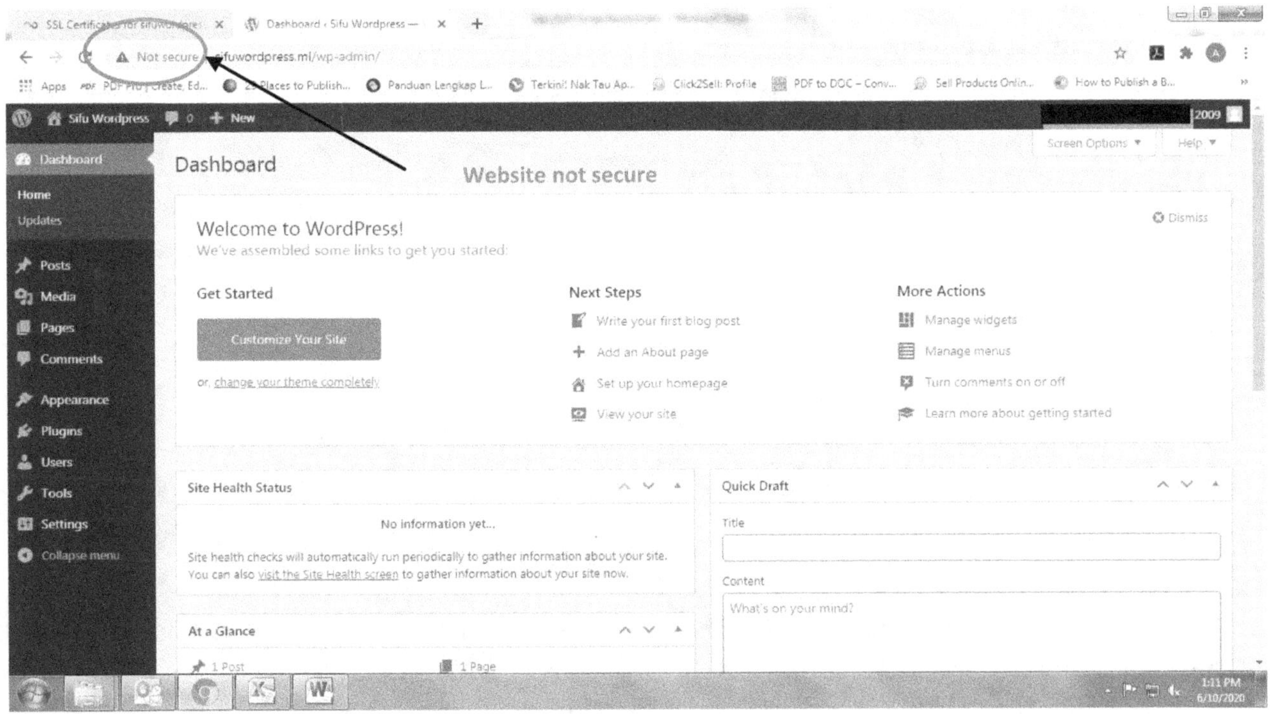

Please follow these steps correctly as the steps to register an SSL certificate are very complex. Follow my steps. If you make a mistake, there will be an error on our cpanel later.

1. Go to Client area > Click on Free SSL Certificates

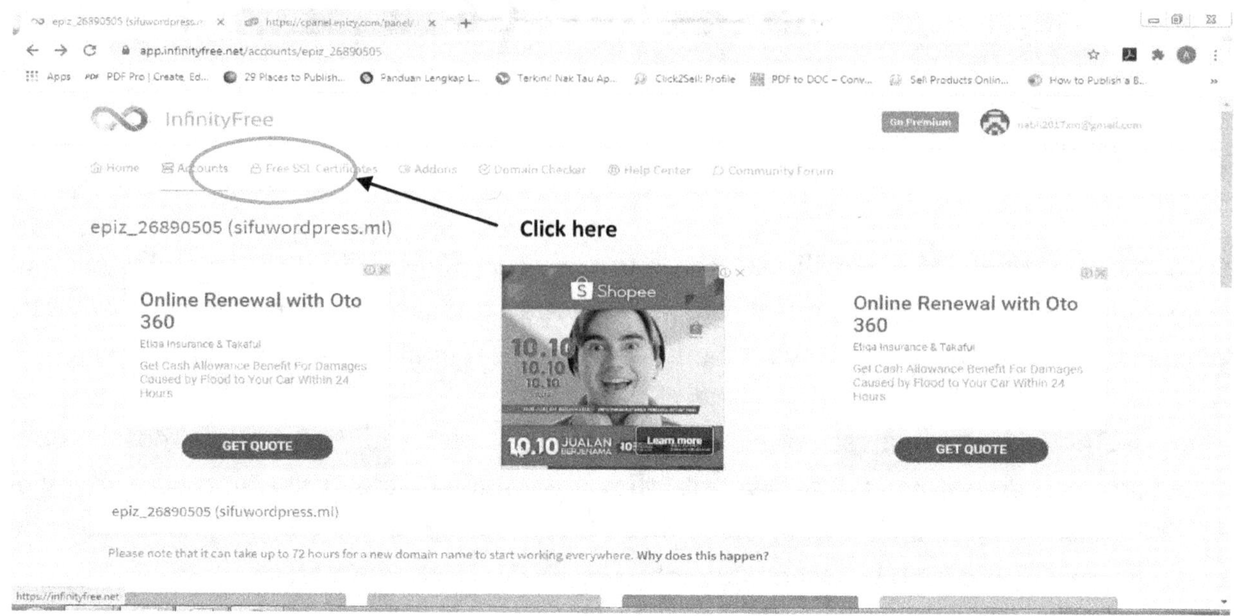

2. Click on **'Add SSL Domain'**

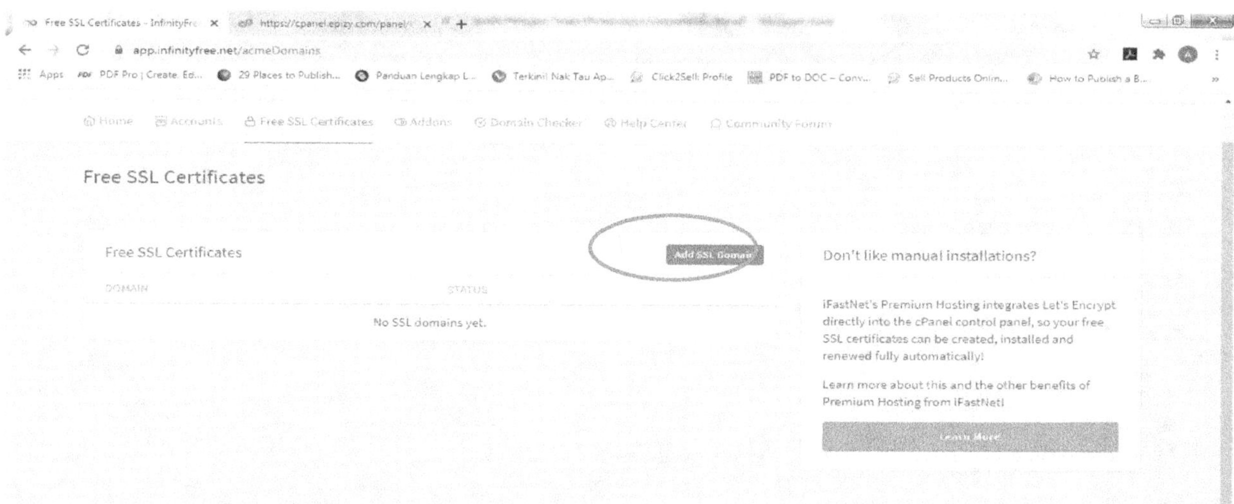

3. Enter your website domain name. For example, sifuwordpress.ml > then, Click on '**Add SSL Domain'**
4. You will be given a record name and Destination. These are the code server which is secure, only for your own website. Different website have different code server.

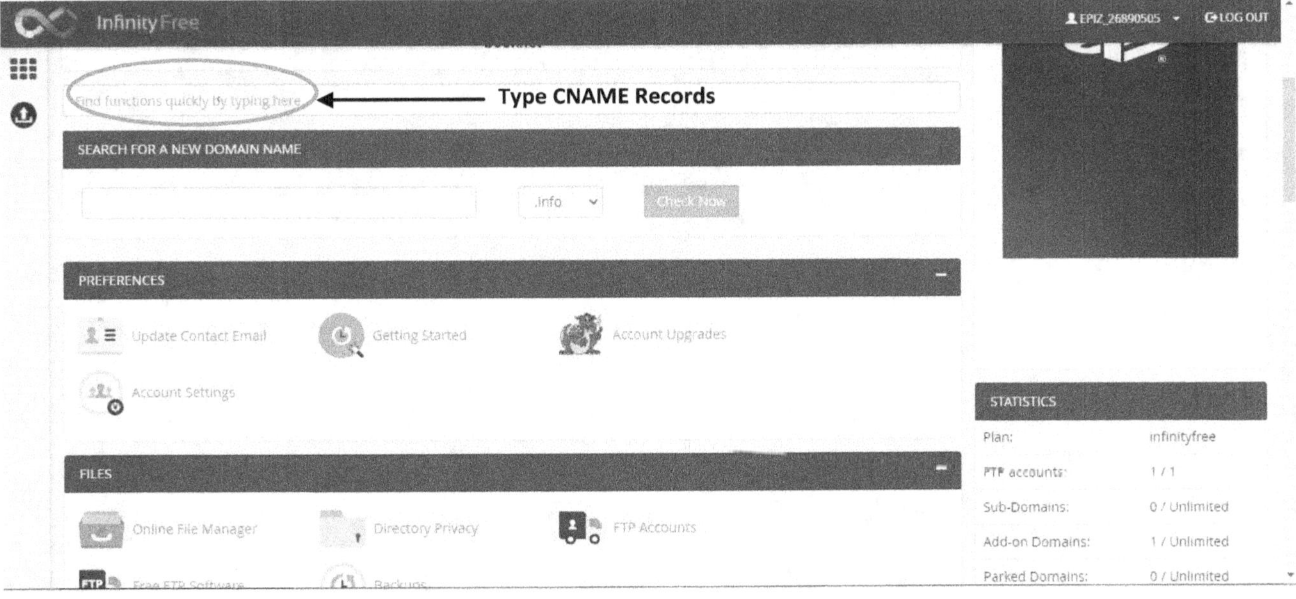

5. Go back to Control Panel (cpanel infinityfree)
6. At search bar function, type CNAME Records > Click on that function

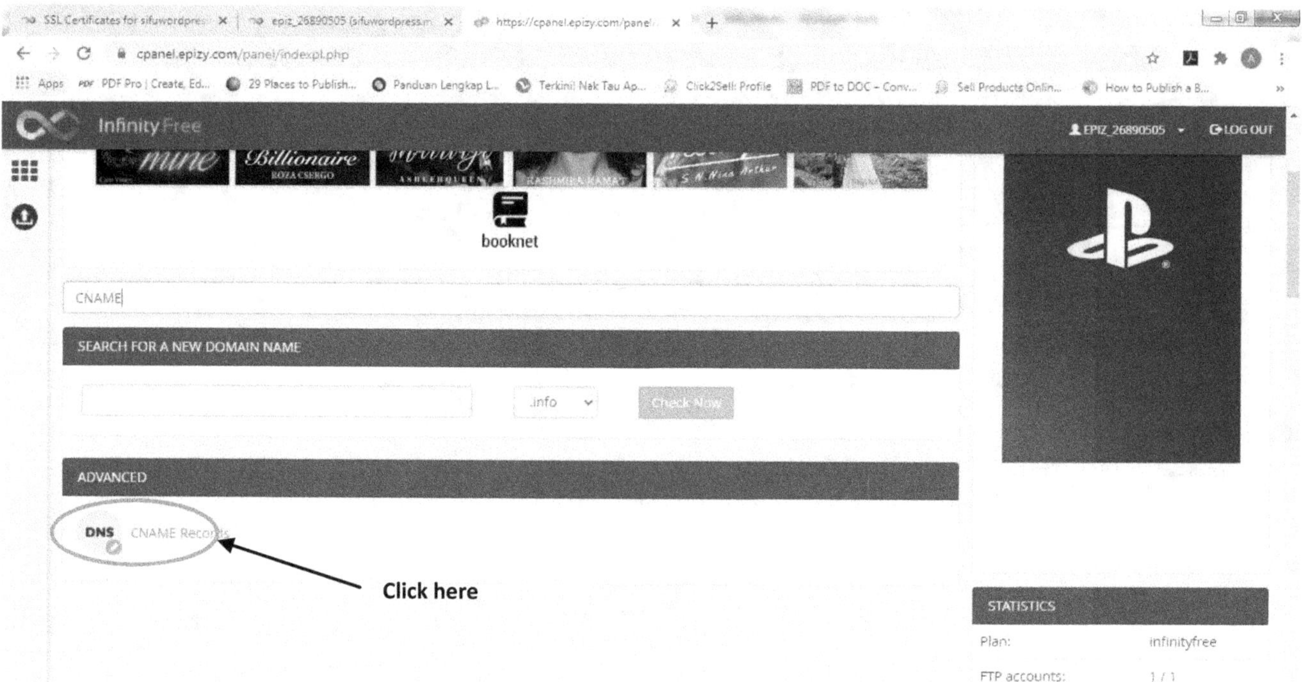

7. You will be taken to menu Custom CNAME Records. There are 2 sections that need to be fill, Record Name dan Destination.

8. Here you need to copy and paste the server code to Cpanel

9. Go to Client area > Copy Record Name 1 from SSL apge > Go to Cnamerecords page > Paste to Record Name section (For more details please follow the steps below. For example, follow the picture below).

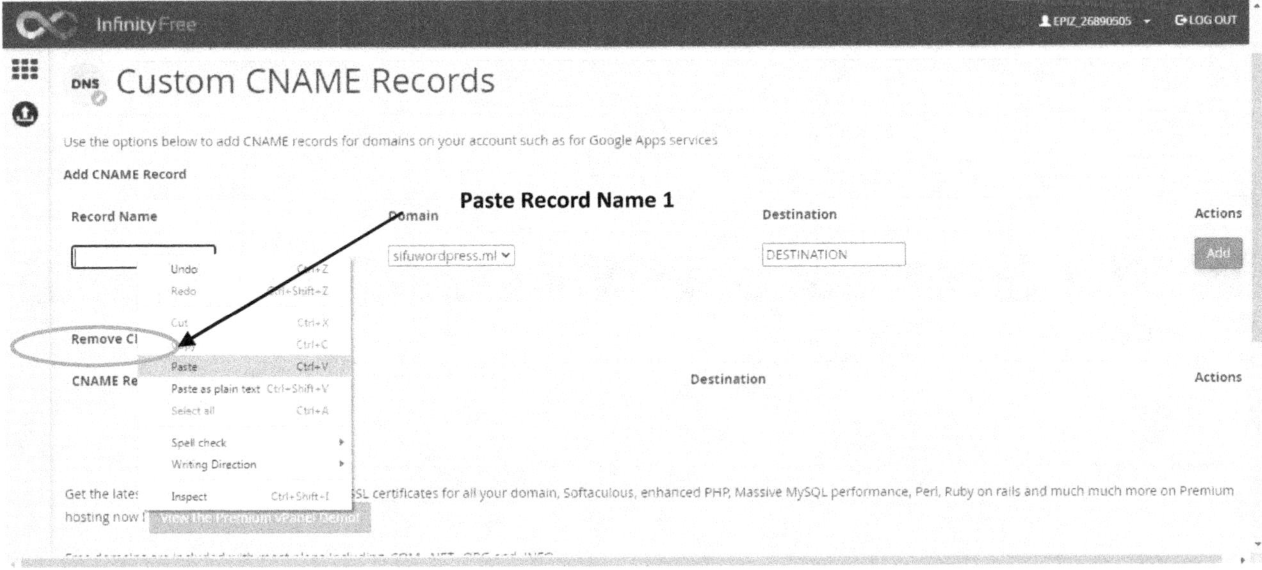

10. Then, copy Destination 1 > Paste to Cpanel Destination

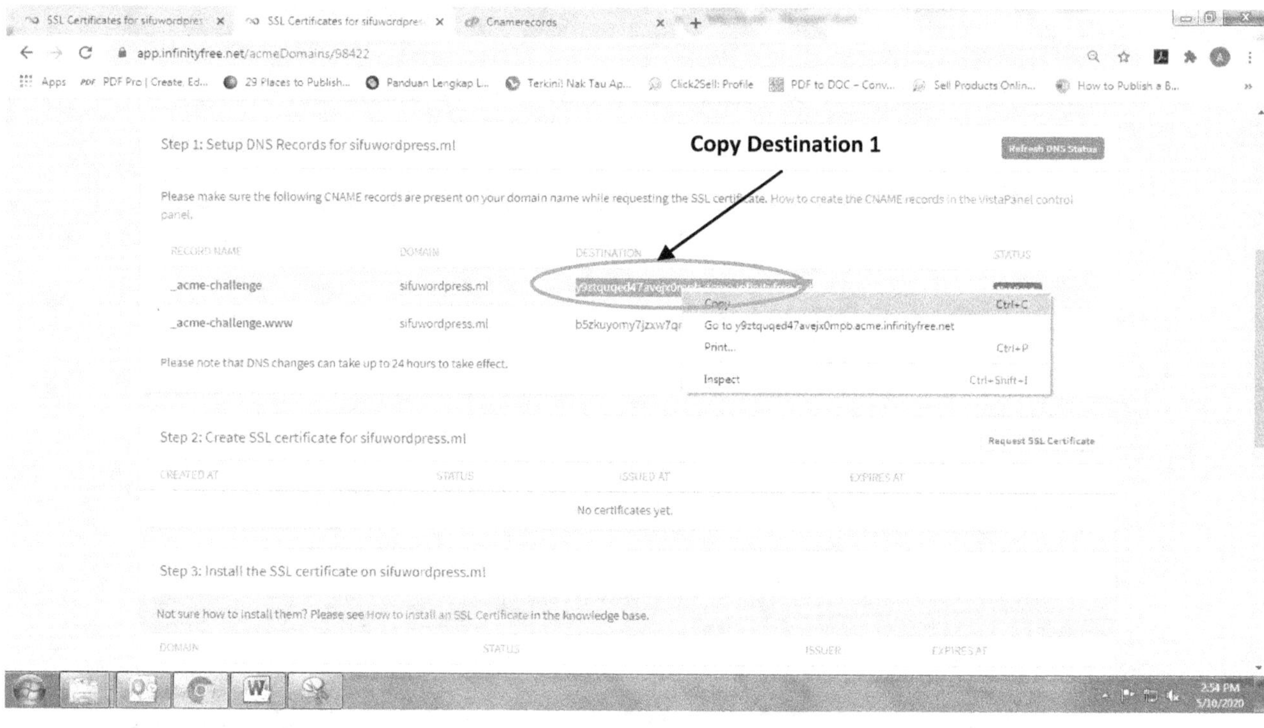

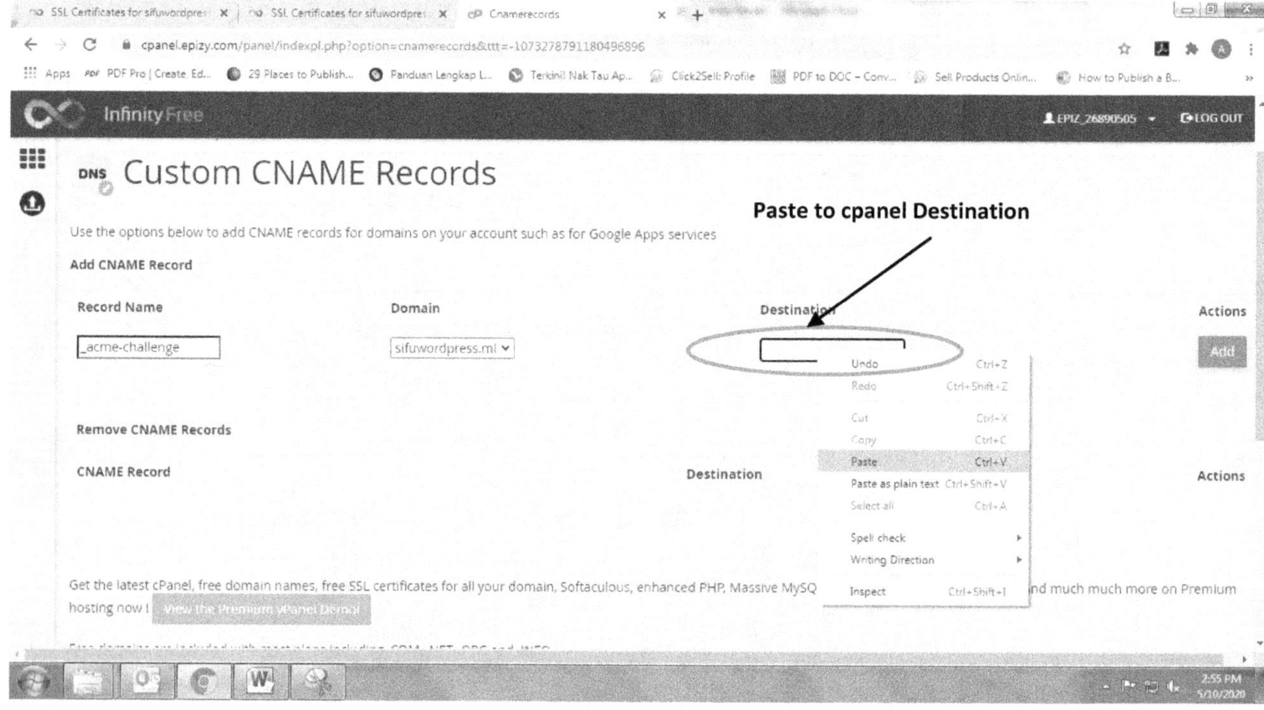

11. Click on Add button.

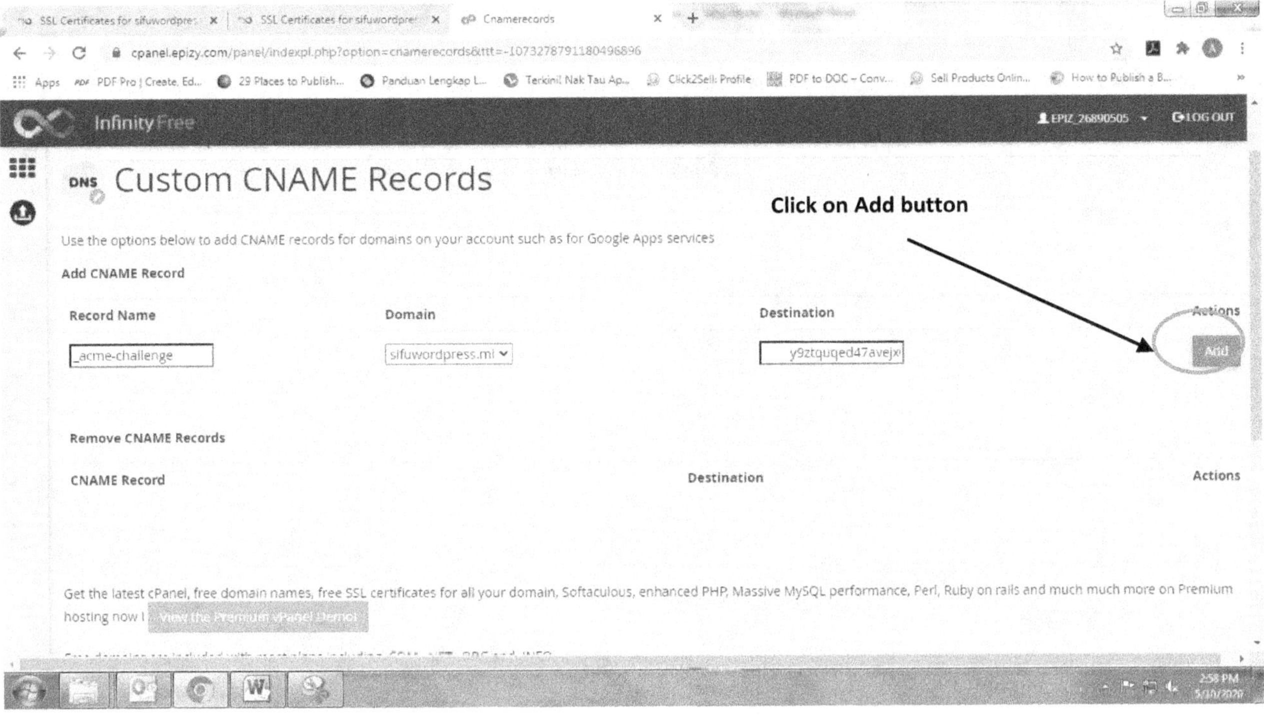

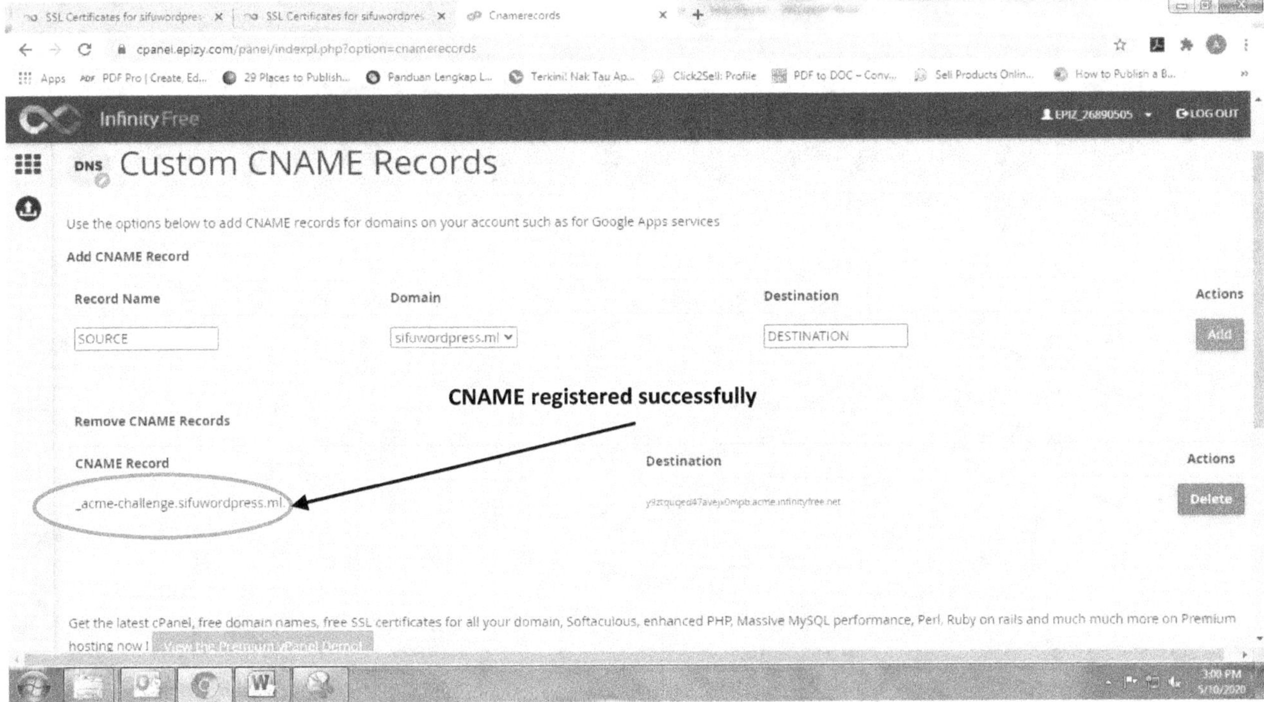

12. Do the same on CNAME Record Name 2 and Destination 2

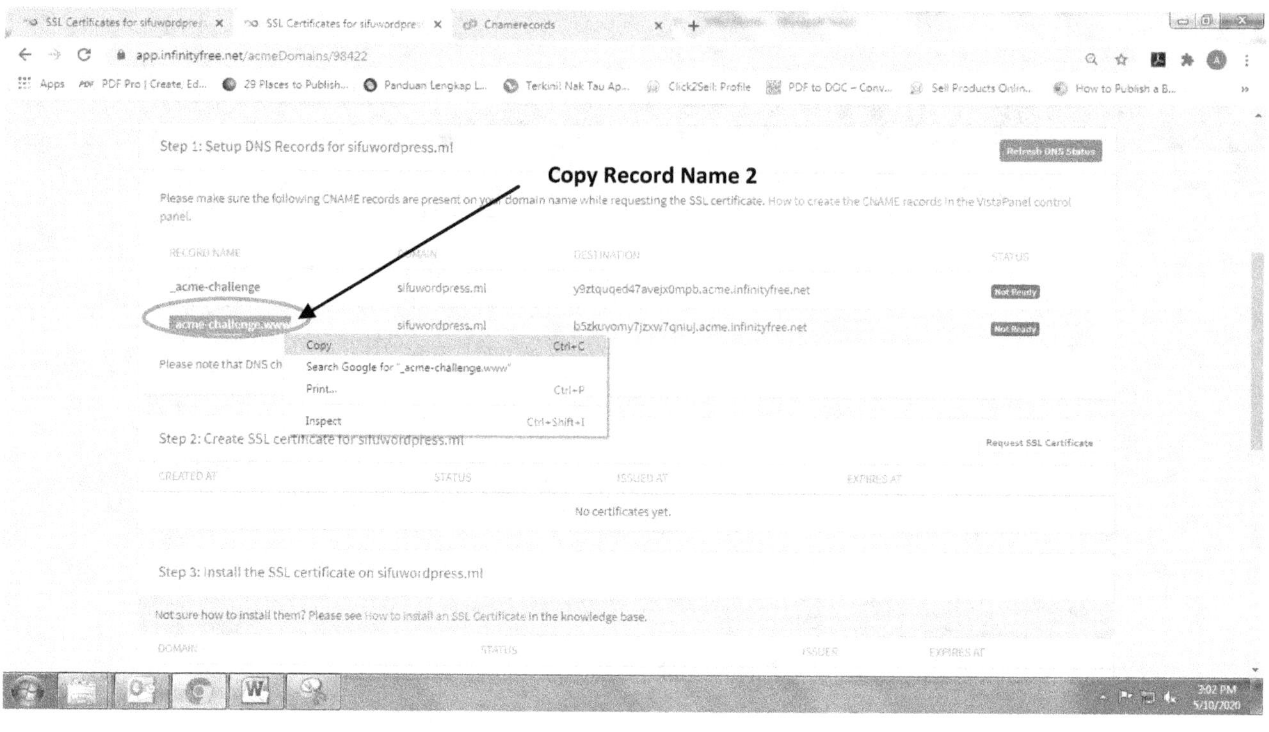

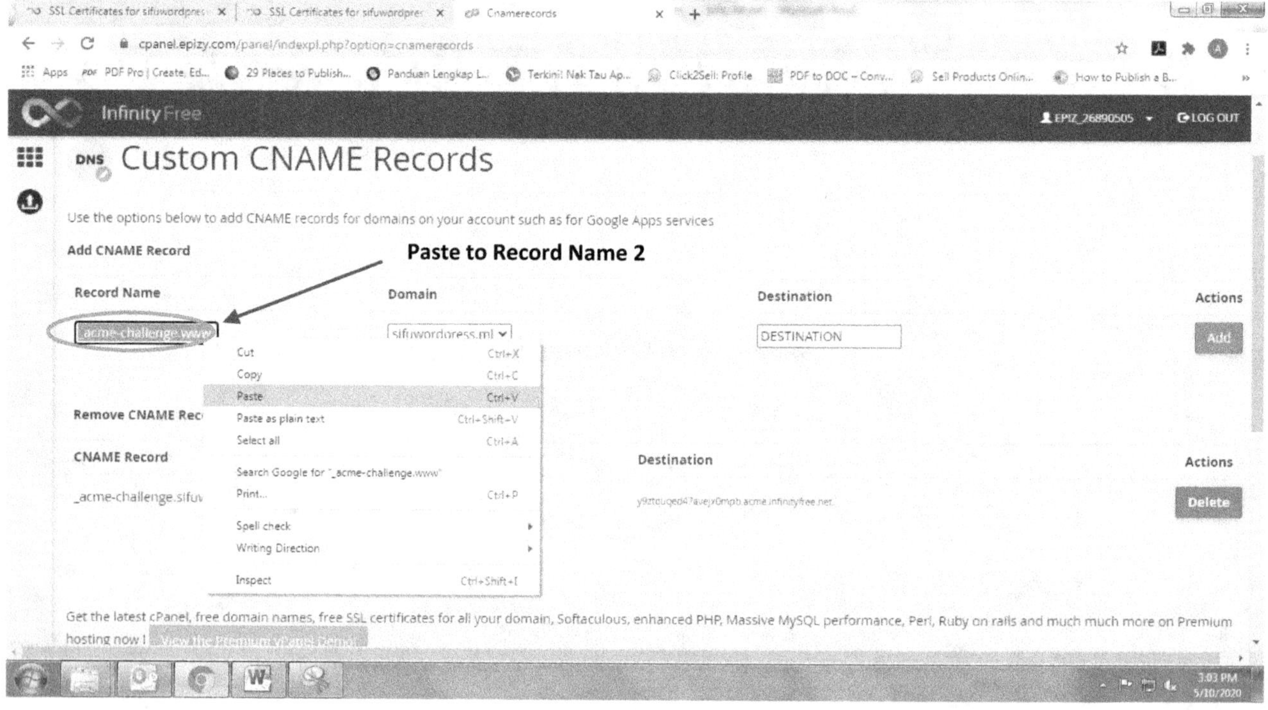

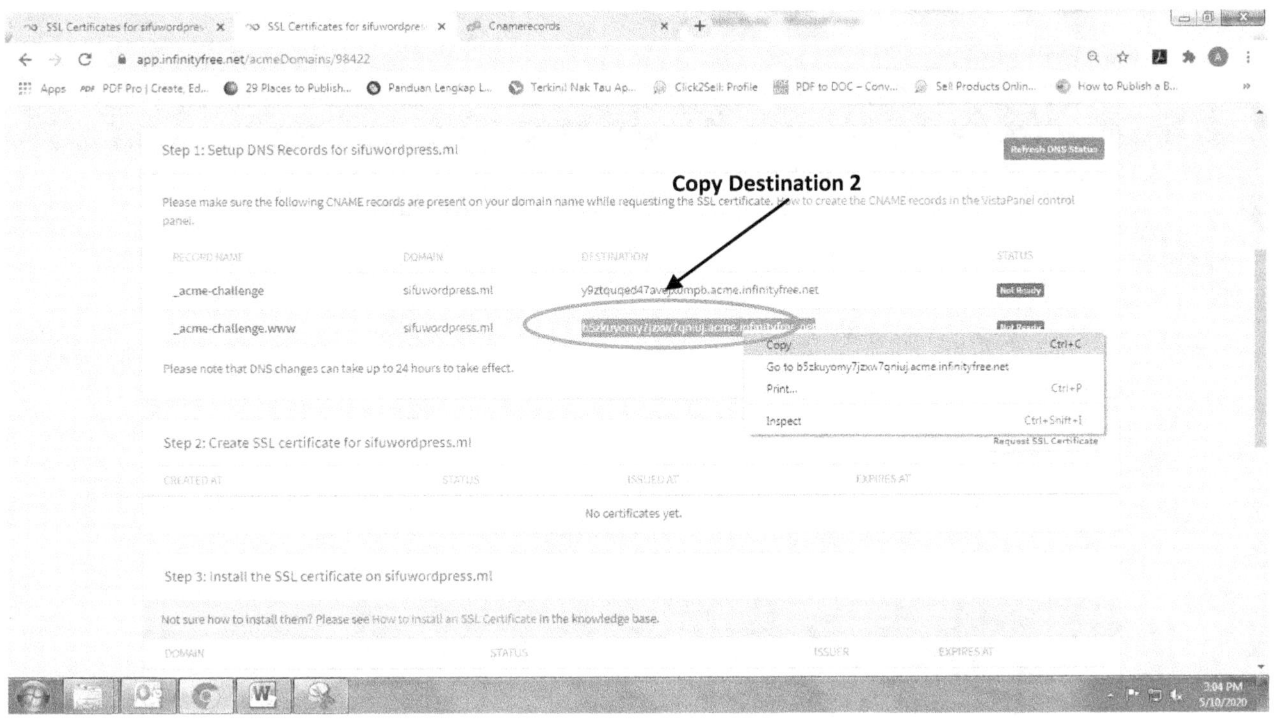

Copy Destination 2
Step 1: Setup DNS Records for sifuwordpress.ml
Please make sure the following CNAME records are present on your domain name while requesting the SSL certificate. How to create the CNAME records in the VistaPanel control panel.
RECORD NAME
DOMAIN
DESTINATION
STATUS
_acme-challenge
sifuwordpress.ml
y9ztquqed47avejx0mpb.acme.infinityfree.net
Not Ready
_acme-challenge.www
sifuwordpress.ml
b5zkuyomy7jzxk7qniuj.acme.infinityfree.net
Copy   Ctrl+C
Go to b5zkuyomy7jzxk7qniuj.acme.infinityfree.net
Print...   Ctrl+P
Inspect   Ctrl+Shift+I
Please note that DNS changes can take up to 24 hours to take effect.
Step 2: Create SSL certificate for sifuwordpress.ml
CREATED AT   STATUS   ISSUED AT   EXPIRES AT
No certificates yet.
Step 3: Install the SSL certificate on sifuwordpress.ml
Not sure how to install them? Please see How to Install an SSL Certificate in the knowledge base.
DOMAIN   STATUS   ISSUER   EXPIRES AT

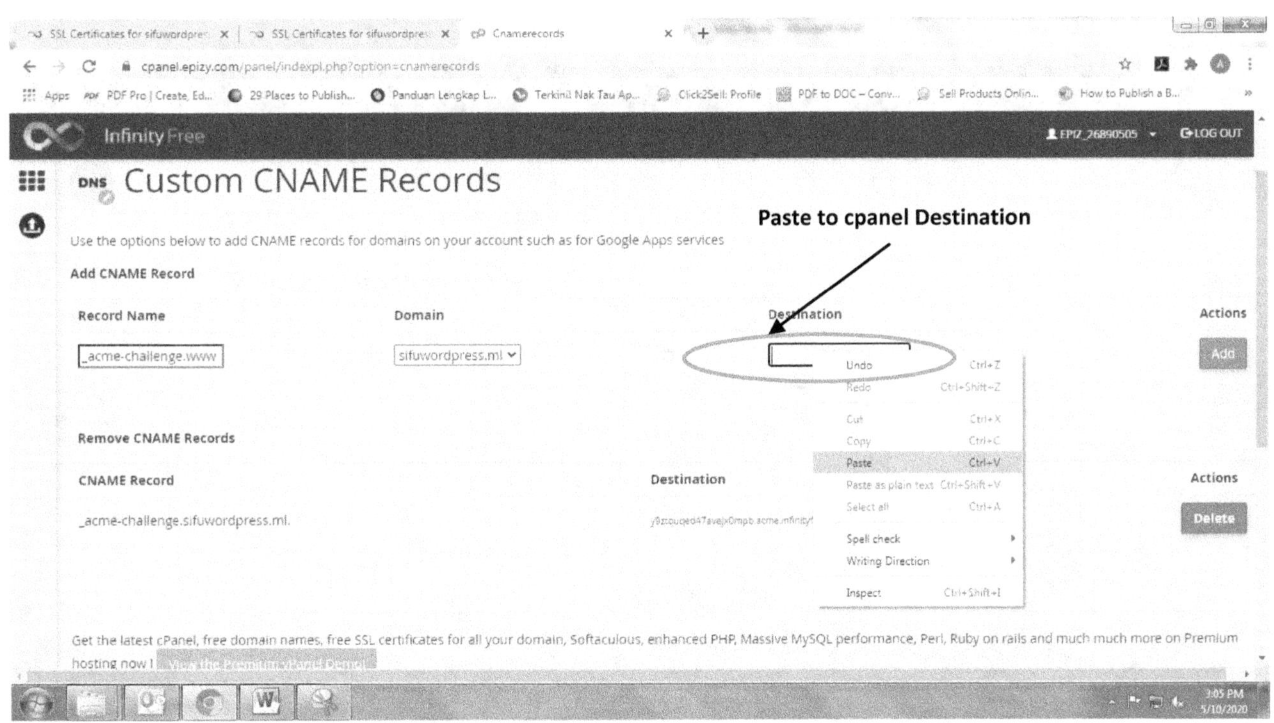

Infinity Free
Custom CNAME Records
Paste to cpanel Destination
Use the options below to add CNAME records for domains on your account such as for Google Apps services
Add CNAME Record
Record Name
Domain
Destination
Actions
_acme-challenge.www
sifuwordpress.ml
Add
Undo   Ctrl+Z
Redo   Ctrl+Shift+Z
Cut   Ctrl+X
Copy   Ctrl+C
Paste   Ctrl+V
Paste as plain text Ctrl+Shift+V
Select all   Ctrl+A
Spell check
Writing Direction
Inspect   Ctrl+Shift+I
Remove CNAME Records
CNAME Record
Destination
Actions
_acme-challenge.sifuwordpress.ml.
y9ztquqed47avejx0mpb.acme.infinity
Delete
Get the latest cPanel, free domain names, free SSL certificates for all your domain, Softaculous, enhanced PHP, Massive MySQL performance, Perl, Ruby on rails and much much more on Premium hosting now !

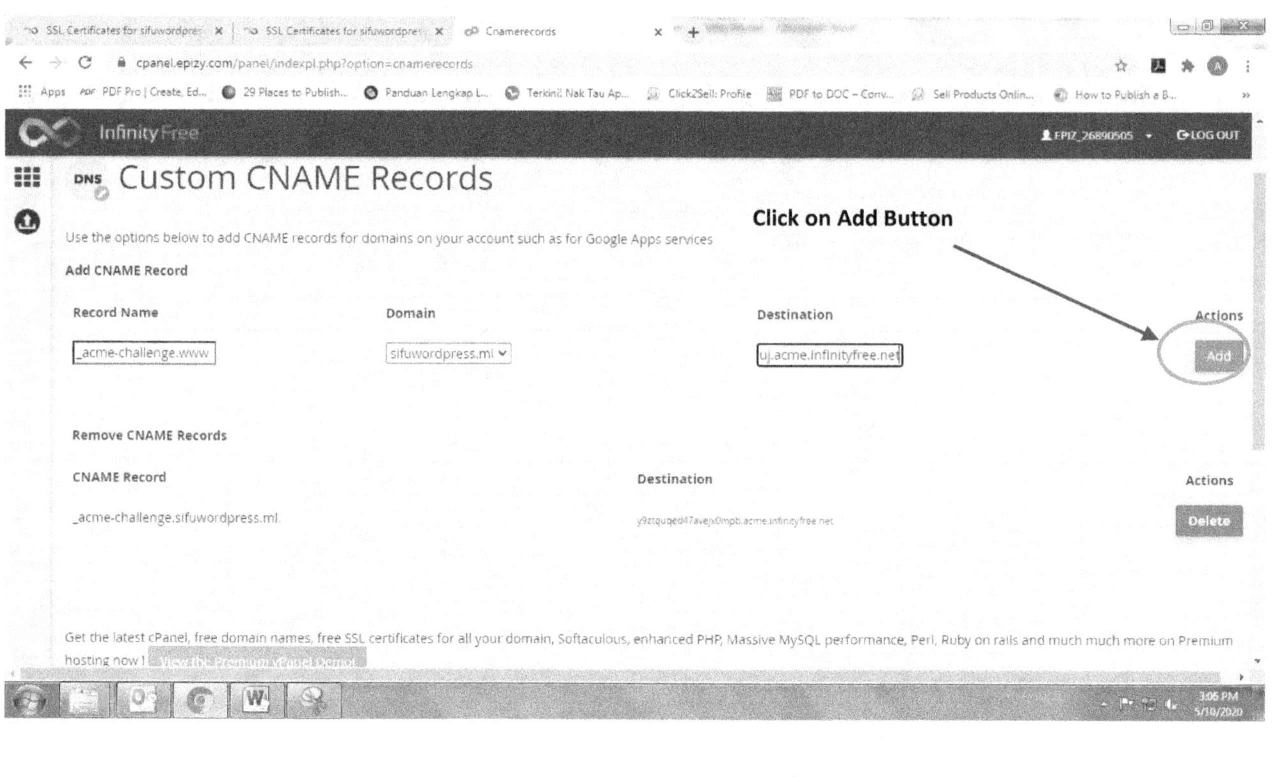

Click on Add Button
DNS Custom CNAME Records
Use the options below to add CNAME records for domains on your account such as for Google Apps services
Add CNAME Record
Record Name
_acme-challenge.www
Domain
sifuwordpress.ml
Destination
uj.acme.infinityfree.net
Actions
Add
Remove CNAME Records
CNAME Record
_acme-challenge.sifuwordpress.ml.
Destination
y9ztquqed47avejx0mpb.acme.infinityfree.net
Actions
Delete

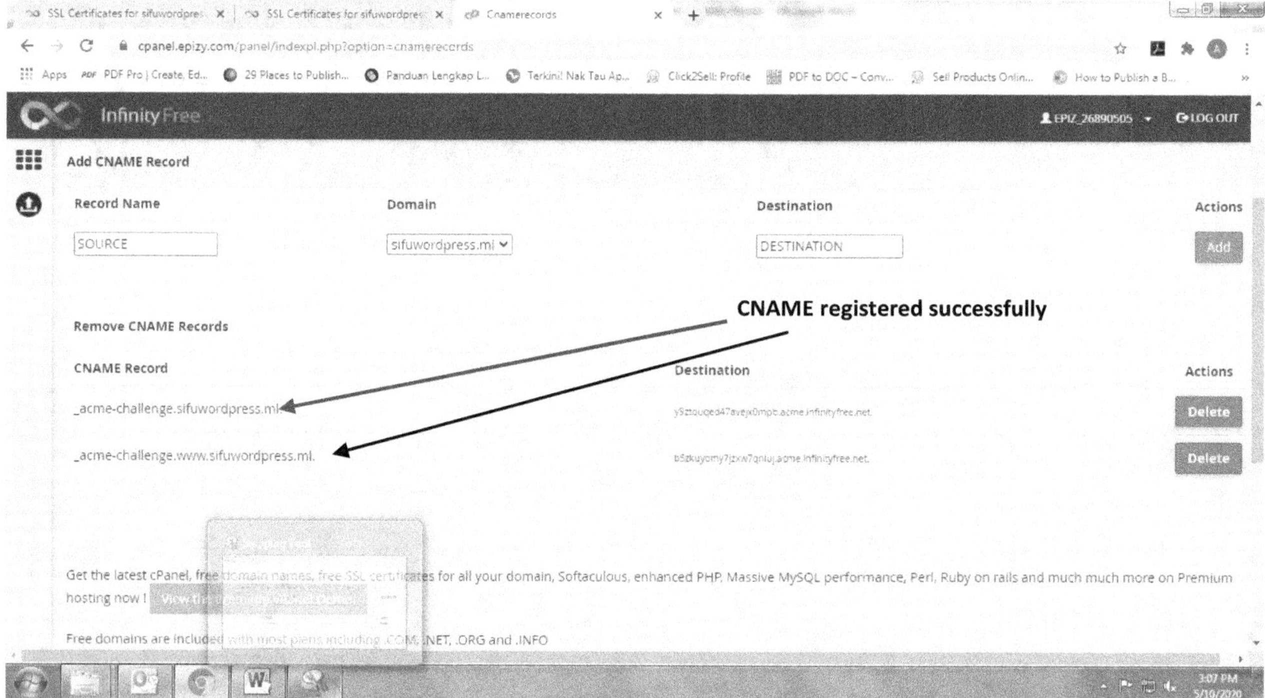

Add CNAME Record
Record Name
SOURCE
Domain
sifuwordpress.ml
Destination
DESTINATION
Actions
Add
CNAME registered successfully
Remove CNAME Records
CNAME Record
_acme-challenge.sifuwordpress.ml
_acme-challenge.www.sifuwordpress.ml.
Destination
y9ztquqed47avejx0mpb.acme.infinityfree.net
u5zkuyomy7jzxv7qnluj.acme.infinityfree.net.
Actions
Delete
Delete

13. Go back to the Client Area > SSL Certificate Menu > Click on **'Refresh DNS Status'**

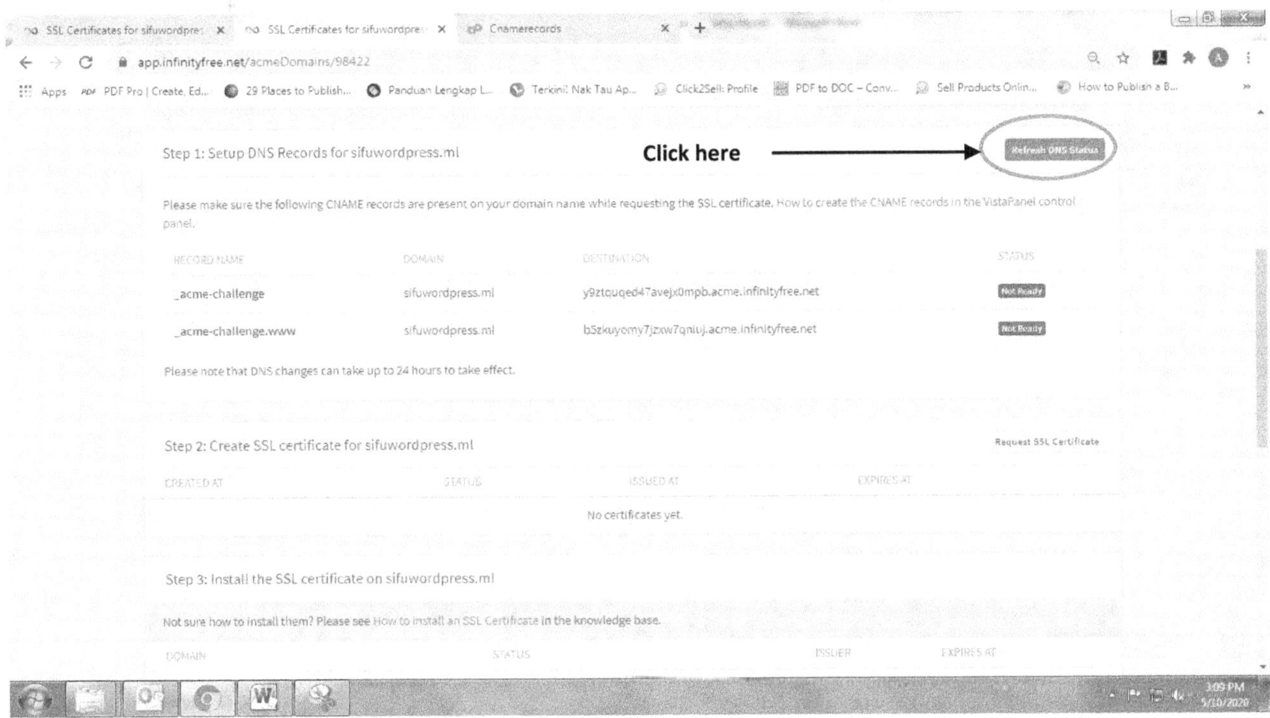

14. A red notification will appear later indicates that your website's DNS takes 24 hours to confirm. This is normal. You will need to wait 24 hours for your website to be verified. While waiting, you can proceed to Chapter 3 to learn WordPress Installation.

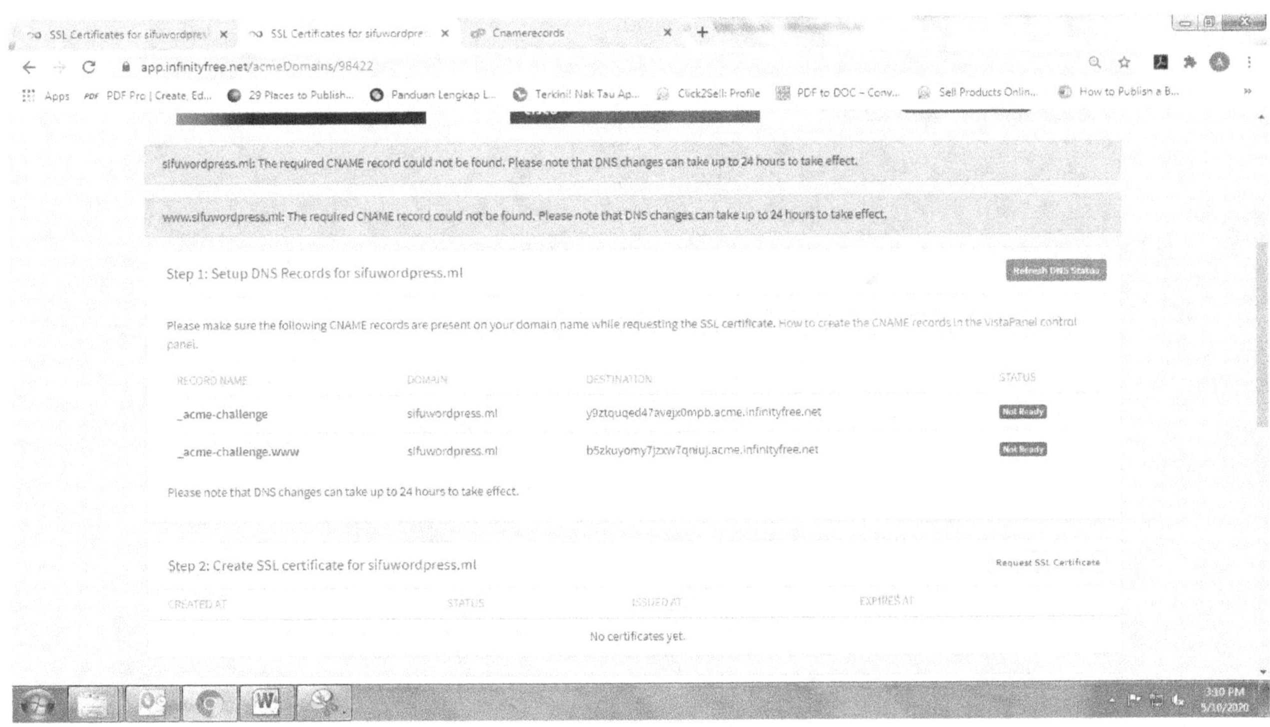

15. After 24 hours of waiting and verification completed. You will see the 'Ready' green status

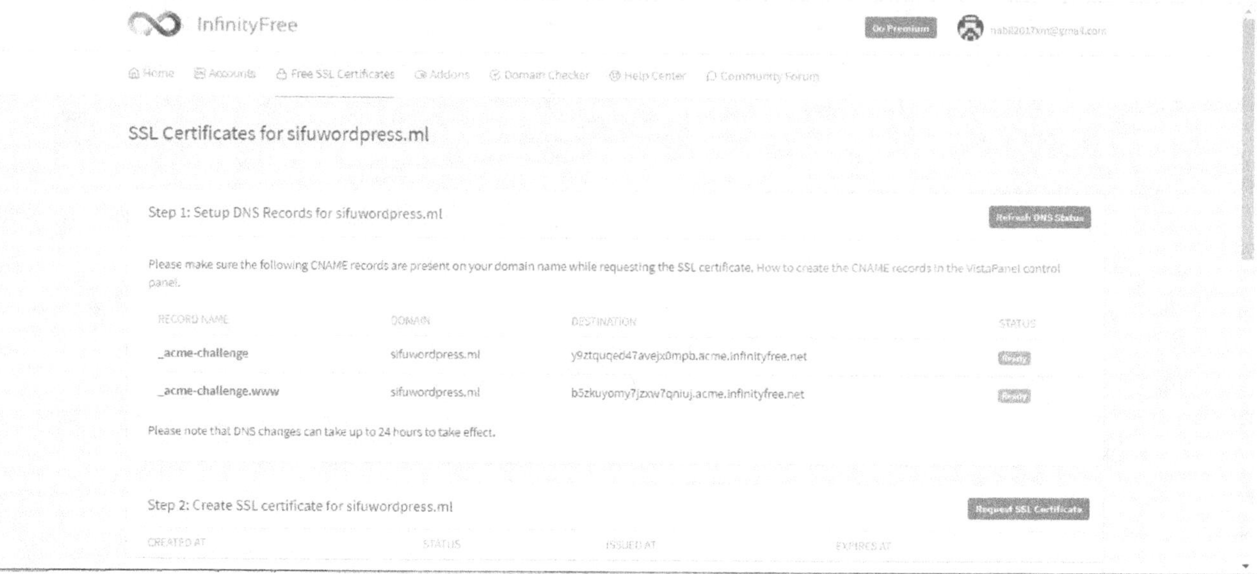

16. Click on **'Request SSL Certificate'**

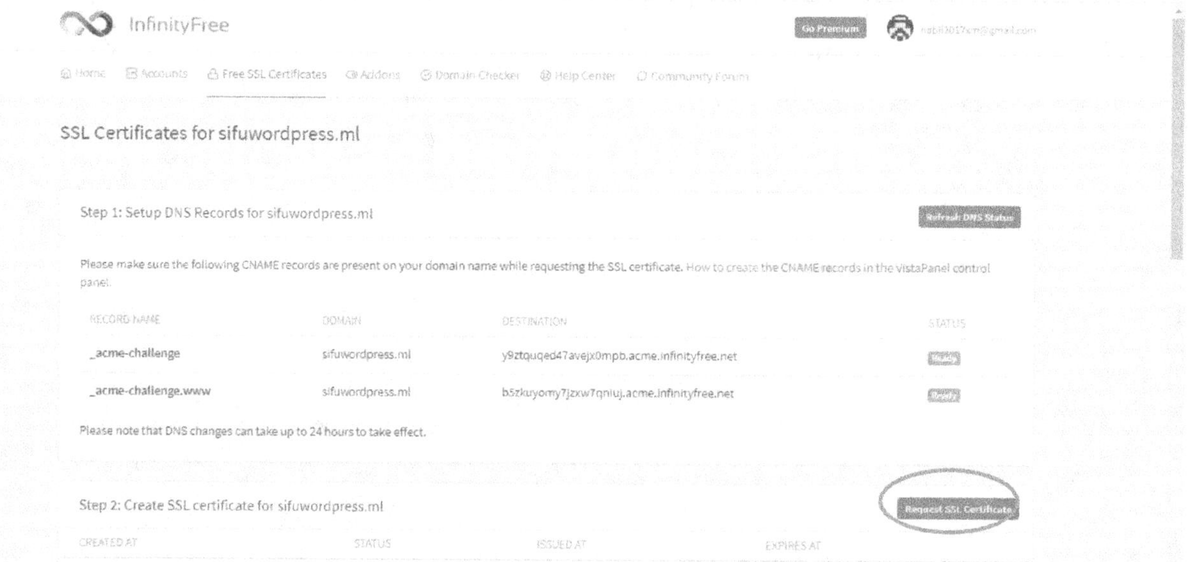

17. SSL Certificate will be pending and will take 3 - 4 minutes. Continue to refresh the page. If it is still pending, refresh this page.

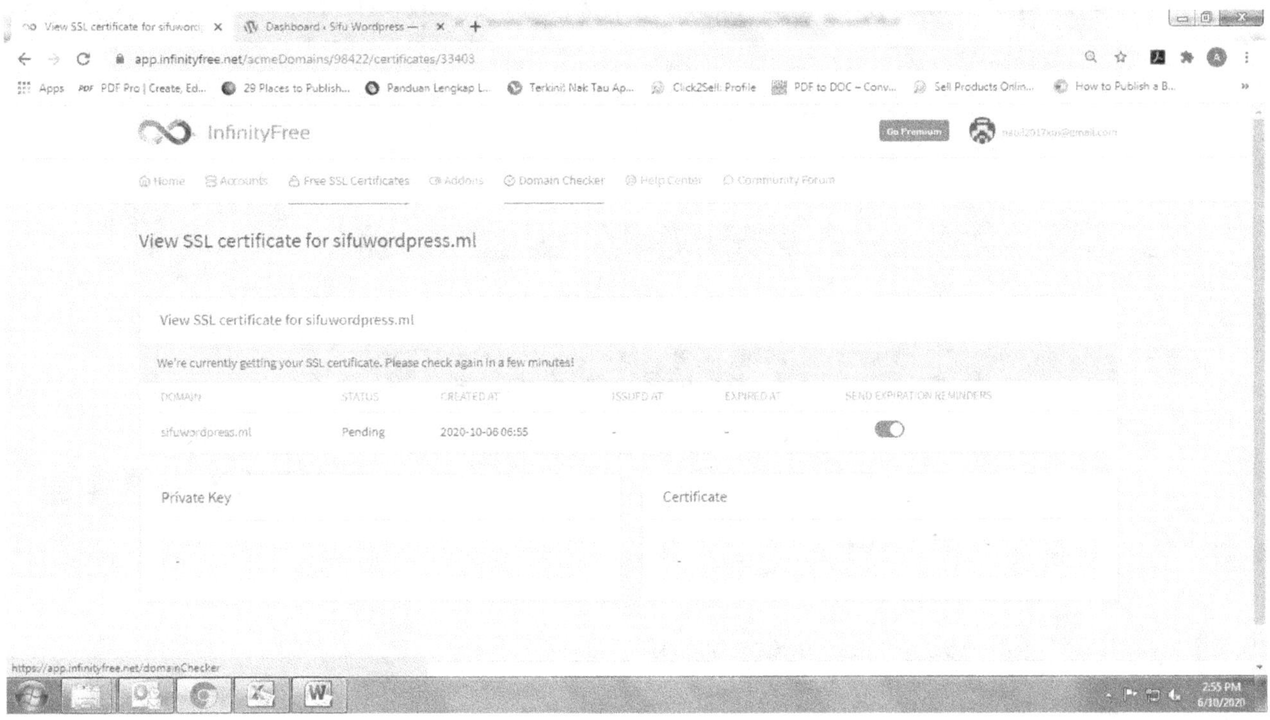

18. After refresh, Private Key and Certificate will appear. This is the Private Key and Certificate that we will copy and paste near the control panel (Cpanel) SSL generator.
19. Right-Click Account> open link in new tab> Click Control Panel
20. In the search function bar, search SSL / TLS> Click on the icon.

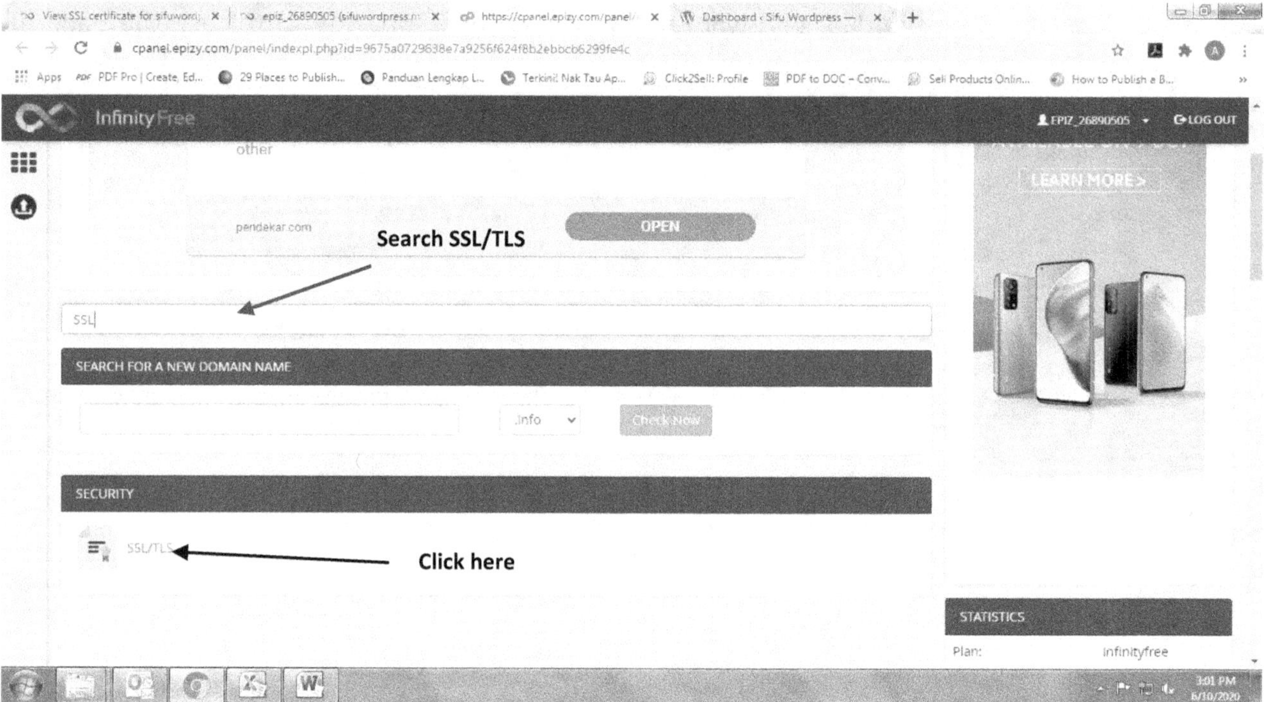

15. Click on 'Configure SSL' > Click on Configure

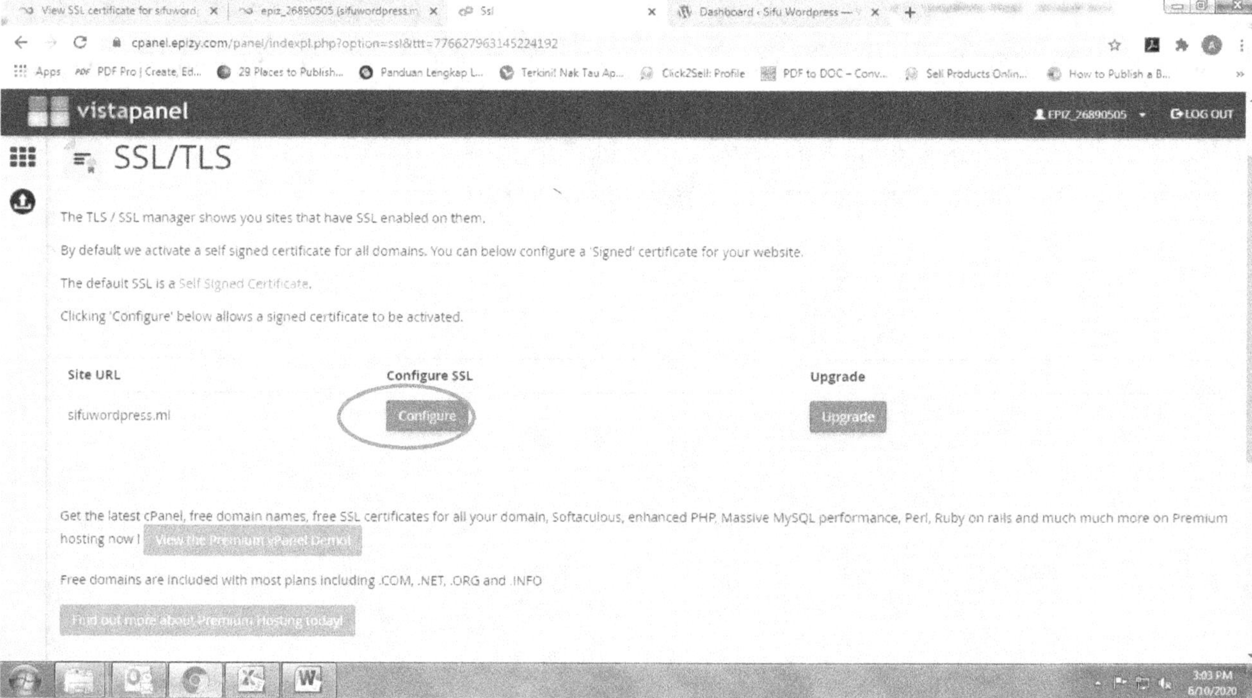

21. Here you need, copy and paste the Private Key and Certificate given earlier.

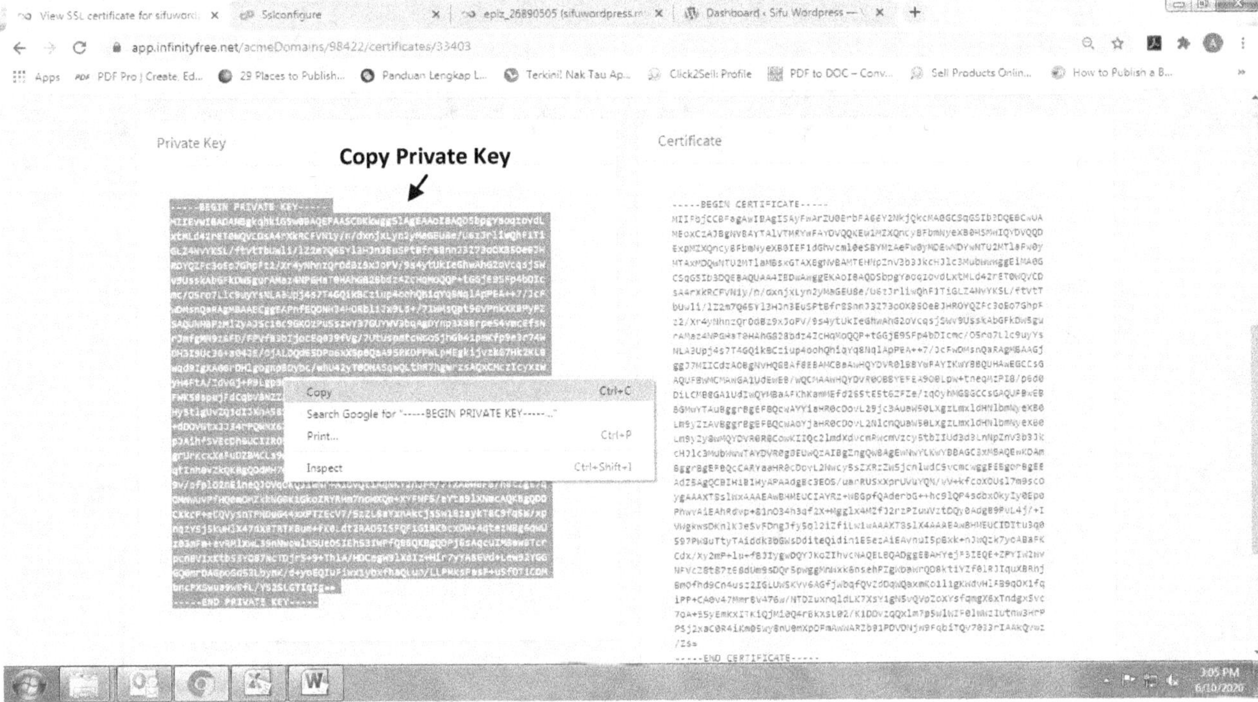

22. Paste in the Private key Cpanel column

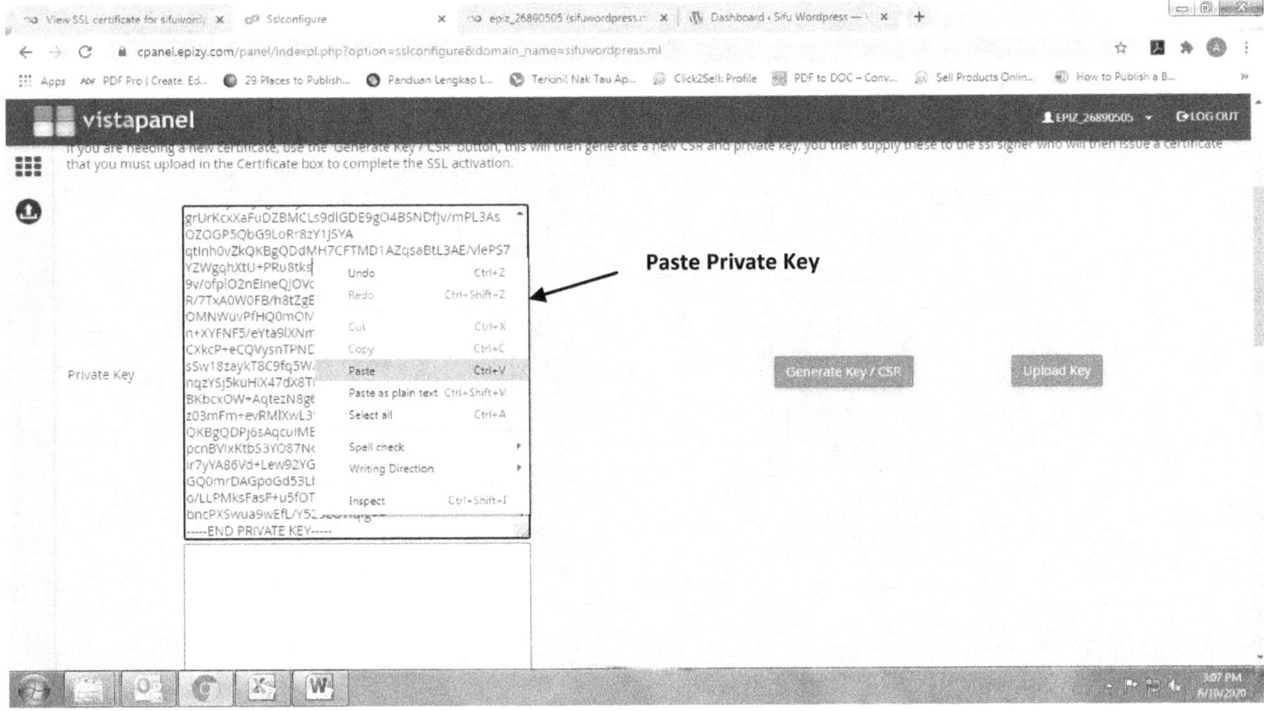

23. Click on 'Upload Key'

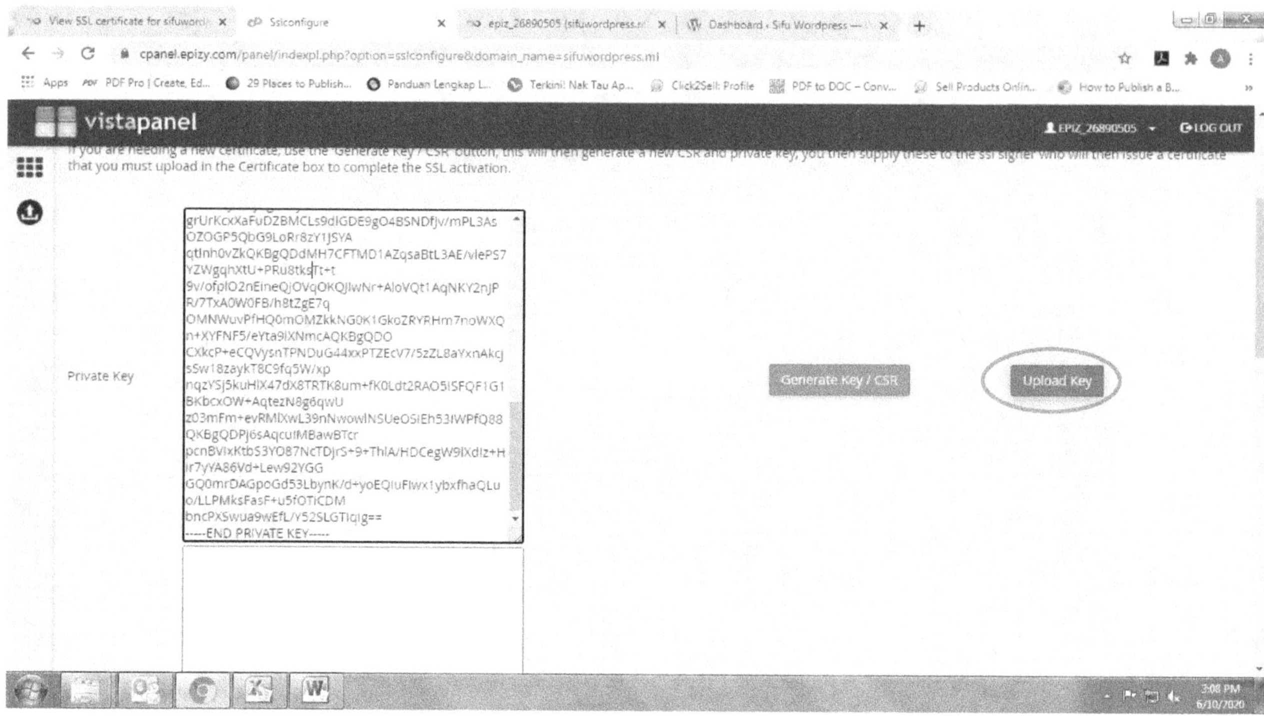

24. After that, copy Certificate

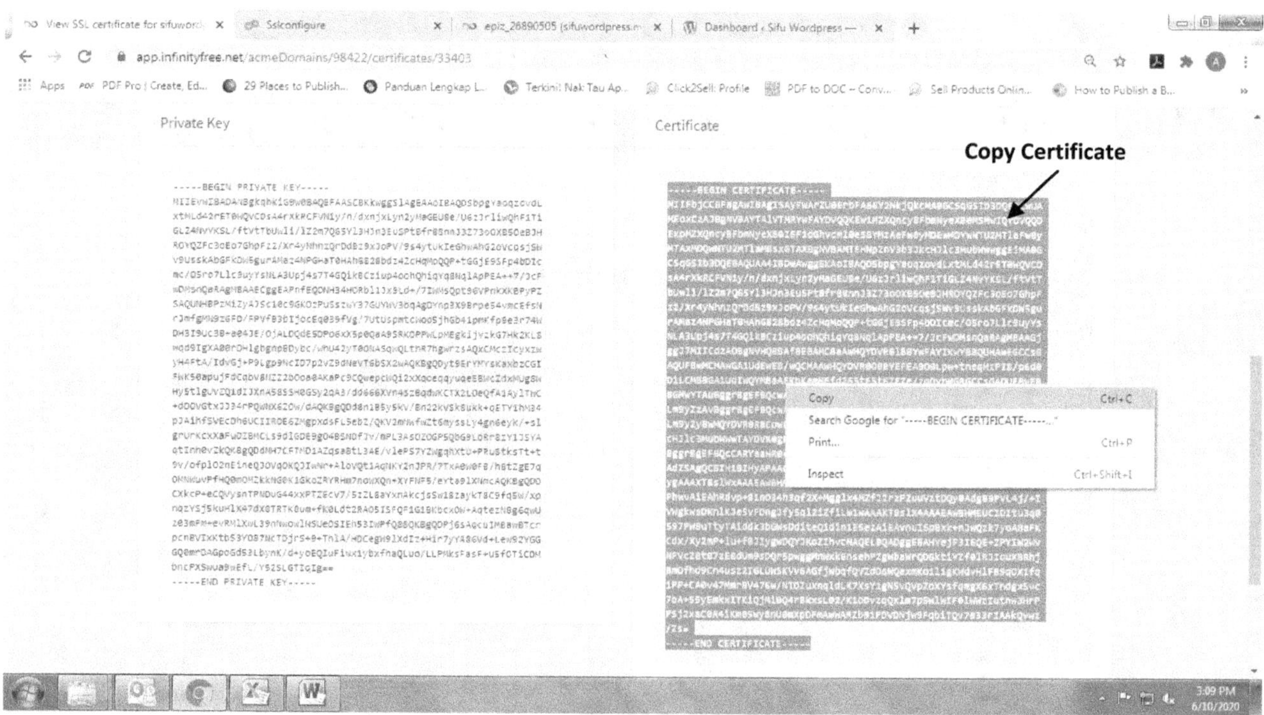

25. Paste Certificate in Cpanel column for certificate

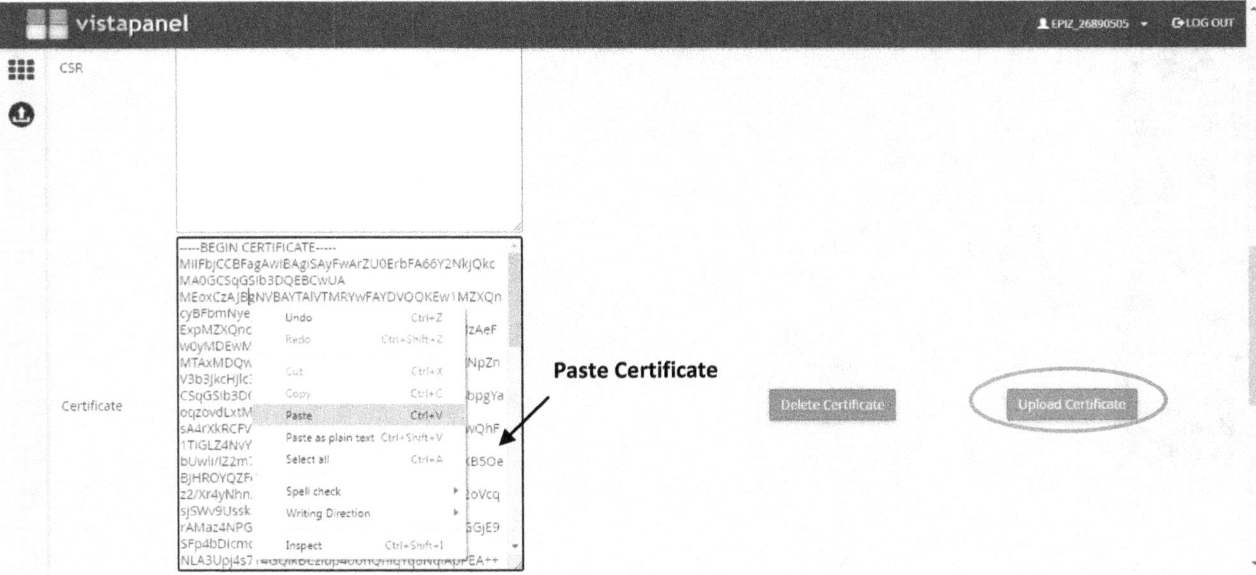

26. Click on **'Upload Certificate'**

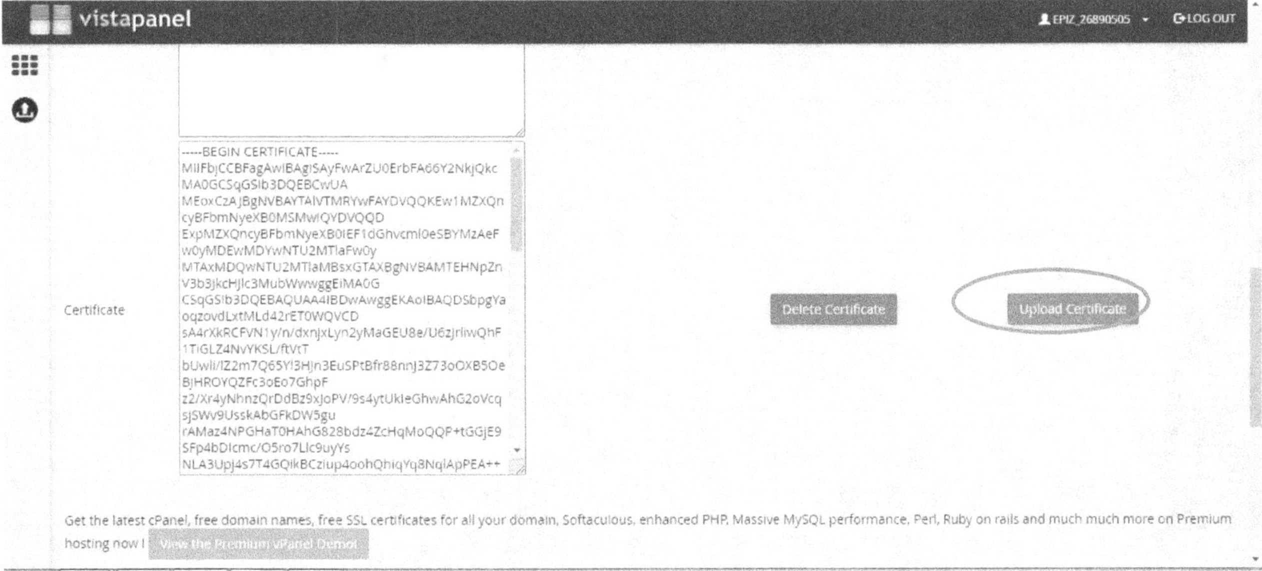

27. Open your WordPress. Go to your WordPress website Dashboard.
28. Go to Plugins> Click on Add New

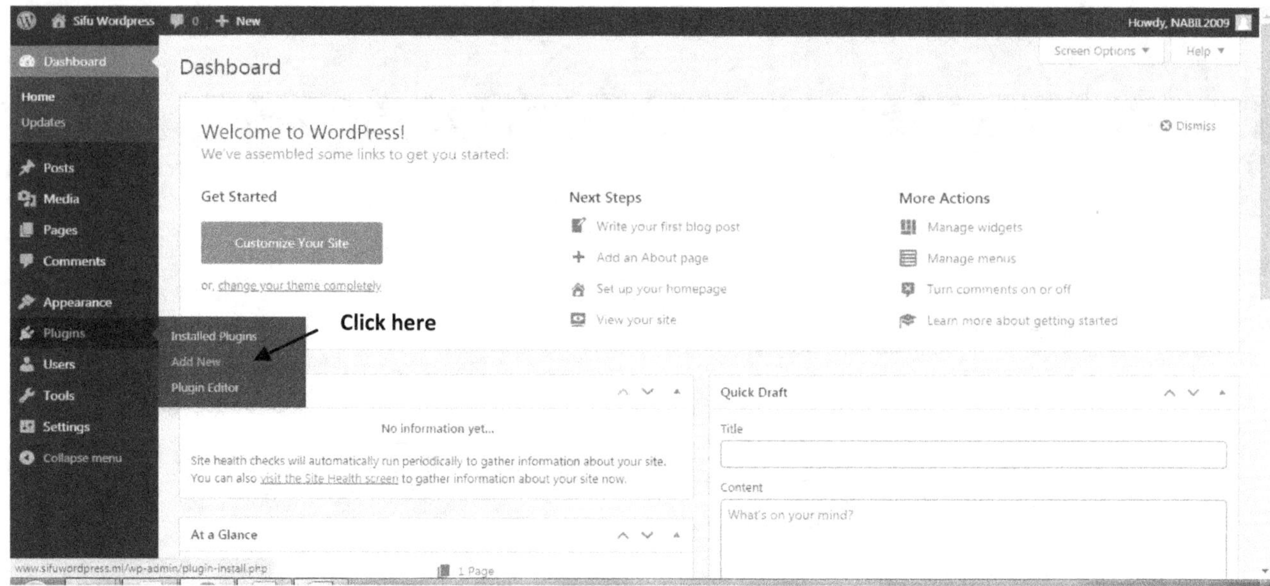

29. Search for 'Simple SSL' plugins

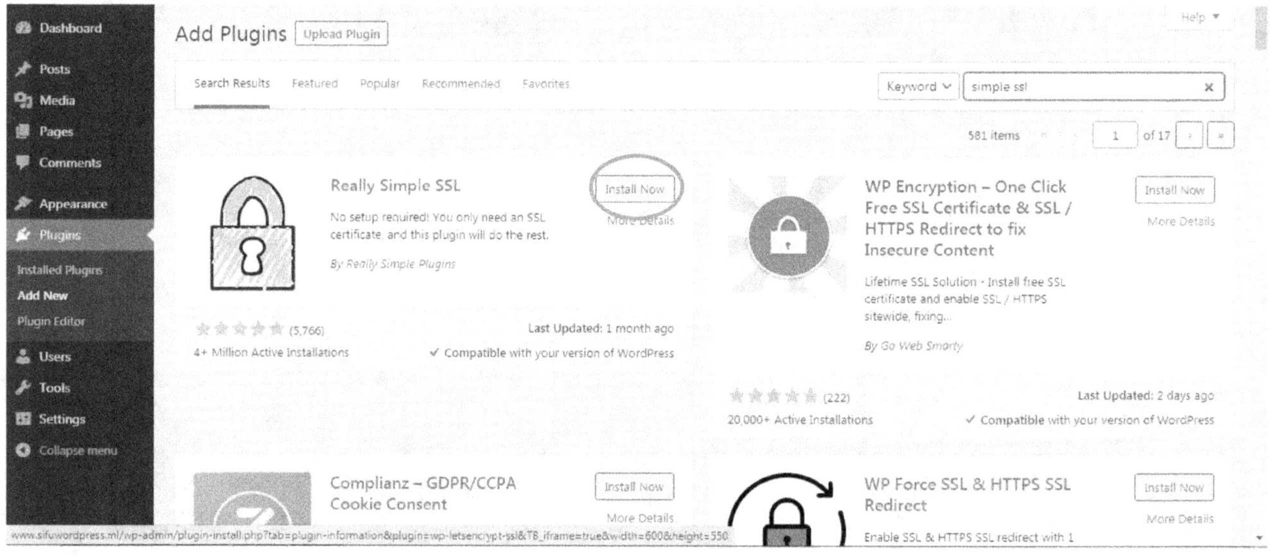

30. Click on Install Now

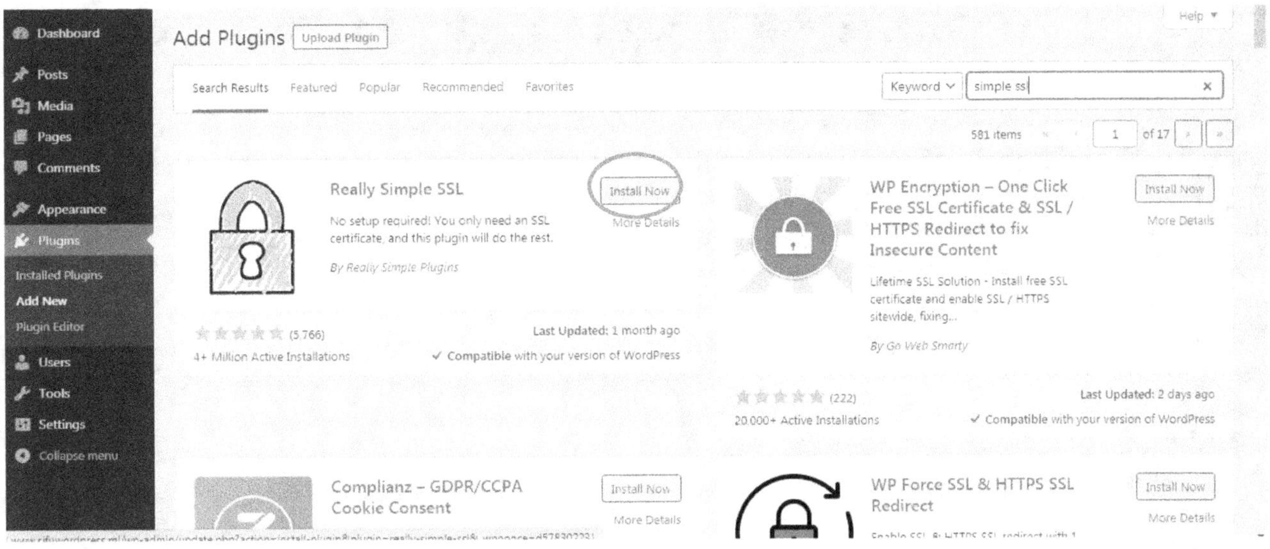

31. Click on **Activate**

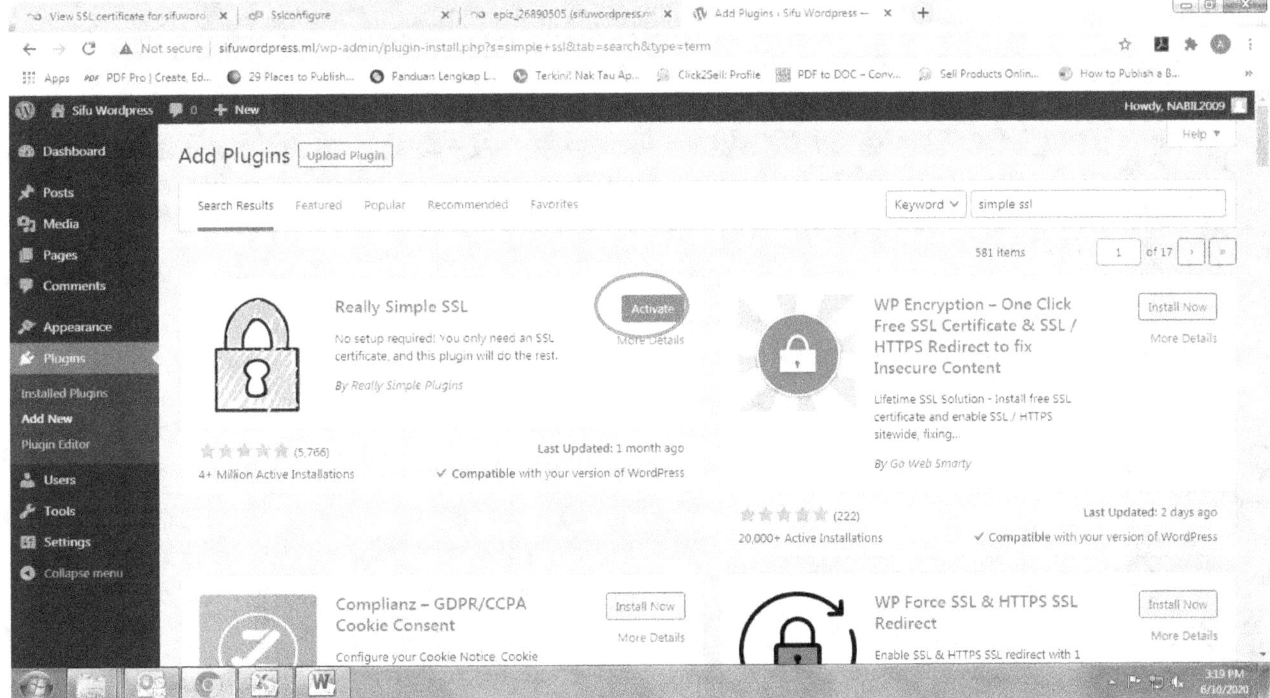

32. Click on **Reload over https**

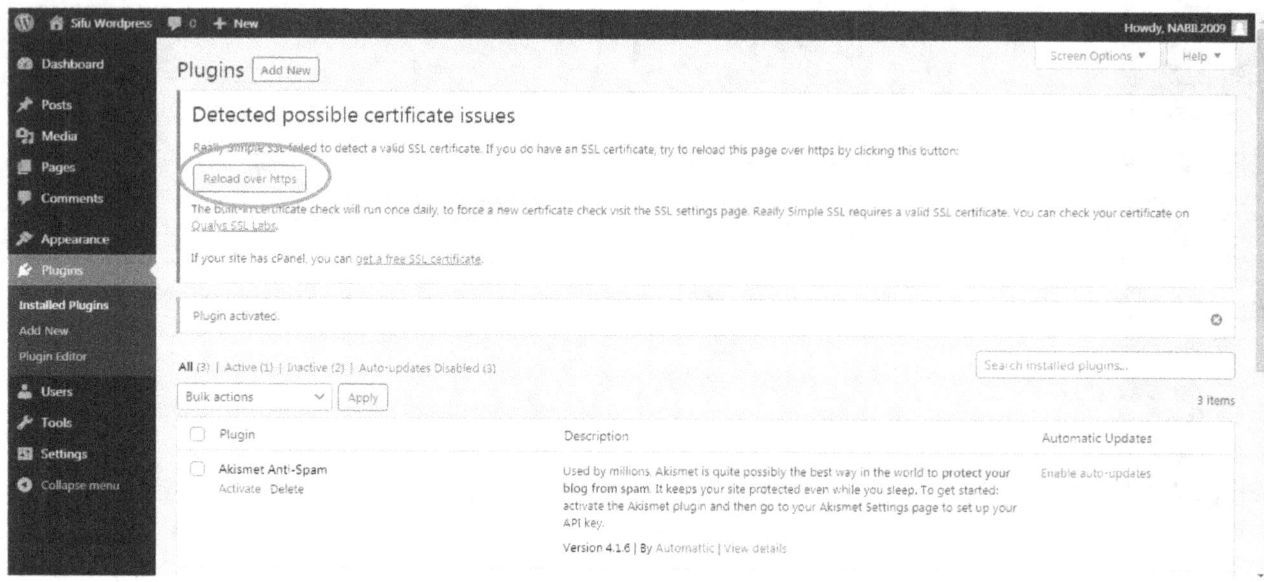

33. You need to Log In again. Log in and you will be taken to SSL activation page.
34. Click on **Go ahead, activate SSL**

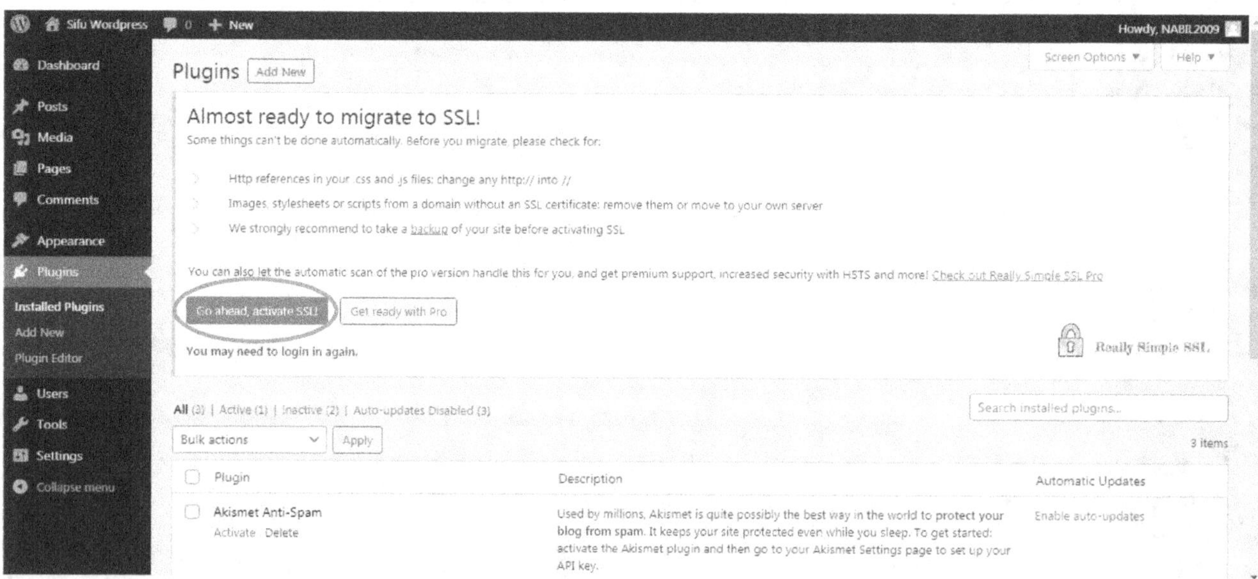

35. Log in to your Wordpress account.
36. Click on **Enable**

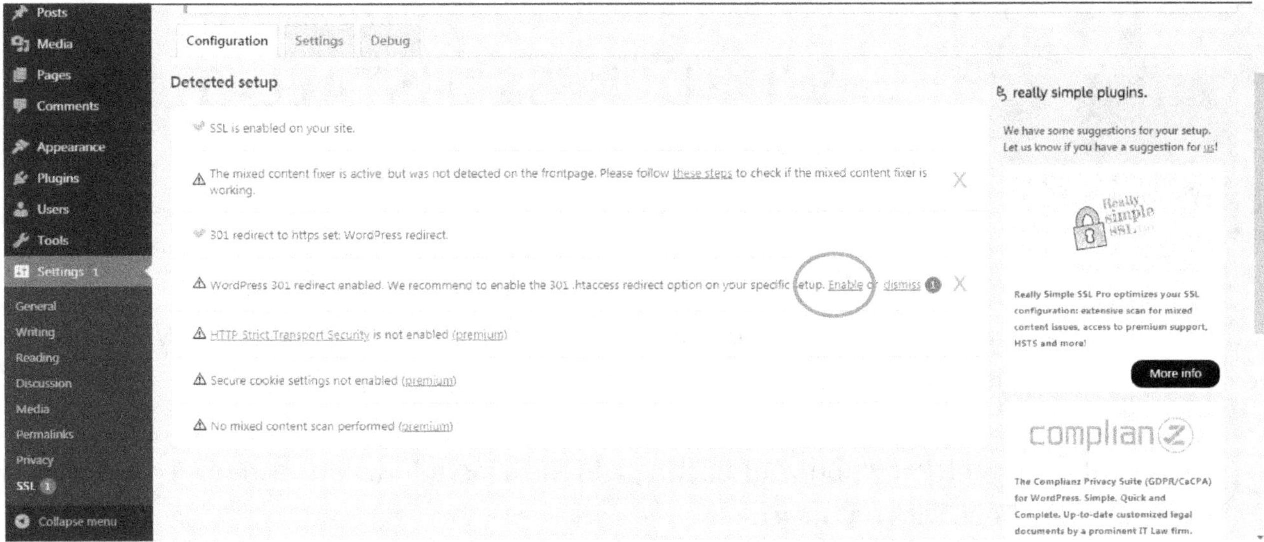

37. Swipe to the right on **Enable 301 .htaccess redirect**

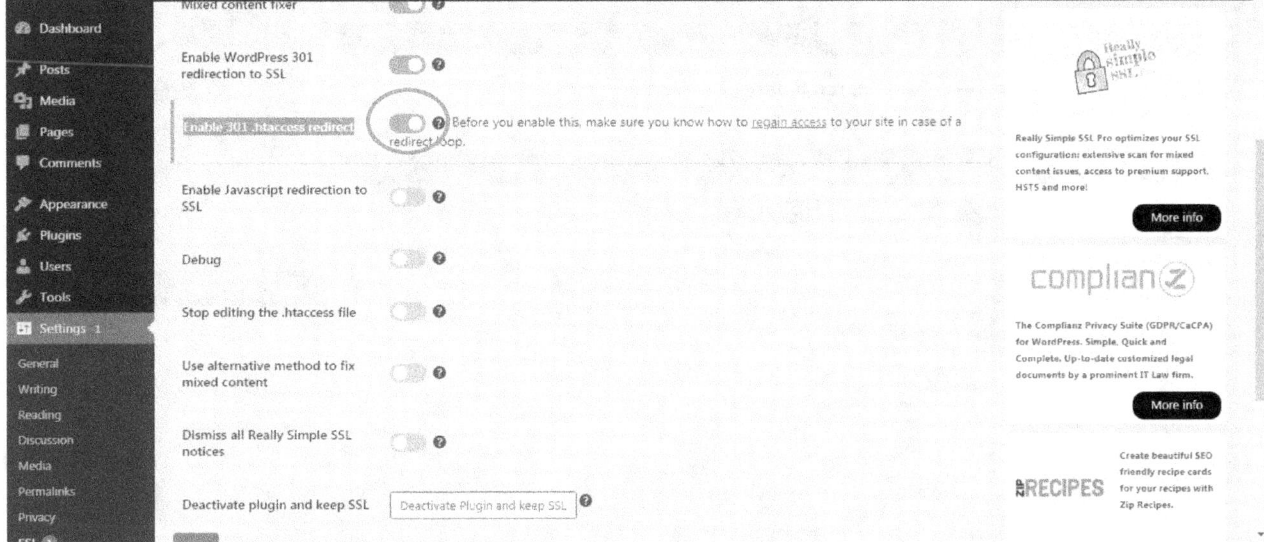

38. Scroll down and Click on **Save**

Congratulations, SSL has been activated. Your website is secure.

WORDPRESS INSTALLATION

Now, the long-awaited time has arrived !. We will install WordPress for your website. WordPress is one of the best web hosting for me because WordPress is easy to use.

1. Go to Control Panel (cPanel) on your hosting > In the search function section> Type **Softaculous Apps Installer**> Then click on the icon

2. It will automatically open a new tab > Go to Top Scripts. Notice a WordPress Logo > Click Install.

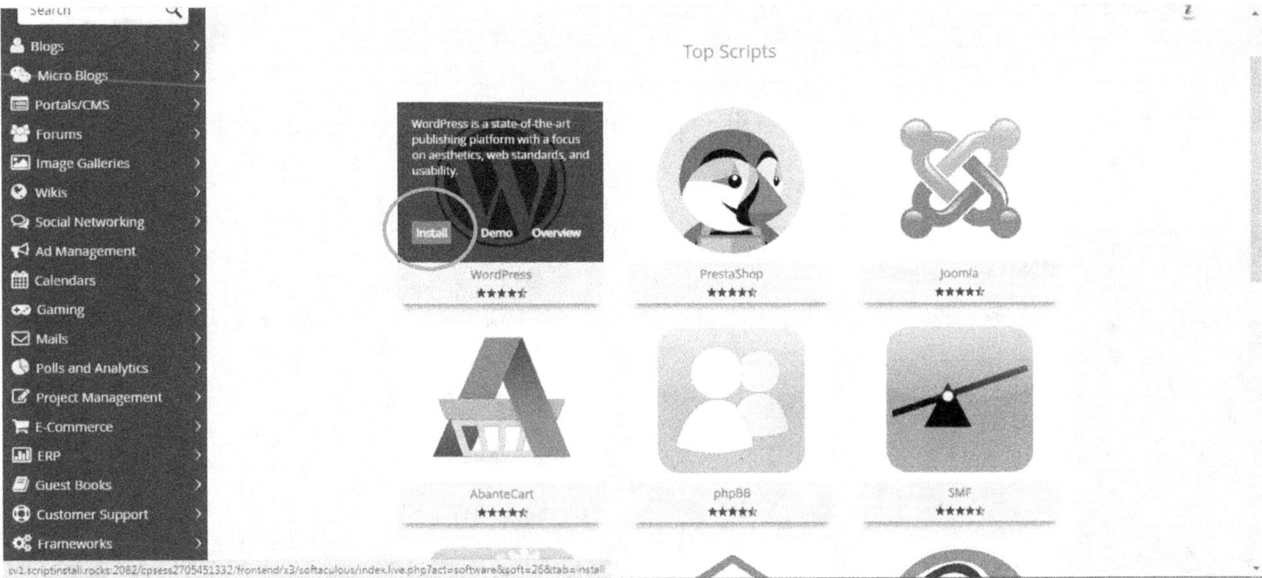

3. You will be taken to the WordPress info section. You need to fill in the relevant information about your website.

4. Choose installation url> http://www. (Important note: We can change to https: // www. After our SSL certificate is confirmed. Do not worry. Check back on our Cpanel whether it has been verified or not. If your site has been verified, continue to Step 15 in Chapter 4.

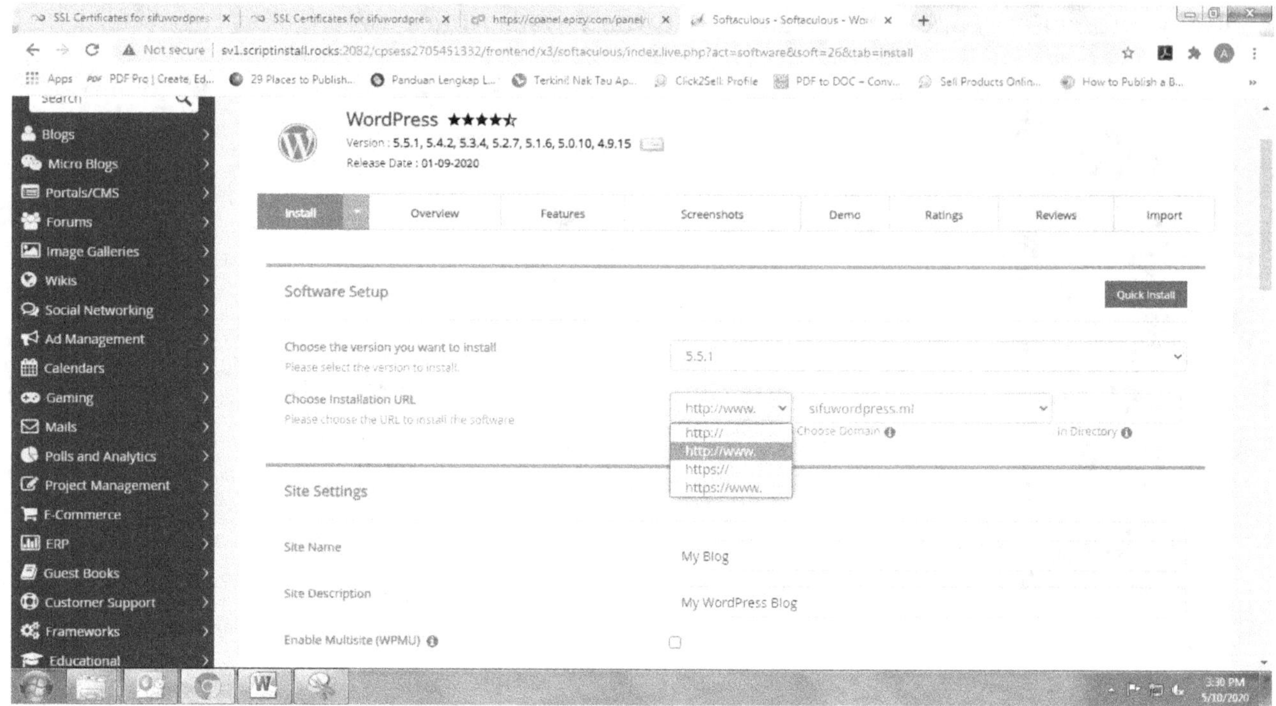

5. In the Site Settings> Site Name> Fill in the name you want to use. I will put the name Sifu WordPress

6. Fill in your username> password> email
7. Select the Language you want to use
8. Under Advanced Options> Auto Upgrade> Do not Auto Upgrade
9. Advanced Options> Table Prefix> wpnx_

10. Scroll down > Click on Install

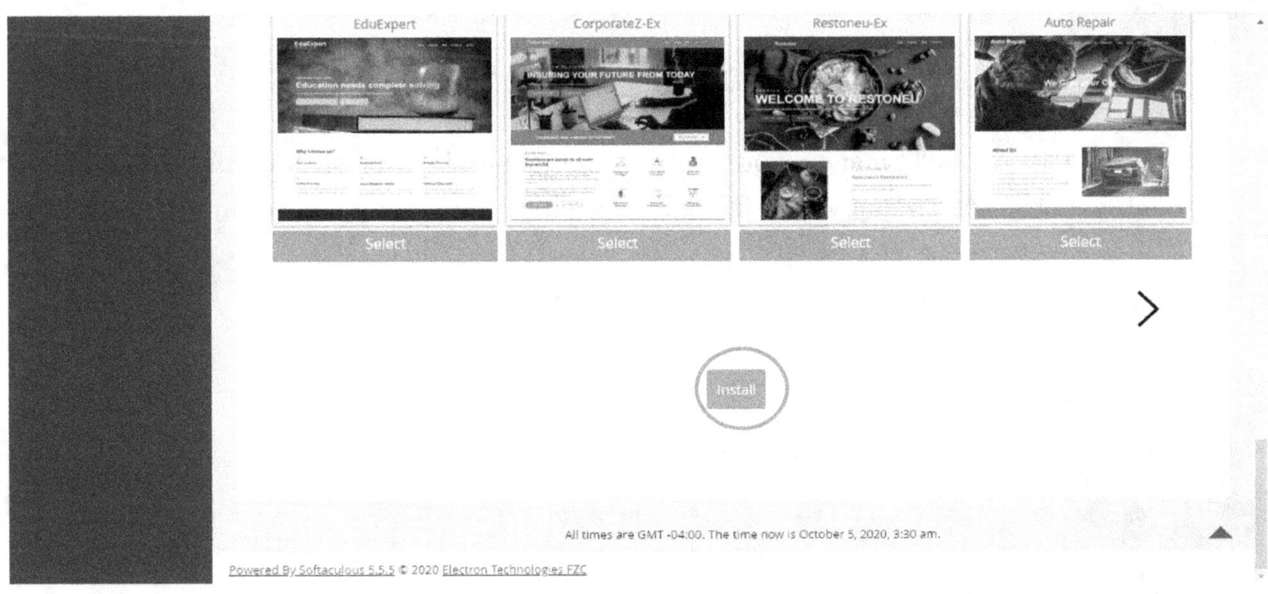

11. You need to wait for a while to install. Take 2 - 3 minutes like that.

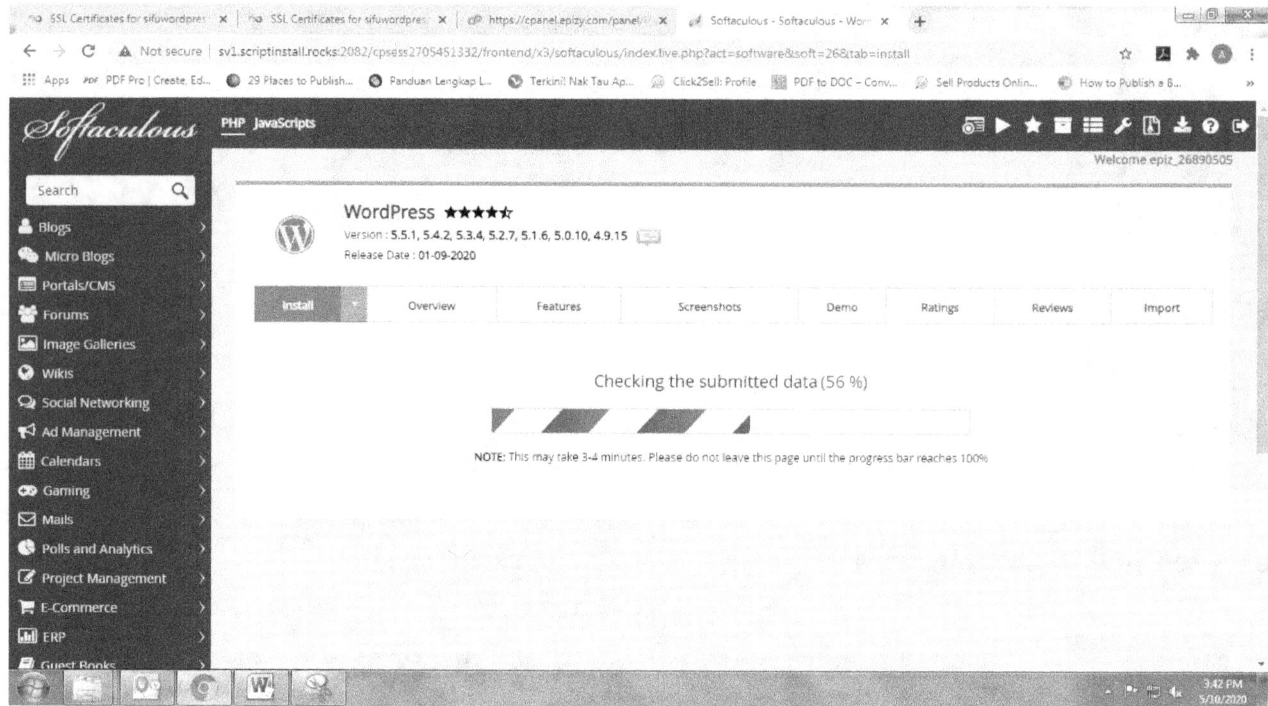

12. After installing. You will be given your website domain and administrative URL. Remember, this admin URL link is the reason we use this link to log in to a WordPress account.

Note: To change to https: // www. , you can follow Step 15 in Chapter 4.

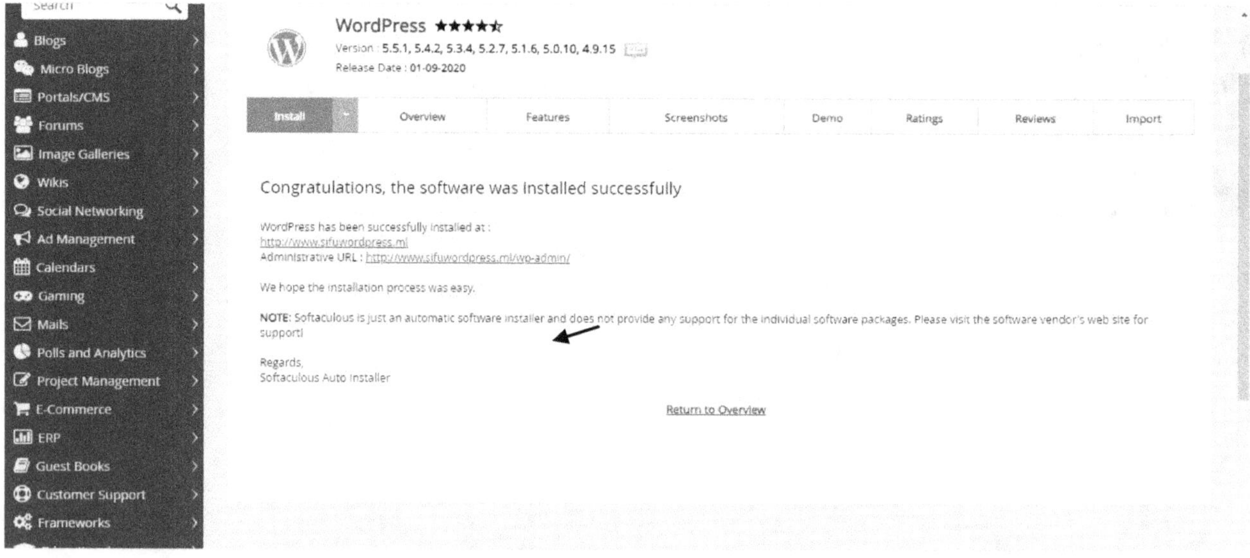

13. Open a new tab window in Google Chrome> type the URL link as you get it.

14. Type <your website> / wp-admin and Log In Username and password.

15. Well done, you already have a WordPress account. Here you will edit and decorate your website according to your liking. We will learn it in the next topic.

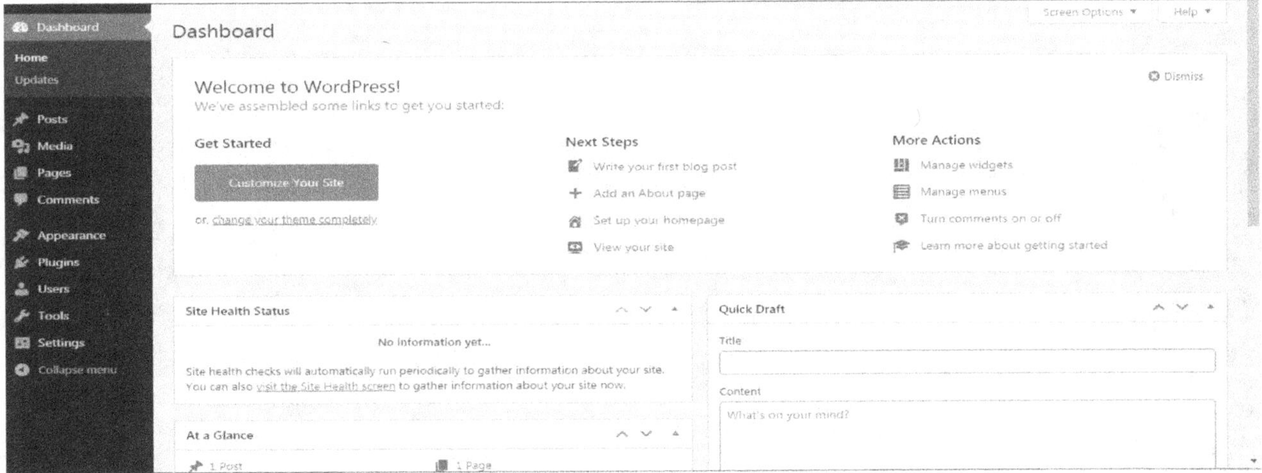

MAKE YOUR OWN WEBSITE

This is the most important topic where I will teach you to 'set up' your website beautifully. Do not worry if you have no experience before, because I will cover all the WordPress knowledge on this topic. First of all, first, log in to your WordPress account using the URL that was sent to your email. My example is as below:

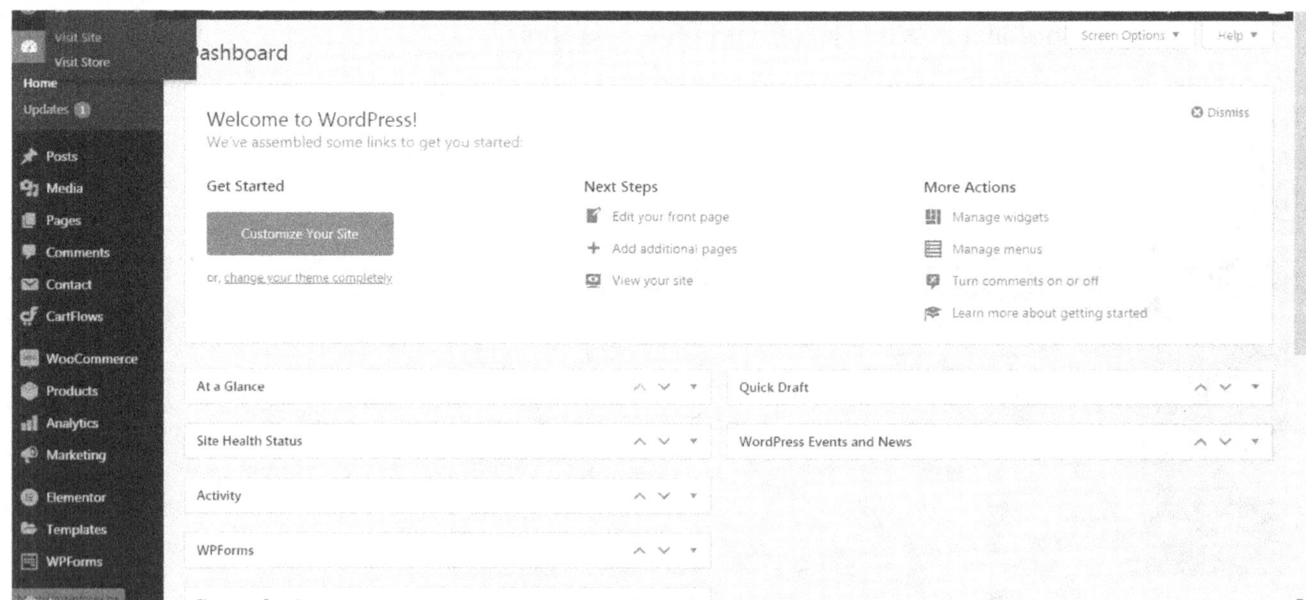

Search URL http: // www. <domain name>. <domain> / wp-admin and press Enter. Then, Log In, enter your 'Username' and password.

You will be taken to the Dashboard. Here is a place to 'control' extensions, plug-ins, and edit your website.

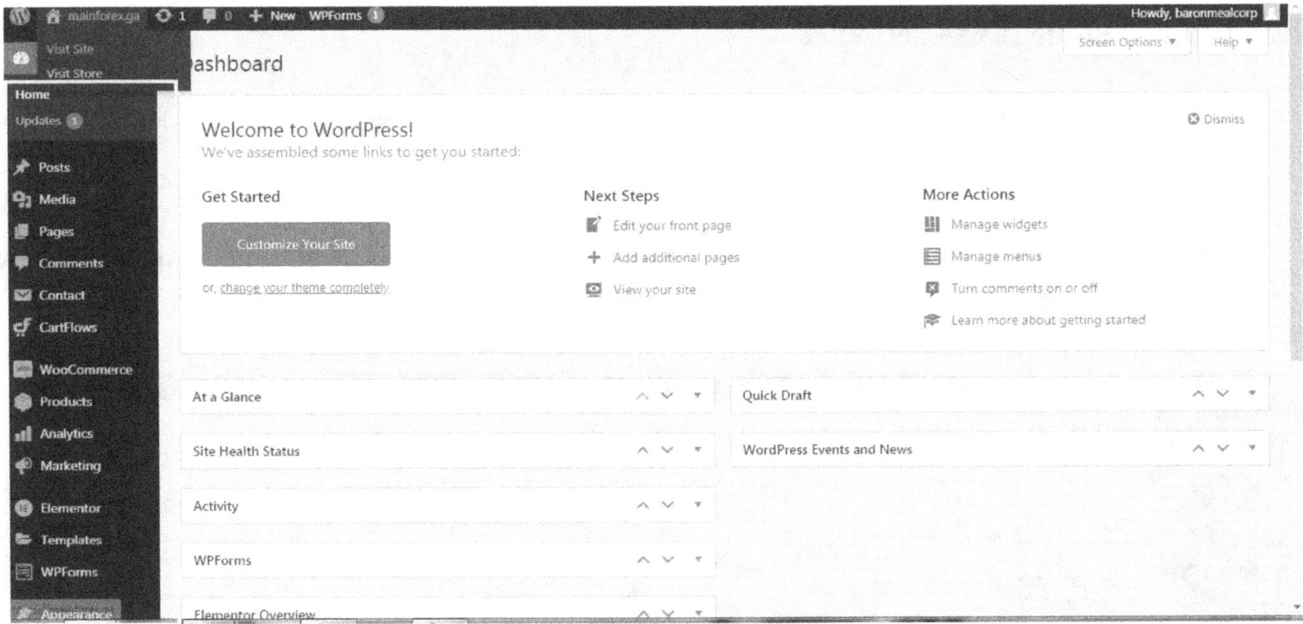

In the left corner, is the panel. I categorize as below:

- **Post -** For control post on the website. Examples of how to edit your Facebook post or status.
- **Media -** To upload pictures or videos in your gallery.
- **Pages -** To edit website pages.
- **Plugins -** Install and activate the necessary extensions.
- **Appearance -** Select and edit themes / Widgets / Templates and editors
- **Users -** To control users who can access/use your WordPress account / Edit profile.
- **Settings -** General Settings / Website Title / Tagline / Time / Date

Well, we consider our website to be like our new home. The important thing before we want to decorate our house, we must need a decoration plan, right? So, we will choose the appropriate themes according to your liking. But before that, you need to choose the necessary items for home decoration that we call Plugins. Plugins are code or extensions that are added to your website and serve to develop WordPress functions.

<u>Elementor – Plugins (Page Builder)</u>

1. Click on Plugins> Add New. There are many types of plugins here and each one has a different role. Some are paid and some are free.

2. Search for Elementor Website Builder> Install> Activate. (Note: Over time, plugins logo will change. So make sure you download the correct plugins).

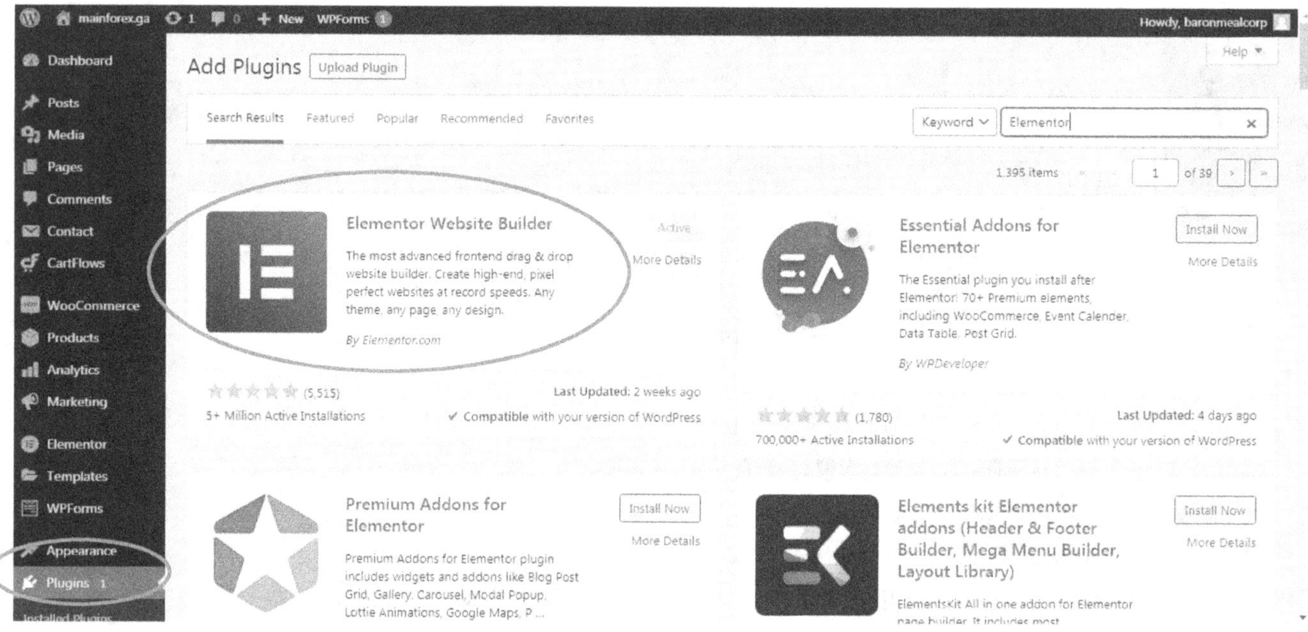

Wordpress Themes : Free Themes (Featured)

Now, we will select themes for our website. Some are free while some are paid. However, if you lack capital, but you want to build an e-commerce website, you can build only with a free theme. It is not impossible to build it, but you have to build from scratch. I will show you one by one.

1. Go to Appearance> Themes. Here you will see free themes for blogs like Blog Mantra or corporate websites like Corporate-Ex, Twenty Nineteen, Twenty Seventeen, and Twenty-Twenty.
2. If there are any that you like, you can go to those themes and Click Activate.

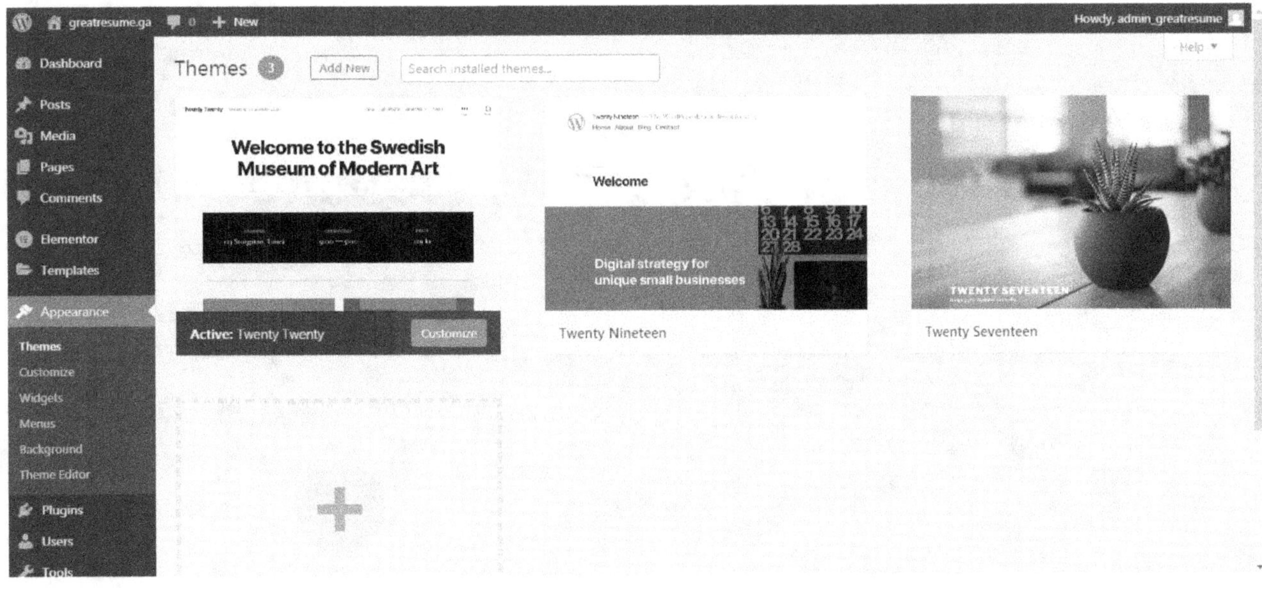

These are all free themes. No hidden fees. It can be used to create simple blogs, landing pages, and websites. If you do E-commerce, I recommend a blank theme as your theme. You need to build your website from scratch.

My objective in publishing this book is to teach beginners out there who are just about to start building their website without any capital. If you already know the basics, then you can create it using paid and trusted domains such as domain hostwinds, 000webhost, and Godaddy.

1. After you are done choosing the theme. In the WordPress menu, Click Appearance > Click on Customize.
2. You will see the task panel on the left side of the customize page

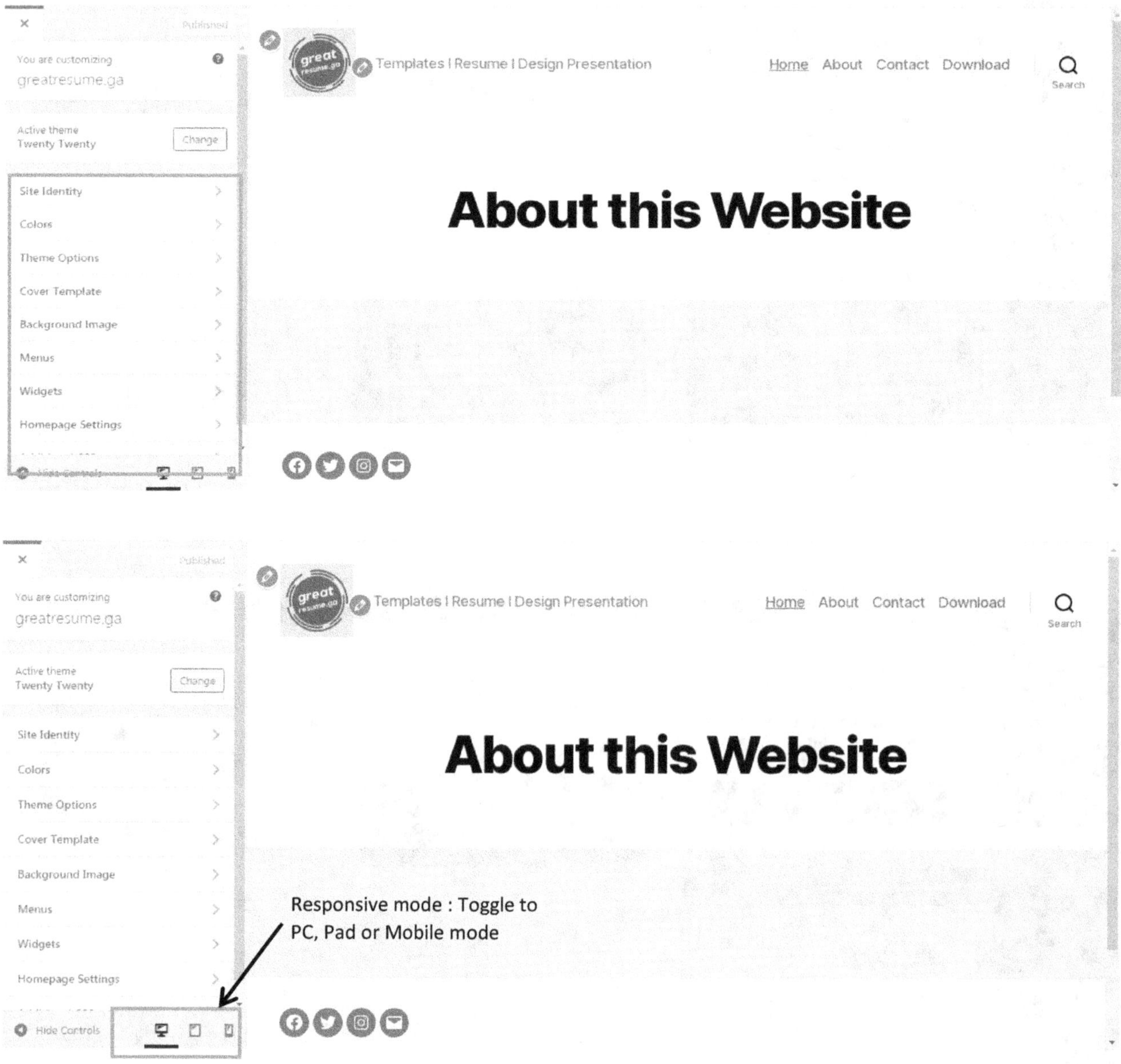

3. This is an example of Twenty Twenty Themes.
4. All free themes have the same settings and functions.

<u>Home page – Set Home page</u>

The homepage is the first page that your audience will see. You can place your product intro or your brand intro with copywriting.

5. Click on Homepage Settings

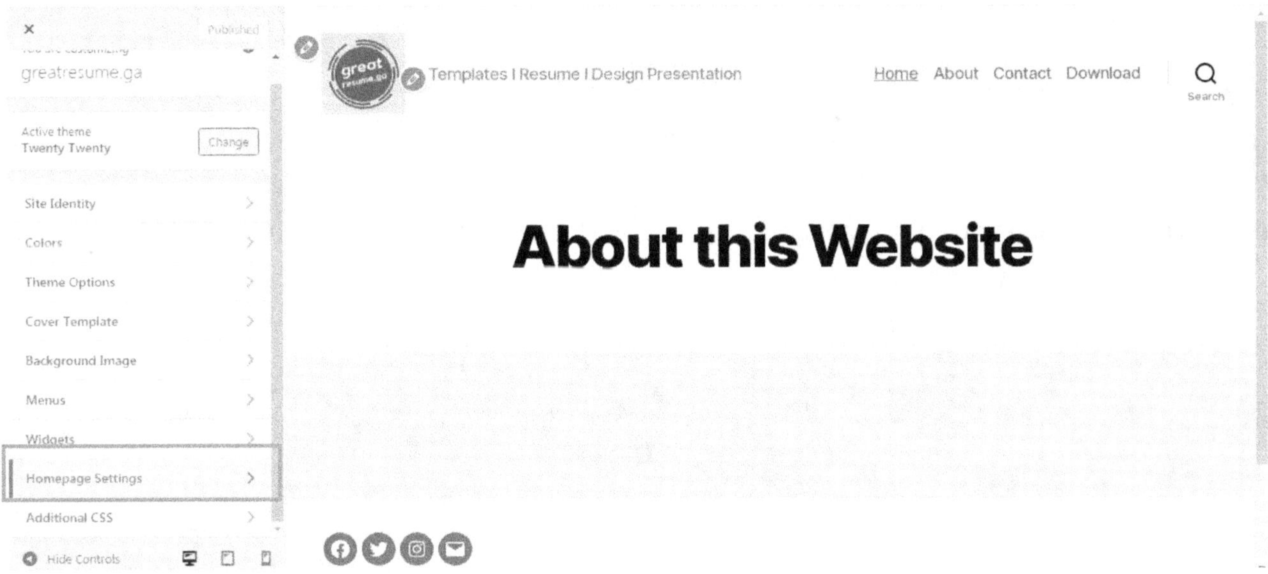

6. Your homepage displays > You can make your homepage to be static, meaning your homepage is not displaying any content other than the page you set.

7. Select which page should be your Homepage and your Post page.

8. Or you can make your homepage to display your latest posts. The updated post from you is will be the first page your audience sees.

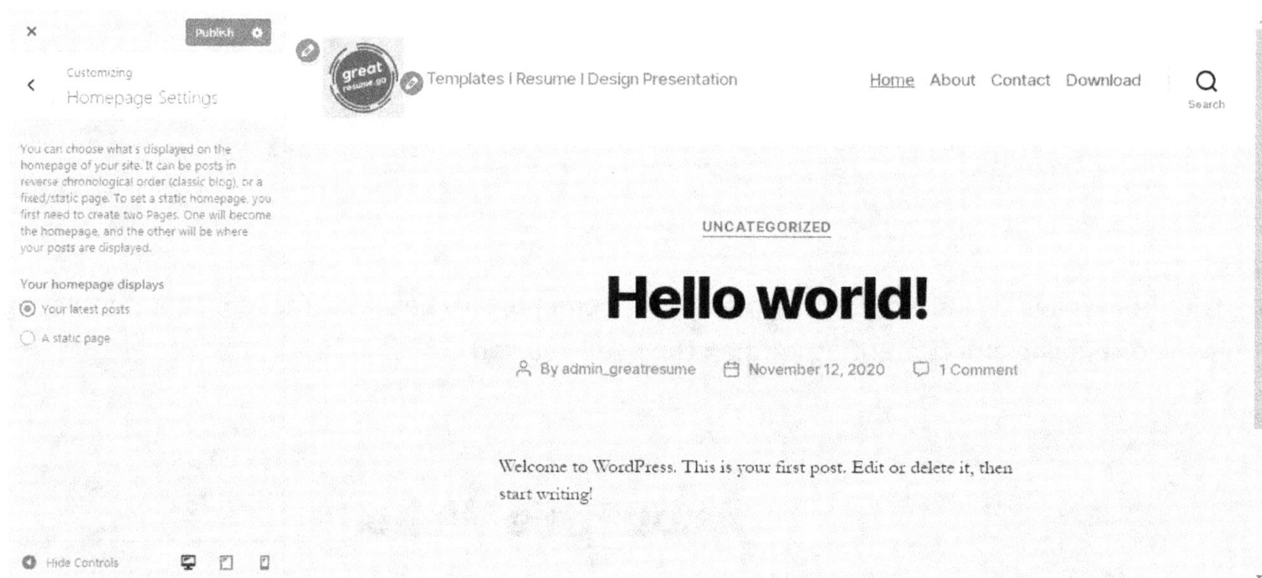

Menus

9. Click on Menus

10. Here, you will be editting Top Menus (Primary) and Social Links Menu (Bottom Menus).

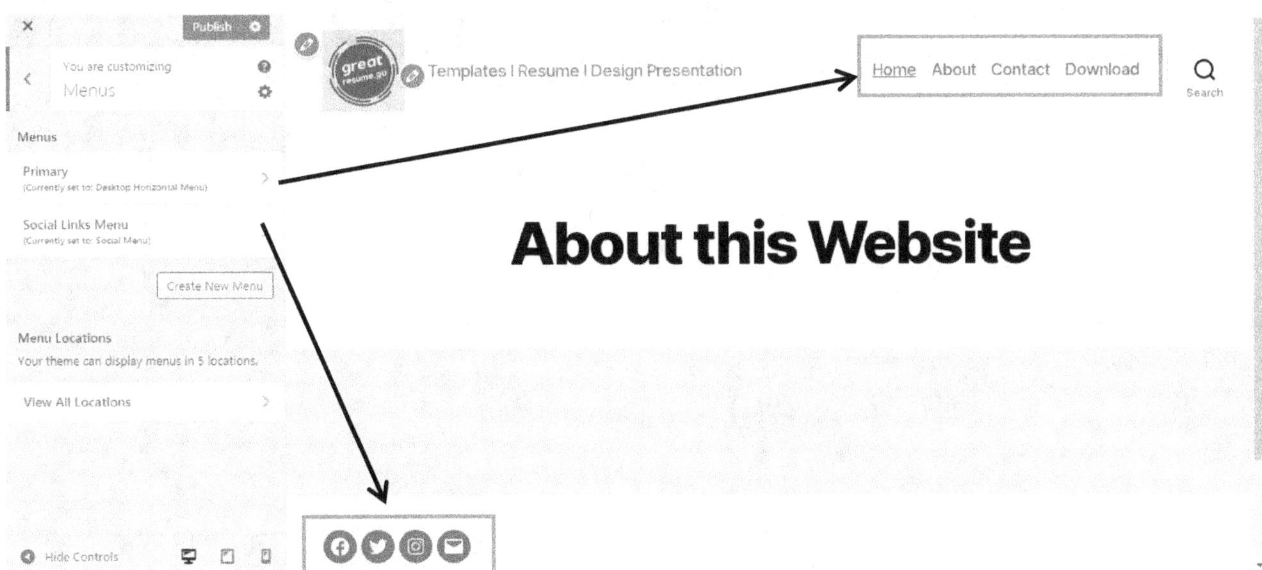

11. You can include any pages you wanted in your menus. To select pages > Click on Primary.

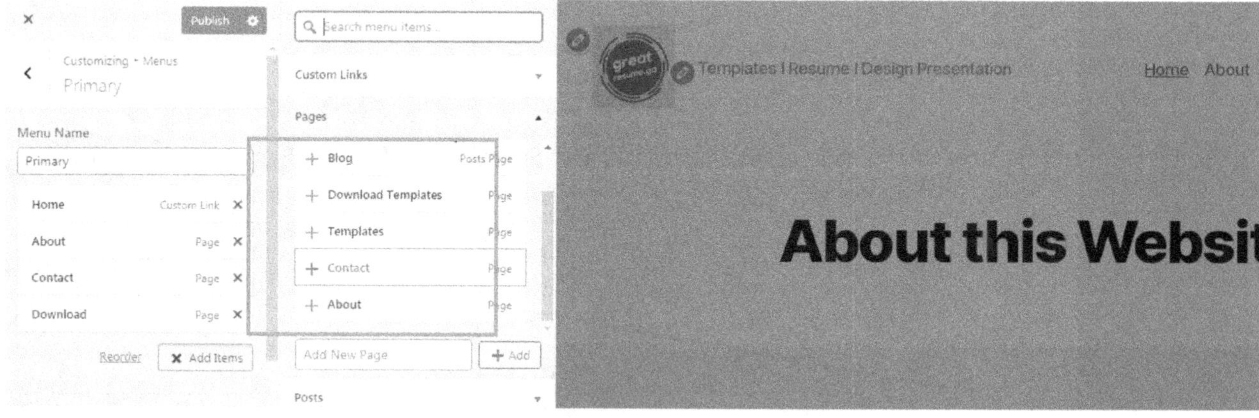

12. If you want to remove a page in your menus, simply click on that page > Scroll sown and you will see Remove > Click on it

13. I will get back to Meuns Setting after finished editing the Home page, Contact page, About page, and Download Page. It is because we need to insert the URL of that page here for it to be directed. To do that, we first must edit these pages. I will show you at the end of this chapter.

Website creation for professional needs such as online store business websites and others certainly needs to be built carefully.Don't just determine the exact theme and domain address.But also a few small details, one of which displays the favicon on the website's display.

Before discussing further, the first thing that you should understand is the definition of what a Favicon is. Favicon itself is short for *"favorite icon"*. The complete definition is a unique icon on a website that functions as the identity of the website. The favicon itself appears in the browser tab and at first glance its size also looks tiny.

Usually, the size of the Favicon will be adjusted to the type of platform used, whether it's Google or iPad and iPhone. The following are the recommended Favicon sizes on several platforms that can be used as a reference during the manufacturing process:

- The Google platform is recommended to use a 96 × 96 size.
- The Opera Coast platform uses a size of 228 × 228.
- The Retina iPad platform for iOS 7 and above uses a size of 152 × 152.
- The Retina iPad platform for iOS 6 and above uses a size of 144 × 144.
- The iPad Mini iOS 7 platform uses a size of 76 × 76.
- The iPad Mini iOS 6 platform uses a size of 72 × 72.
- The iPhone Retina platform for iOS 7 and above uses a size of 120 × 120.
- The iPhone Retina platform for iOS 6 and above wears a size of 114 × 114.

Follow the following steps:

1. Click on **Site Identity**

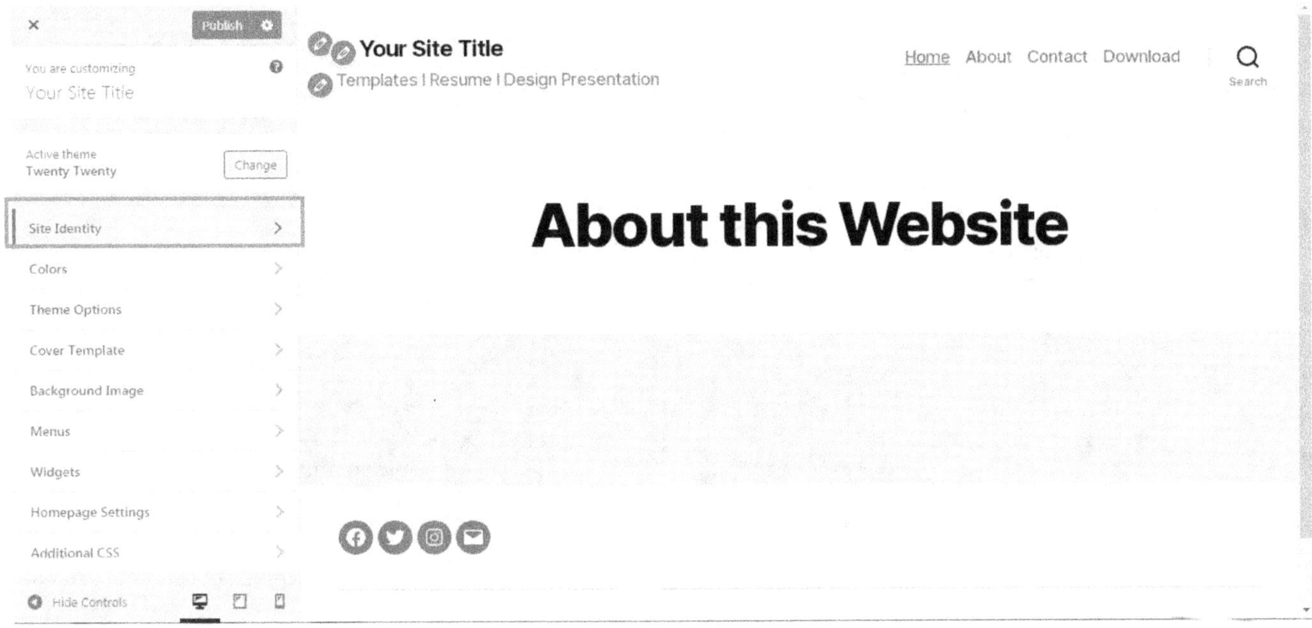

2. This is where to set up you website titles, logo and Favicon. Enter the title of your site under Site Title. Enter/Edit your tagline or you can leave it be.

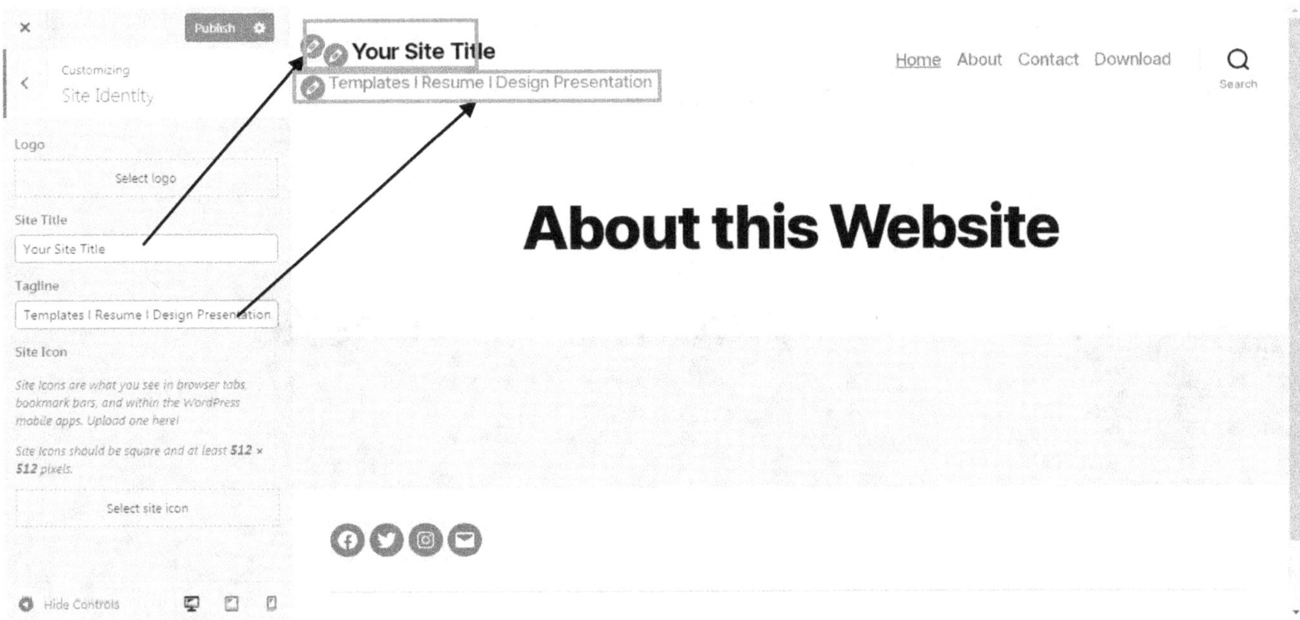

3. You can upload and insert a logo into your website. Click on **Select logo** button

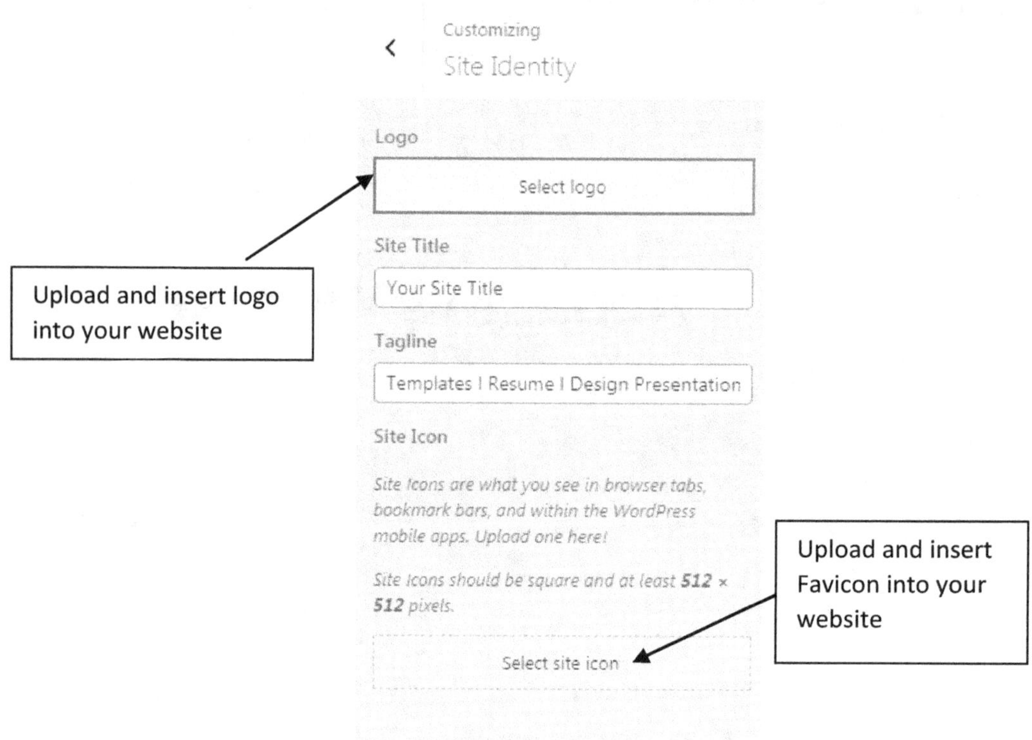

4. Click on **Select site icon** to upload and insert Favicon into your website.

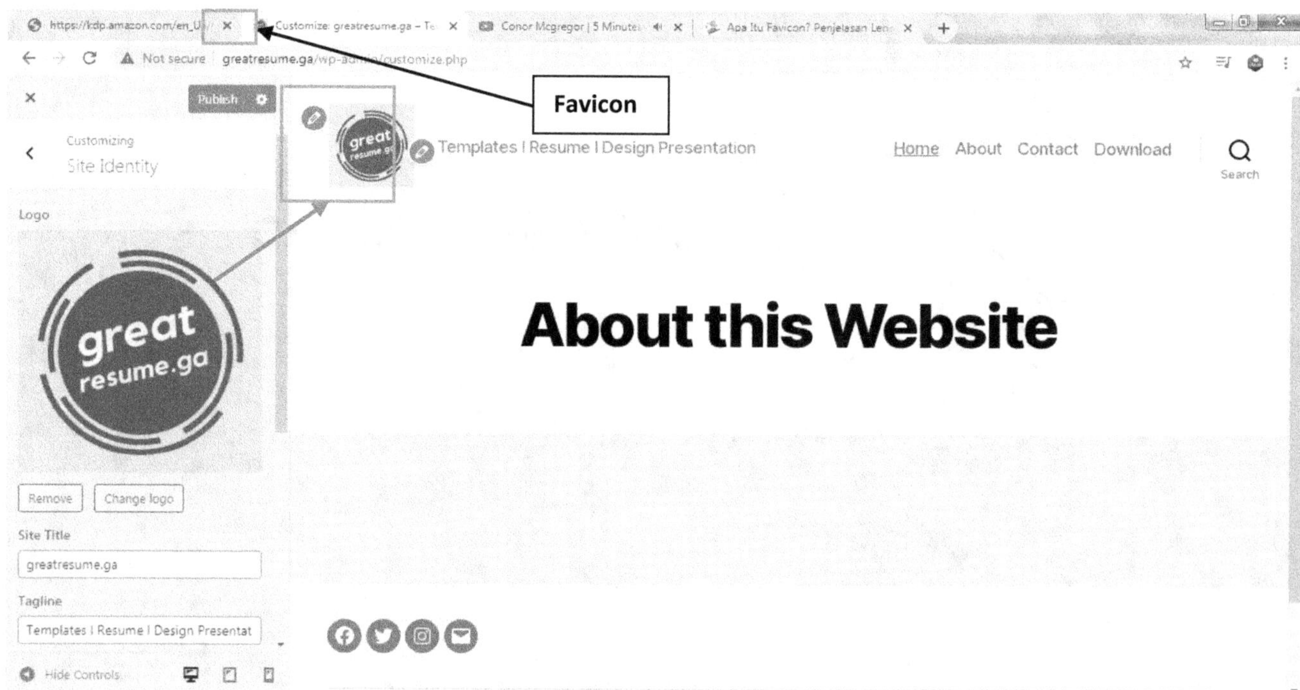

5. You may choose the color of your website to suit your taste.
6. Click on **Colors >** Select any colors you want.
7. In Theme options, you can change the settings of your themes
8. In Cover Templates, you can change the settings of your background and color background text.
9. In Background Image, you can upload and insert background picture on your site.
10. You can customize your widgets > Go to Widgets.

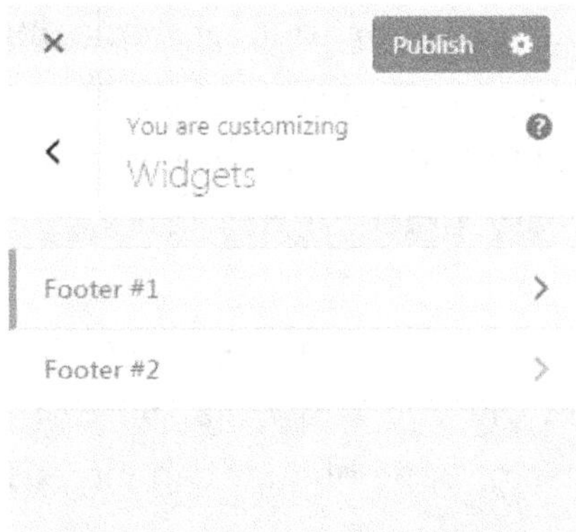

11. You will see **Footer #1** and **Footer #2**. This display the placements of widgets on your site.
12. Footer 1 is on the left on your web page while Footer 2 is on the right or vise versa (depends on the theme used).
13. You can add widgets like images, calendar, video, categories, Meta, Navigation Menu and recent posts on your website.
14. Don't worry, you can also add and edit widgets using Elementor. It's easier. I will show in the next chapter. Select any colors you want

EDITTING WITH ELEMENTOR – PAGE BUILDER

Elementor Page Builder is a live page builder or tool for managing, designing the web, etc. with real-time/live that also provides high-end page design features, high capacity, and Elementor page builder is something new from WordPress. Elementor Page Builder is perfect for you who are a beginner who can help you in creating a website that is easy, practical, and fast.

I like to use Elementor because of its mobile-friendly features. With responsive mode, it is easy for me to update the content of the website. Did you know that 50% of internet users use mobile phones to surf the internet? So, here the best use of page builder can increase the SEO ranking of our website on Google.

In this guide I will show you steps by steps, to edit your pages/posts with Elementor. But first, install Elementor and activate plugin.

1. Go to your pages tab > Click on Edit.

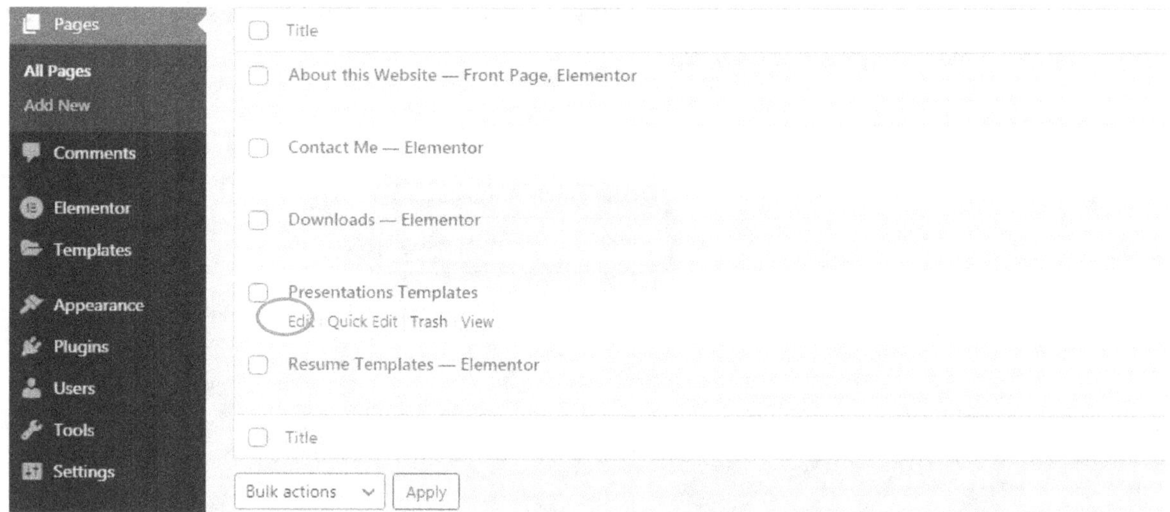

2. Click on Edit with Elementor.

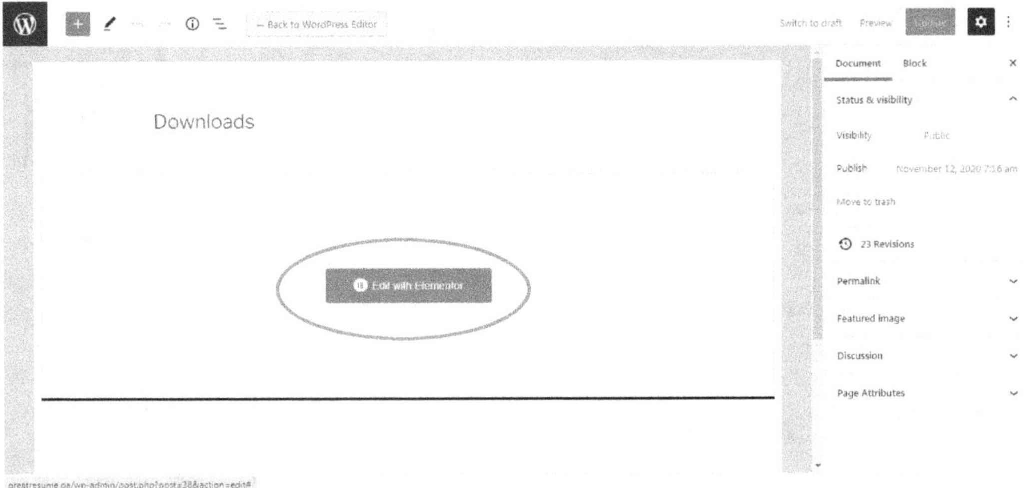

3. You will be taken to Elementor page builder.
4. You can only edit on that particular page that you have selected. If you want to edit another page, you need to exit to Dashboard and select other pages to edit.

You will notice on the left side of page is the widgets options. By using Elementor, you can:

- Edit Text/Header
- Upload and insert images
- Upload and insert videos from youtube
- Adding buttons and icons (etc. buy now buttons, contact us buttons)
- Adding testimonial sections
- Adding tabs selection
- Adding social icons, html options
- Adding sidebar and read more archive

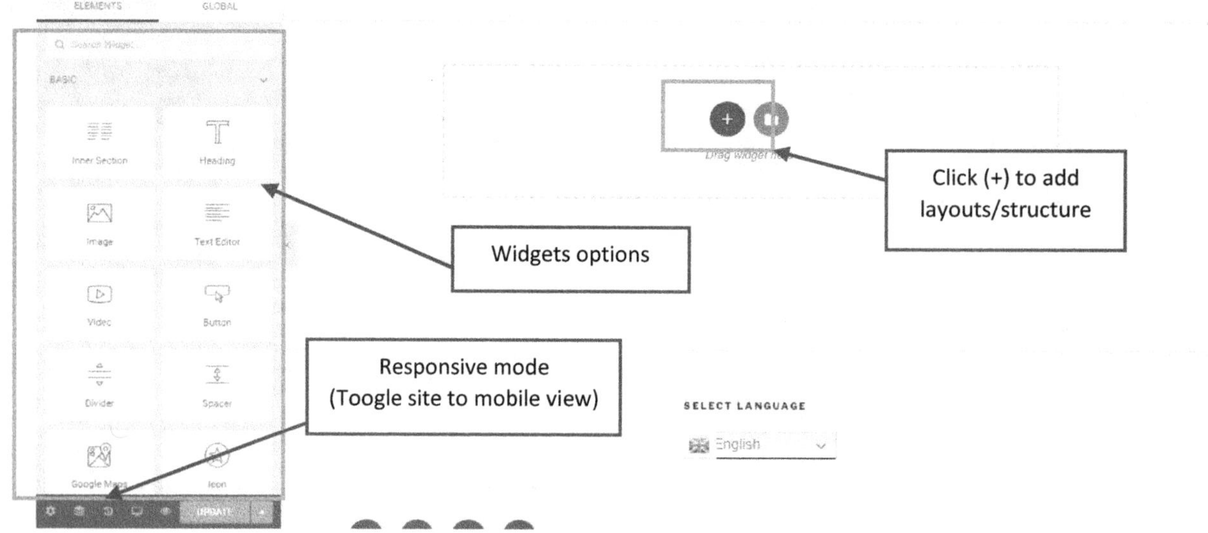

5. First, Click on (+) icon > Select your structure.

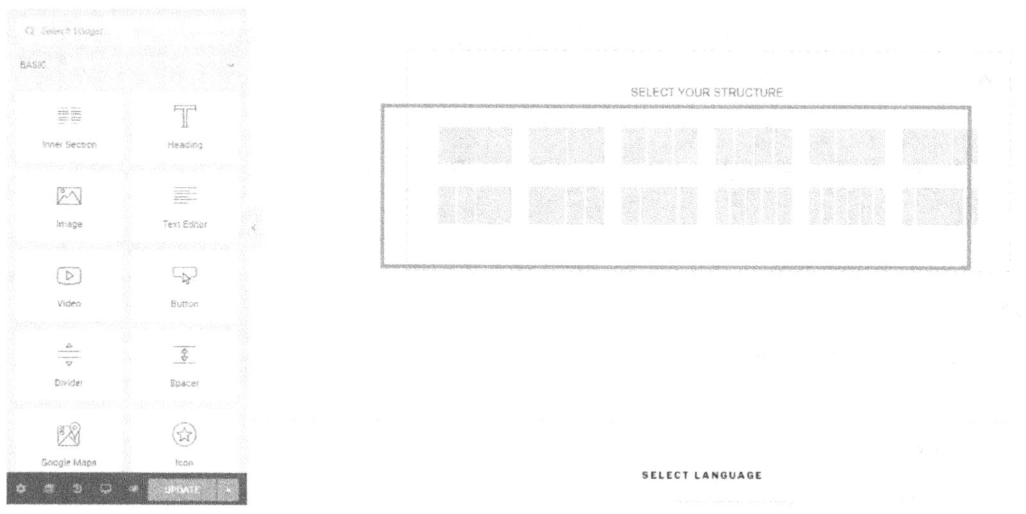

6. Click on the (+) inside the structure to add widgets
7. Simply drag from widgets house to the structure.

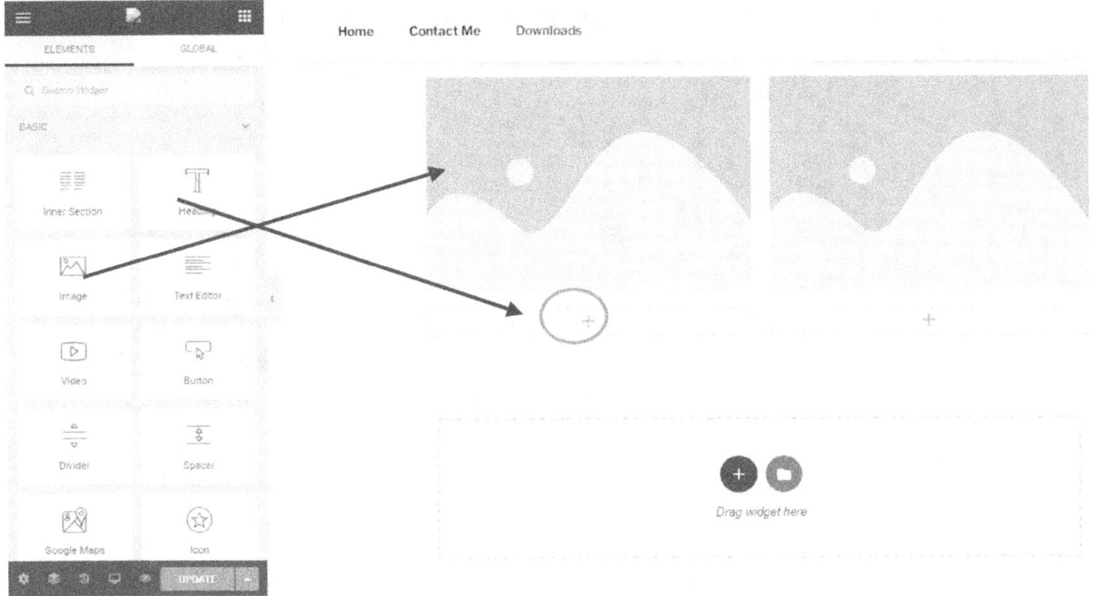

8. Try to add Heading widgets into the structure.
9. You will notice the settings on the left side of the panel. This is where to edit the appearance and style of the widgets.
10. There are three tabs in the setting. Content, Style and Advance.
11. The first tab is Content settings. This is where you can edit alignment of the text and the text content (See on the next page).

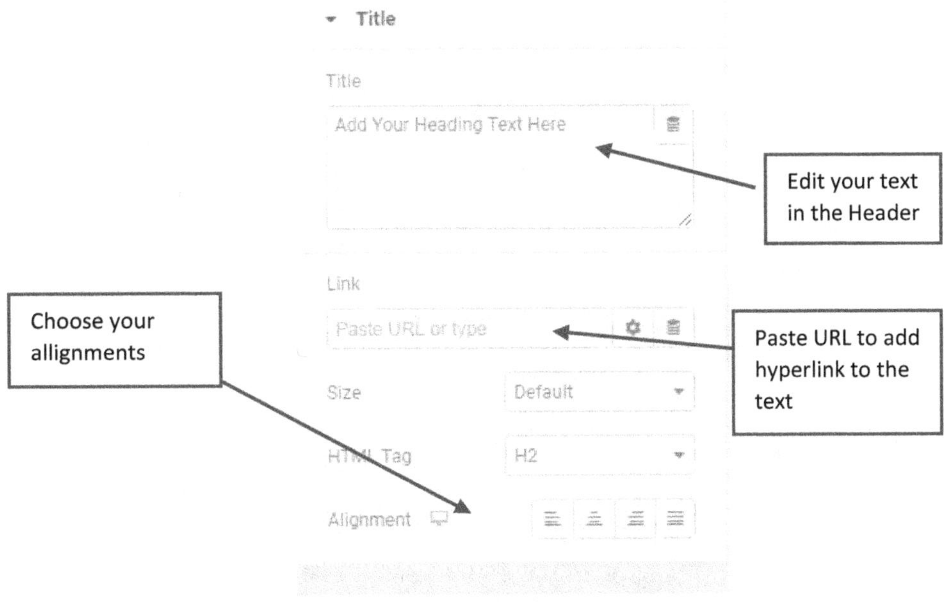

12. In second tab, you can edit Text color,typography (the size of the text) and text shadow.

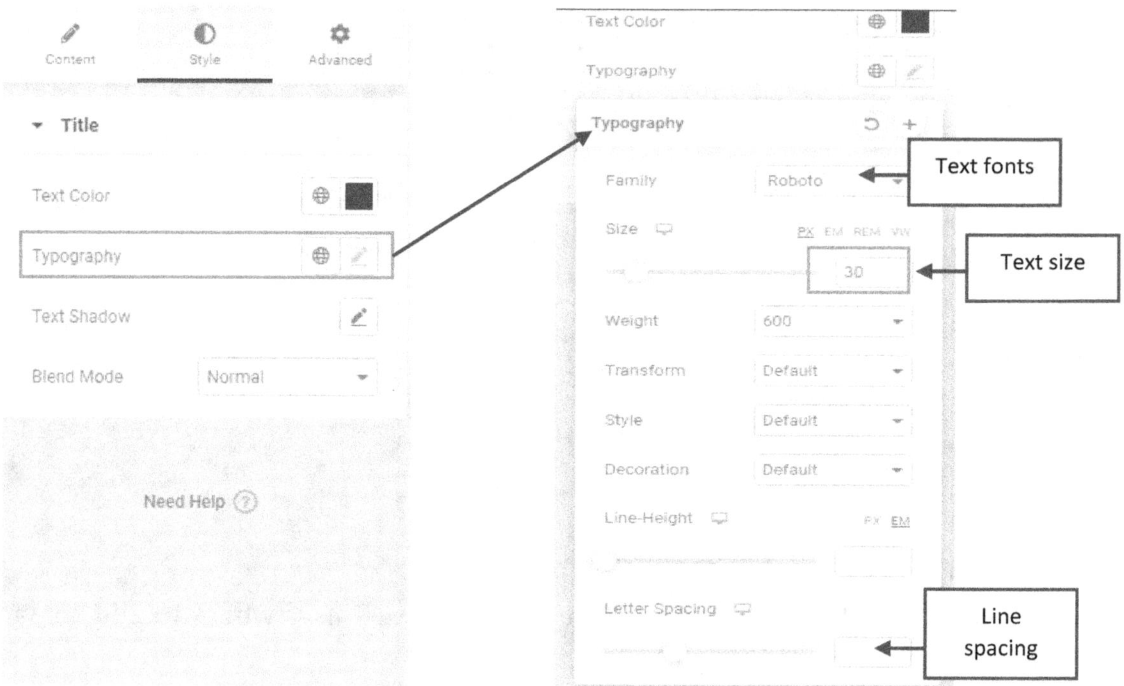

13. In third tab, advance options such as animations, motion effects and positioning can be edited.

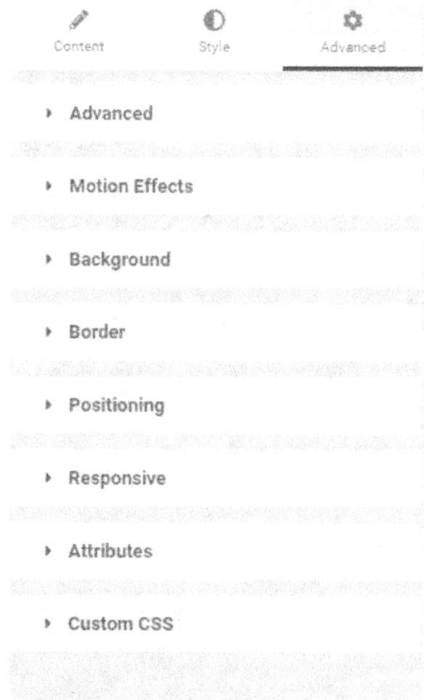

14. To add buttons widget. Simply drag widget into structure > Click on that widget.

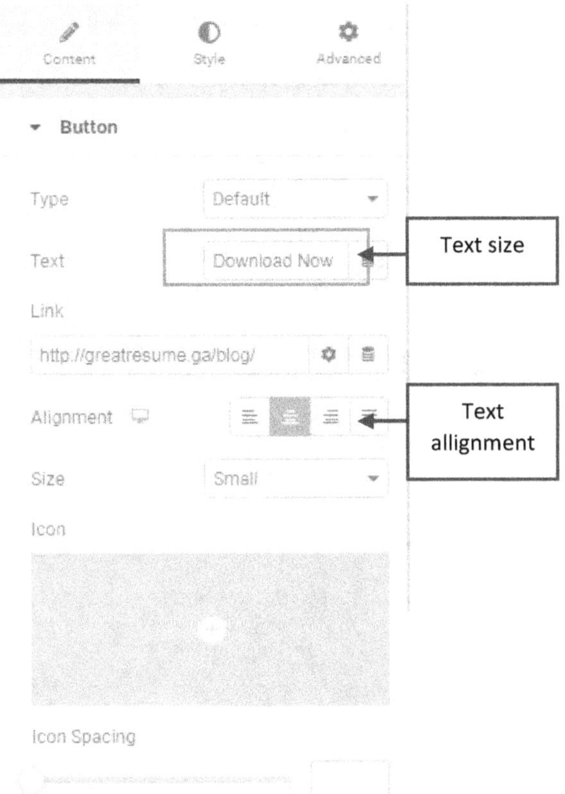

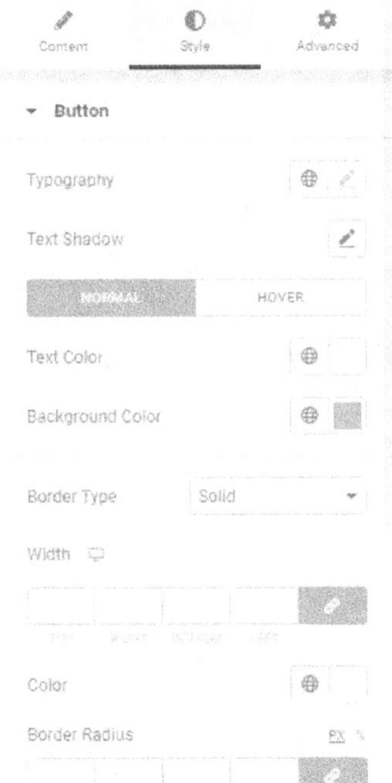

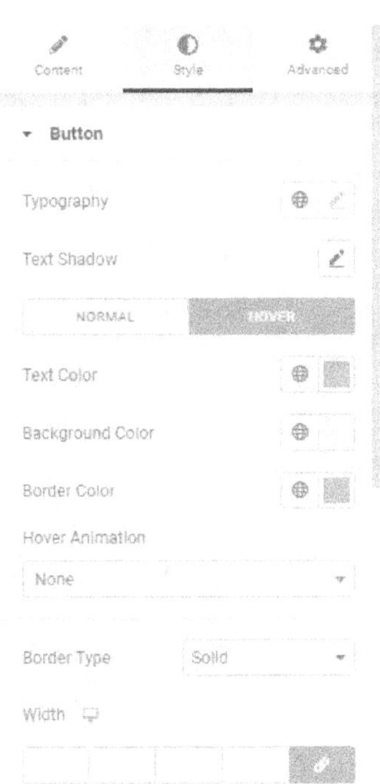

Presentation Templates

Resume Templates

SOCIAL MEDIA & WHATSAPP GENERATOR

As we all know, social media plays an important role in online business. In Malaysia, the most popular platform and many Malaysians use to connect is via WhatsApp, followed by Facebook. Throughout my online business, I have met all kinds of customers' needs for closed deals. There are types of customers who directly continue to pay on the website (auto-payment), there are those who want to ask first about the product and then buy. Some want to look at Facebook pages first. Most rarely, some customers communicate through email.

So, we as traders need various platforms to connect with customers by serving and educating our "potential clients" about our products/services. New customer satisfaction. So here, the generator for WhatsApp is the answer. How to make it? We see the step-by-step tutorial below.

1. Go to plugins > Click on Add New
2. Search for Callbell in search bar
3. Click on Install Now and start to activate the plugin

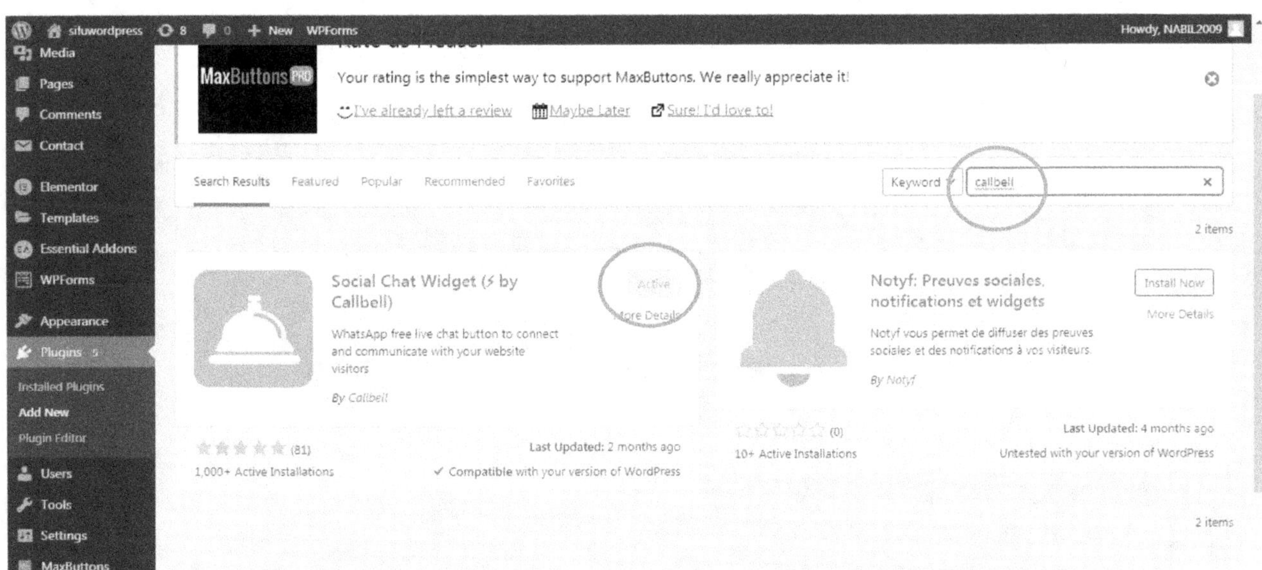

4. After activating, you find the installed plugins in the Menu and Click on Callbell

5. Click on Callbell Dashboard

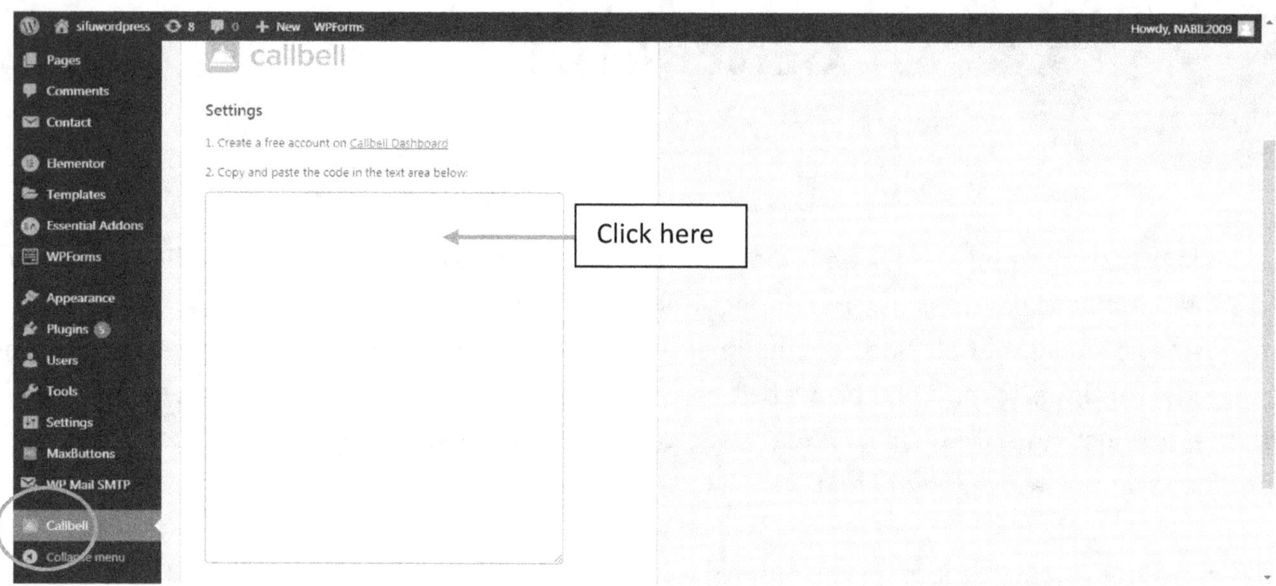

6. You will be directed to the Callbell page. Sign Up account. And verify your email with the sent link.

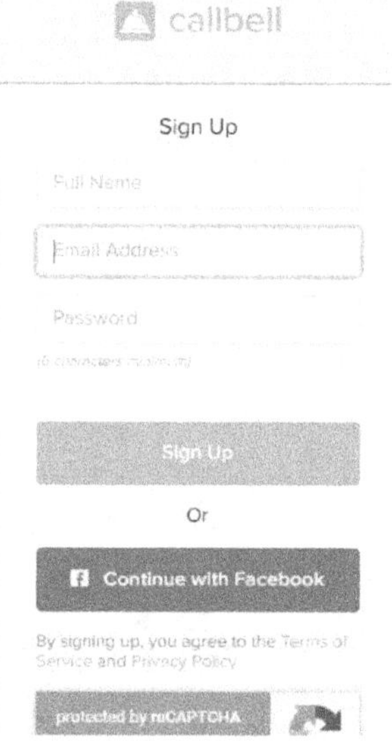

7. Choose which platform you want. Messenger, WhatsApp, Instagram, or Telegram. You can put all that stuff on your website.

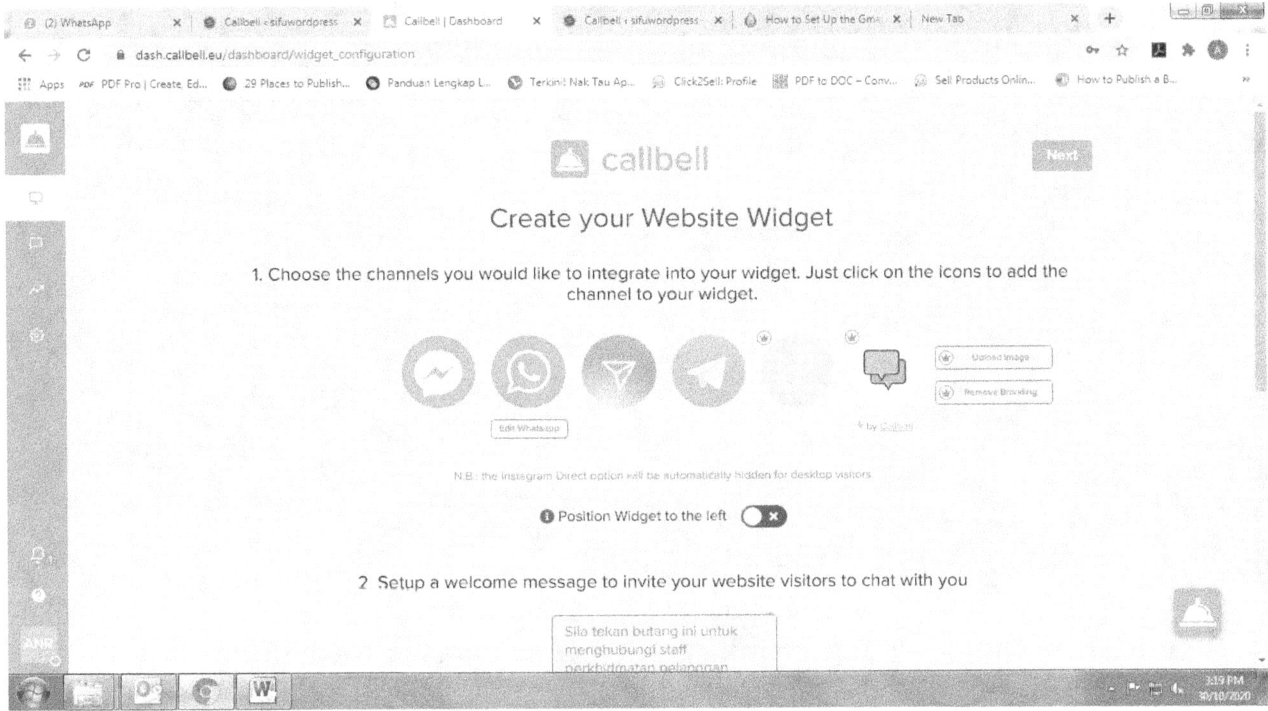

8. For Facebook Messenger. Click on the messenger icon and Connect with Facebook to log in

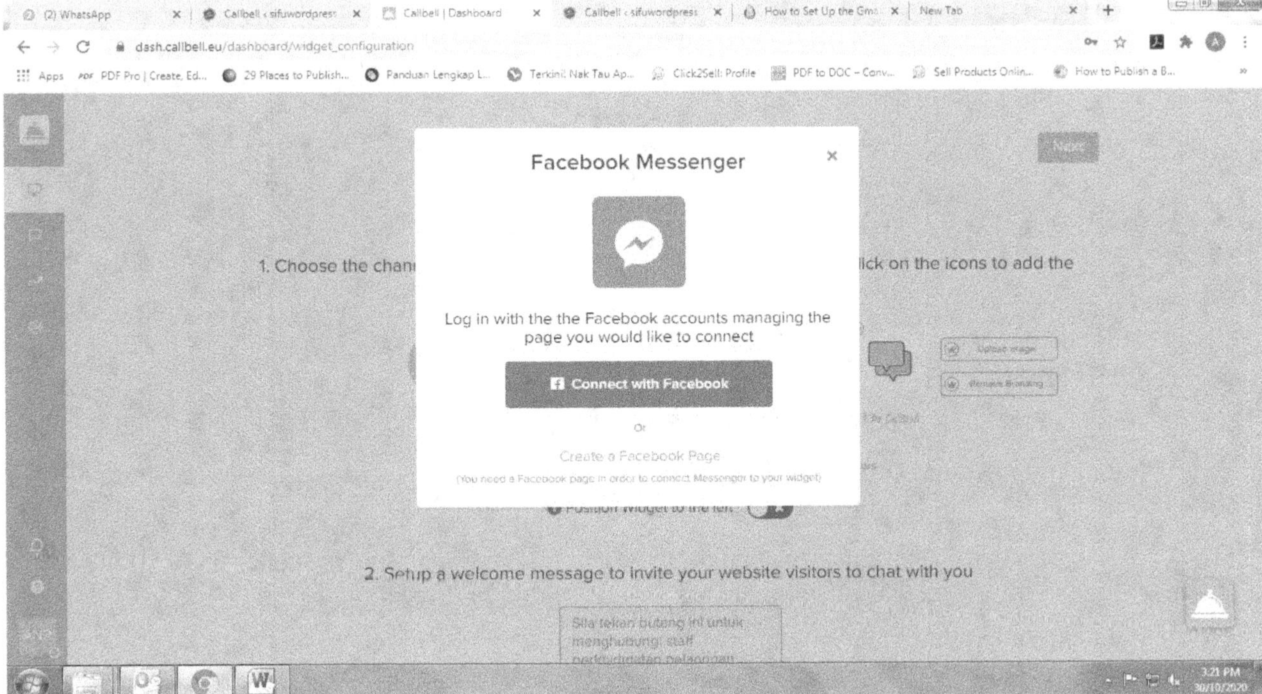

9. For Whatsapp. Click on the WhatsApp icon and enter your phone number starting with your +(country code). Click Save / Save changes

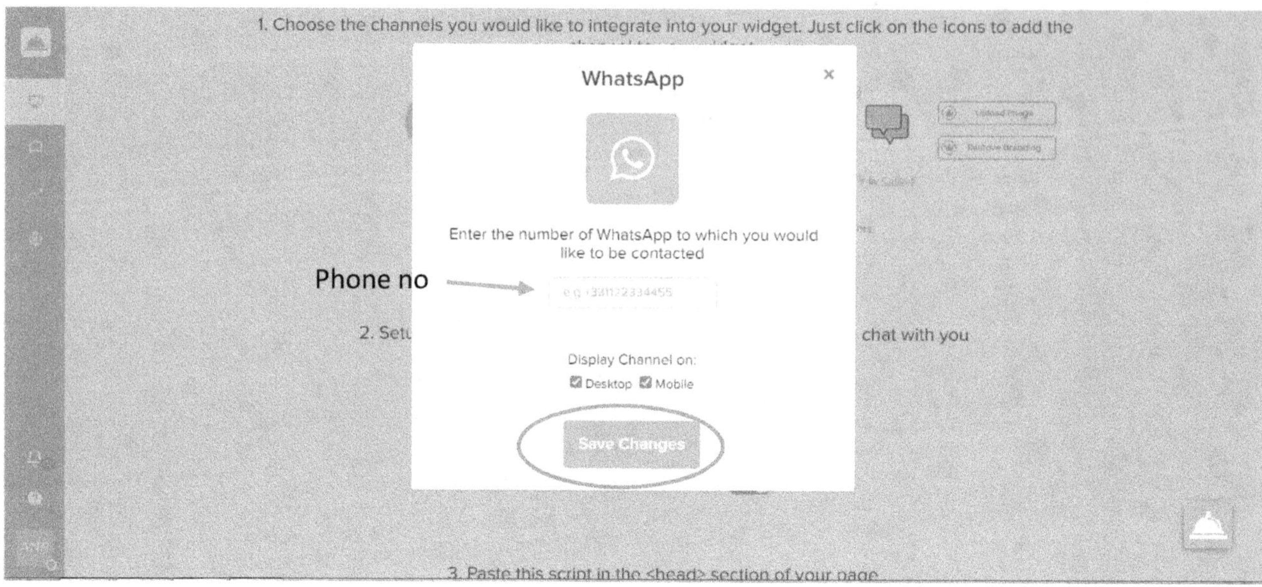

10. For Instagram. Click the Instagram icon. Enter your Instagram account username and Click Save Changes.

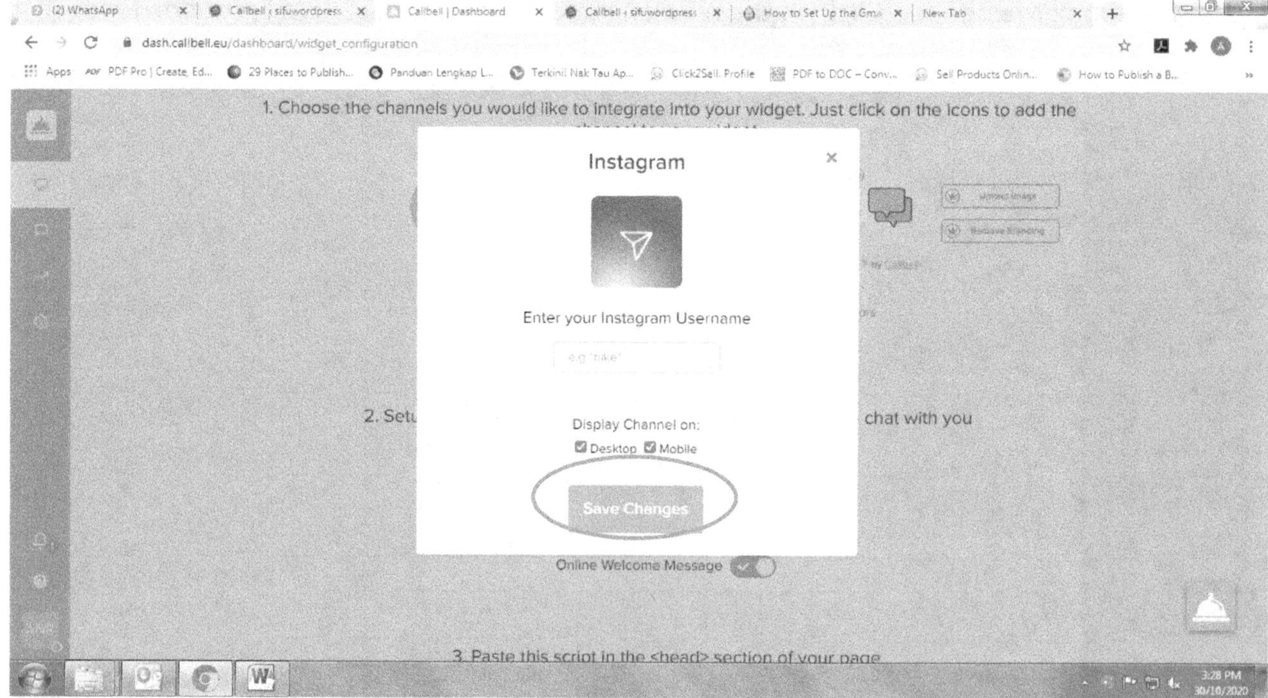

11. For Telegram. Click the Telegram icon. Enter the Telegram username and Click Save Changes

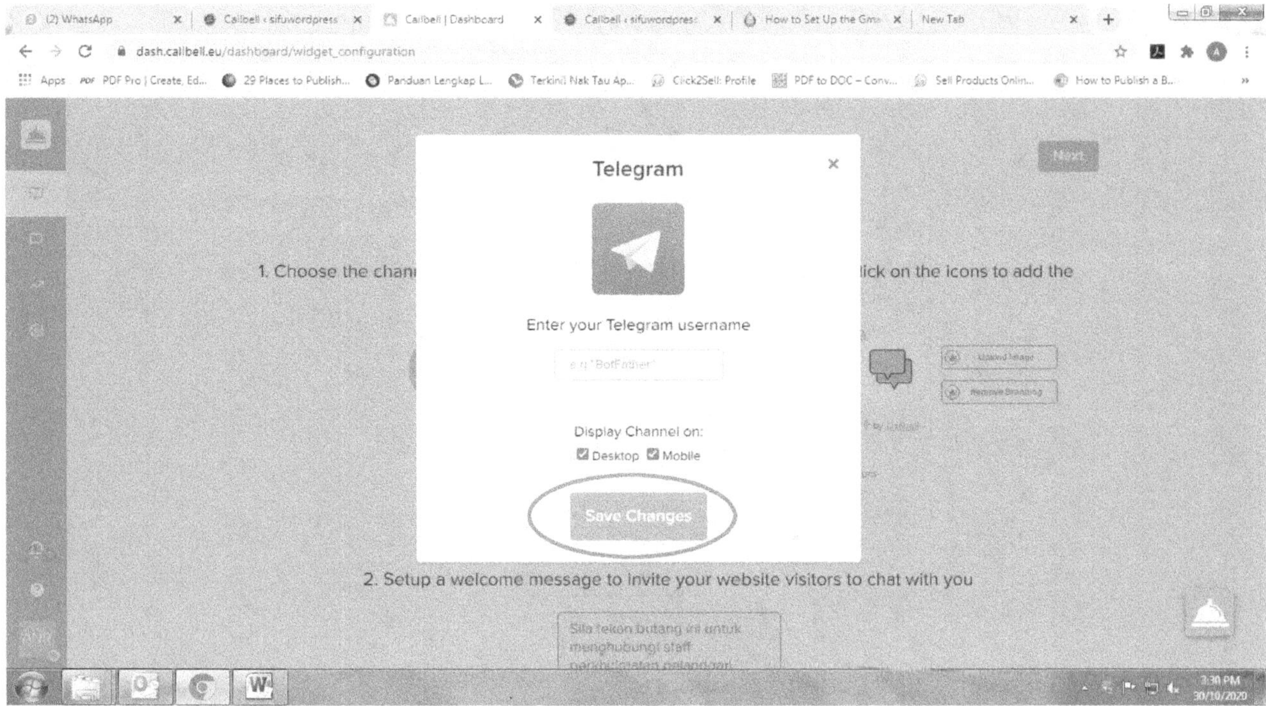

12. Scroll down. Tick-Right in the **"Position Widget to the left"** section if you want this widget to be on the left side of the site. Untick it, will make this widget be on the right side of your site. Follow the order that suits your theme.

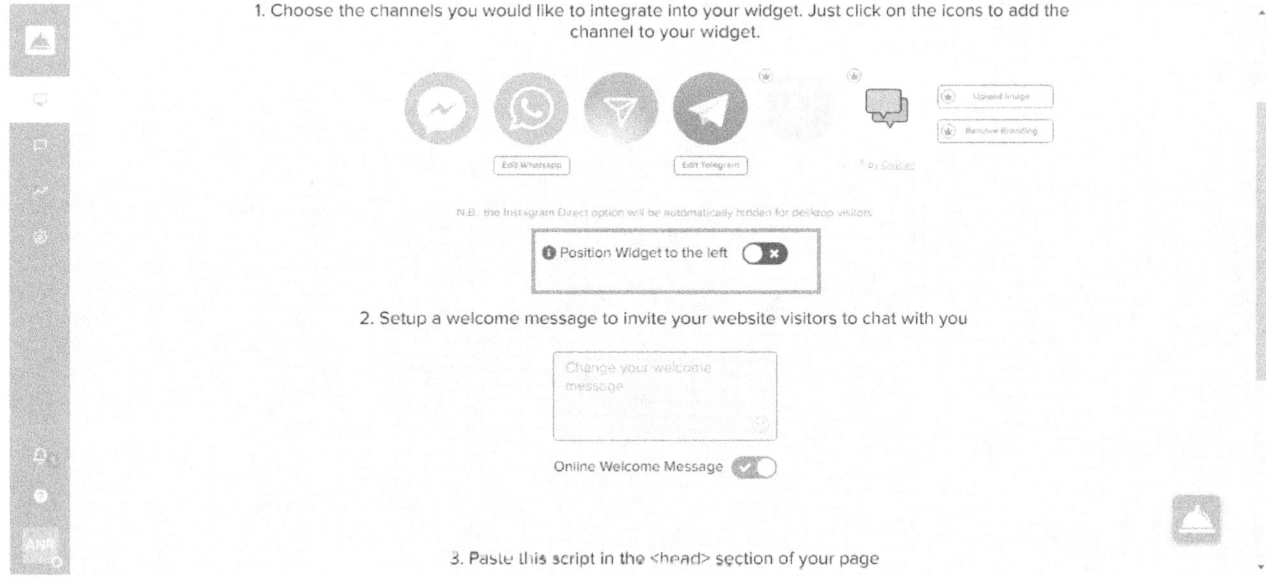

13. In the welcome message section. Enter a welcome message for this widget. For example, "thank you for visiting our website. Click here to contact our service staff ".

14. When done, click on "Copy code to Clipboard"

15. You have copied the clipboard earlier. Go to the Callbell menu in WordPress again.

16. Paste the clipboard in the text box.

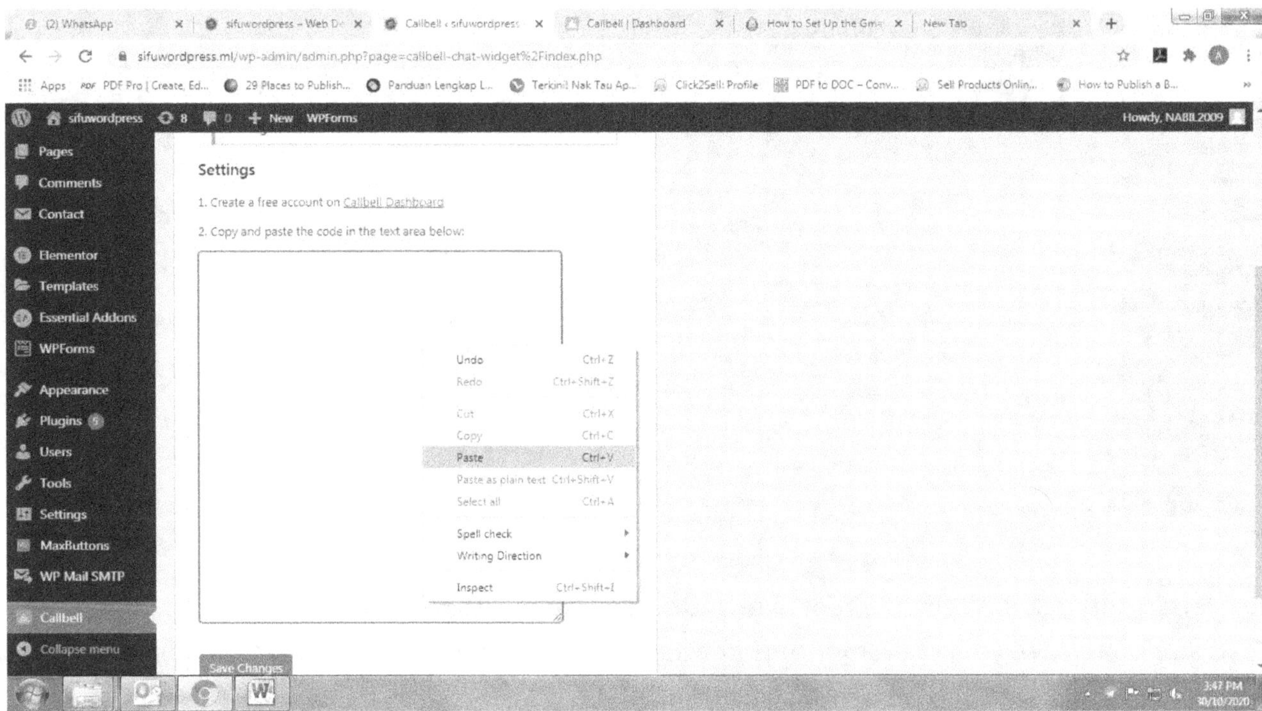

17. Click on **Save Changes**

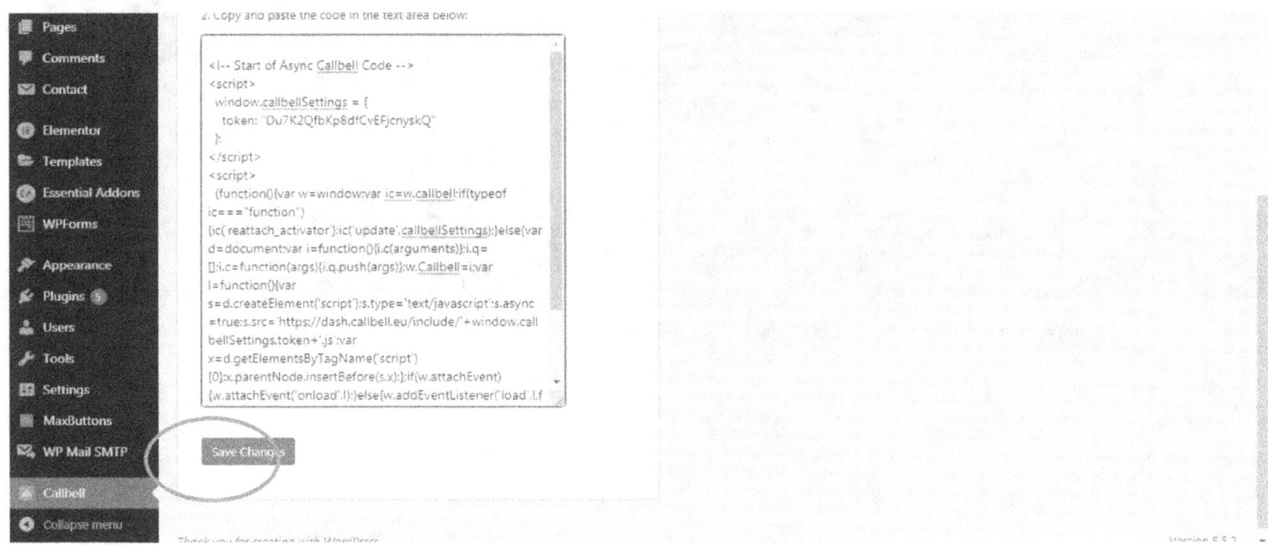

18. Open your site. Click on visit site

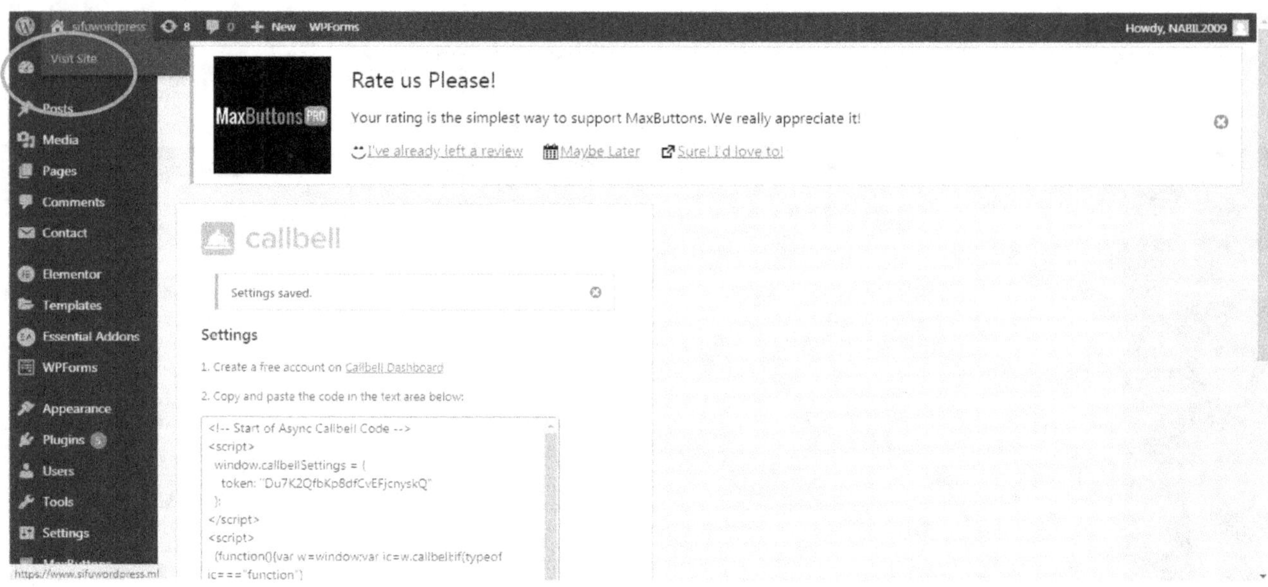

19. Here is the result. Welcome message and widget generator WhatsApp, Facebook, telegram, and
Instagram. Now, your customer or potential client or audience can contact you directly (direct)

If the audience presses this button, the contact button like this will come out later.

Note: To change or edit your information in Callbell can takes up 1 to 2 days to update.

WAY TO BUILD AN EMAIL ADMIN LIST– EMAIL SUBSCRIBER

Many businesses overlook the importance of having a direct relationship with their audience. By asking audiences to subscribe to your email list, you can increase traffic, make more sales, and establish good relationships with your audience. Remember, any audience can be your clients one day. They may only look at the post on your website, not buy at first. But if you update your attractive offers, ridiculous packages, lucky draws, or great promotions, they will buy it one day. Not only can you get their email, but you can also get their phone numbers.

Indirectly, you already have a database list of your potential customers or who are already clients. Everything is fully automated. No need, reply to WhatsApp anyway. Have you ever opened any website on Google, and suddenly pop-up appear to enter your information such as name and email. If yes, that is what we are going to do on this topic. Usually, to get the data about your audiences, you must come up with an offer after your audience subscribes to your website. Examples of offers such as:

- Free Ebook or sample ebook (Suitable for those who sell services)
- Testimonials of your product/service
- Discount coupons
- Promotions (for example Out of stock sales
- Free-trials

If you are one of the above offers, the audience will subscribe to your website.

For that, there are two ways to get a subscriber audience. You can use both of these methods to suit your niche website.

Method 1: Create WPForms (Registration/Contact Us/Offer)

1. Go to Wordpress Menu> Go to Plugins> Click Add New
2. Find the Contact Form with WPForms and WP SMTP mail by WPForms
3. Click Install> Click Activate

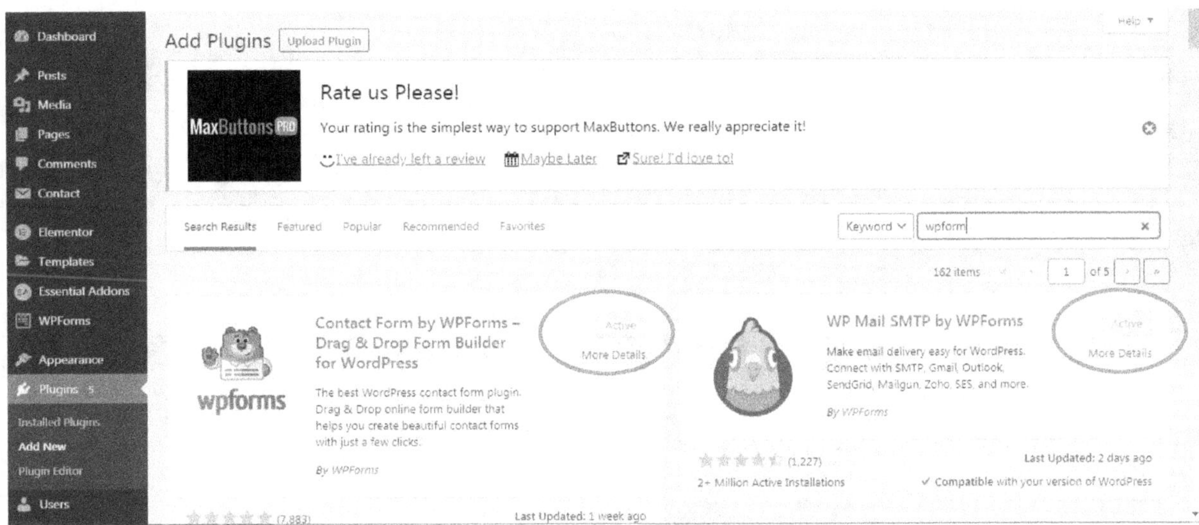

4. After activating the plugins, in **Menu** > Click **WPForms** > Click **Add New**

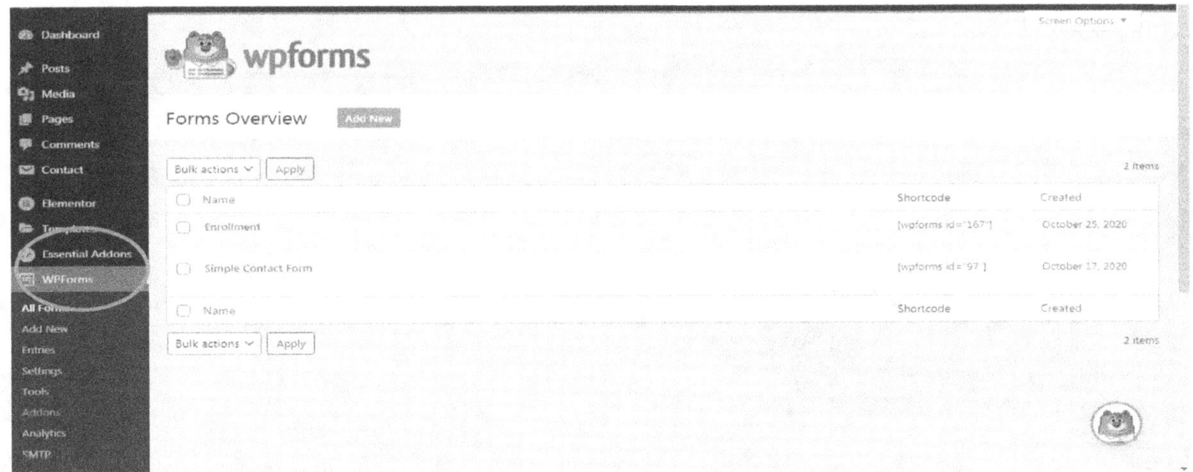

5. You will be taken to the WPForm page.

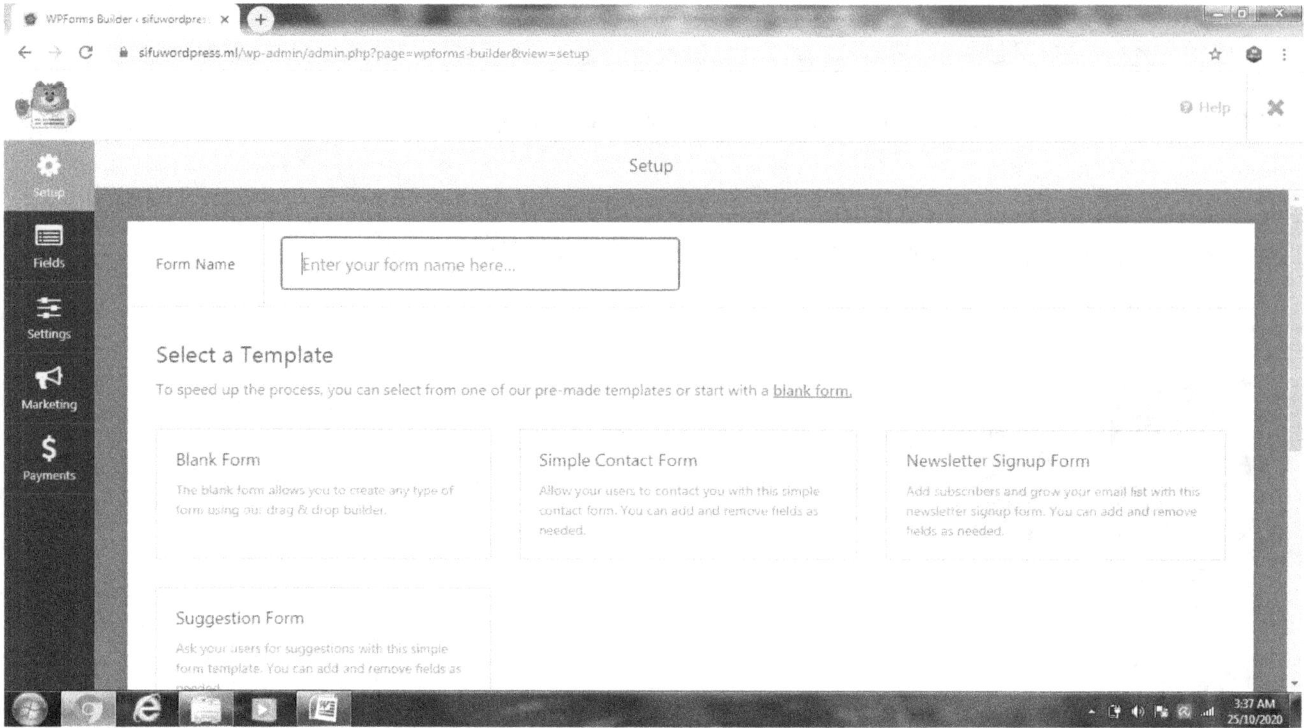

6. Under **Form Name**> You can put the name of the form title you created. For example, "Register / Contact us".

7. Go to Blank Page> Click Create a Blank Form

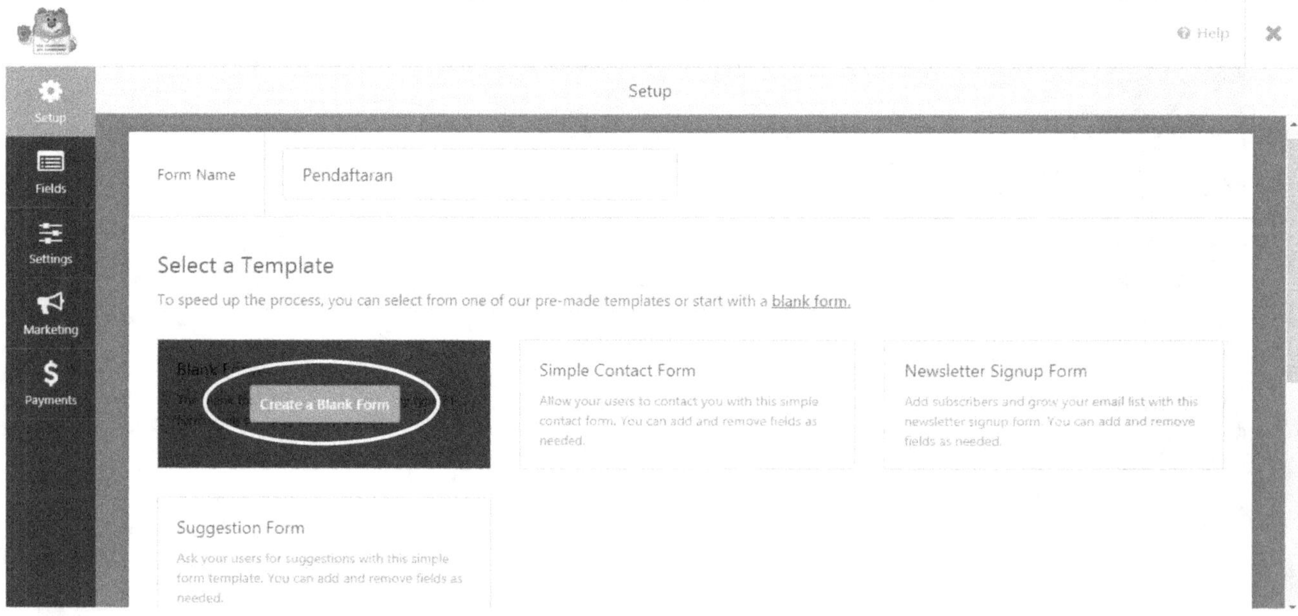

8. In Blank Form, many Fields can be included.

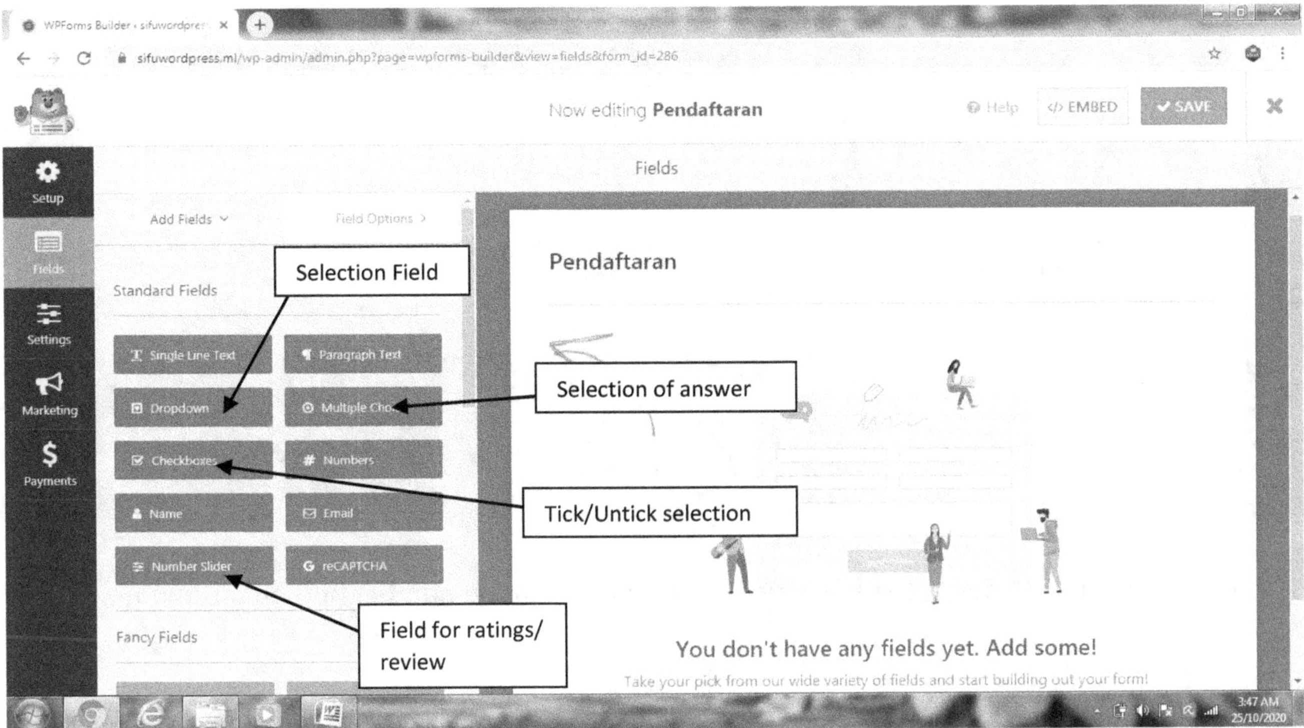

9. We will be using Single Line Text> Click on the Field> Click on Column content

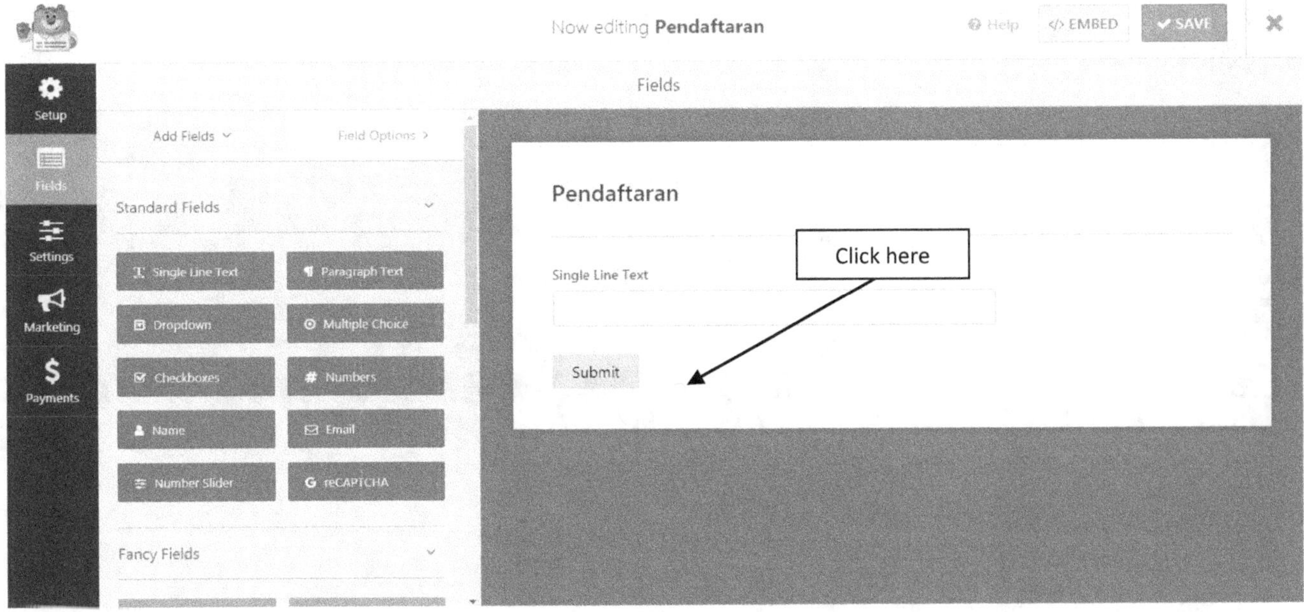

10. You need to edit labels and settings.
11. In the label space, type Name> Tick on Required for red star (*).

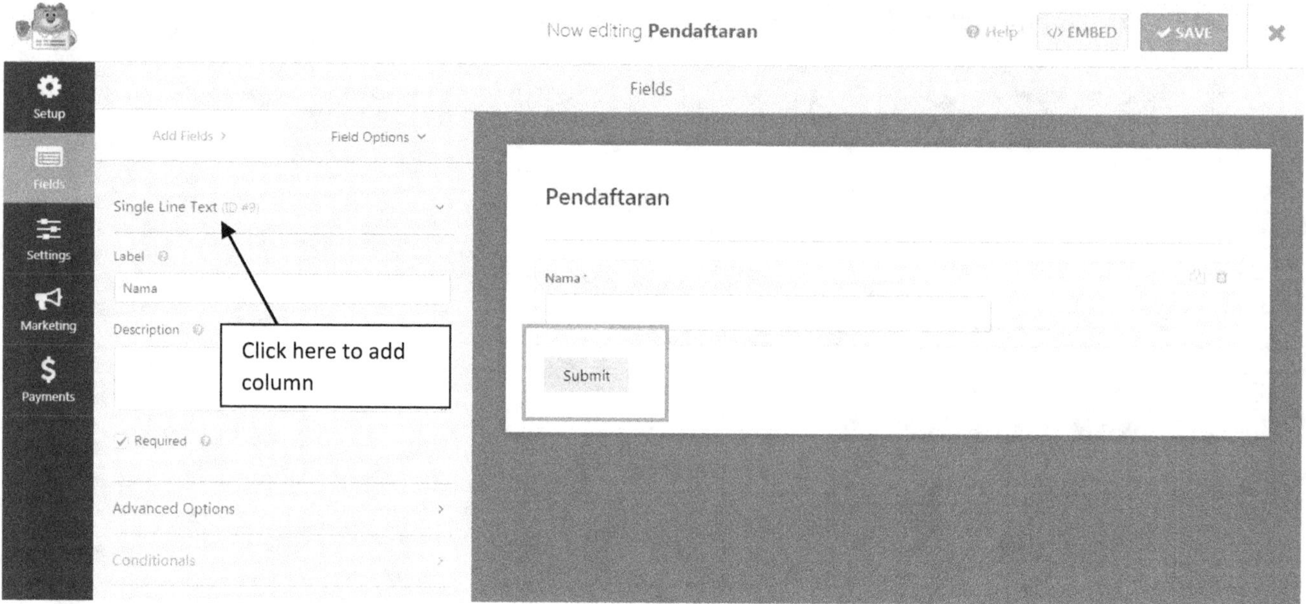

12. Then, Add Field to add a column. This time enter the phone number and email column.

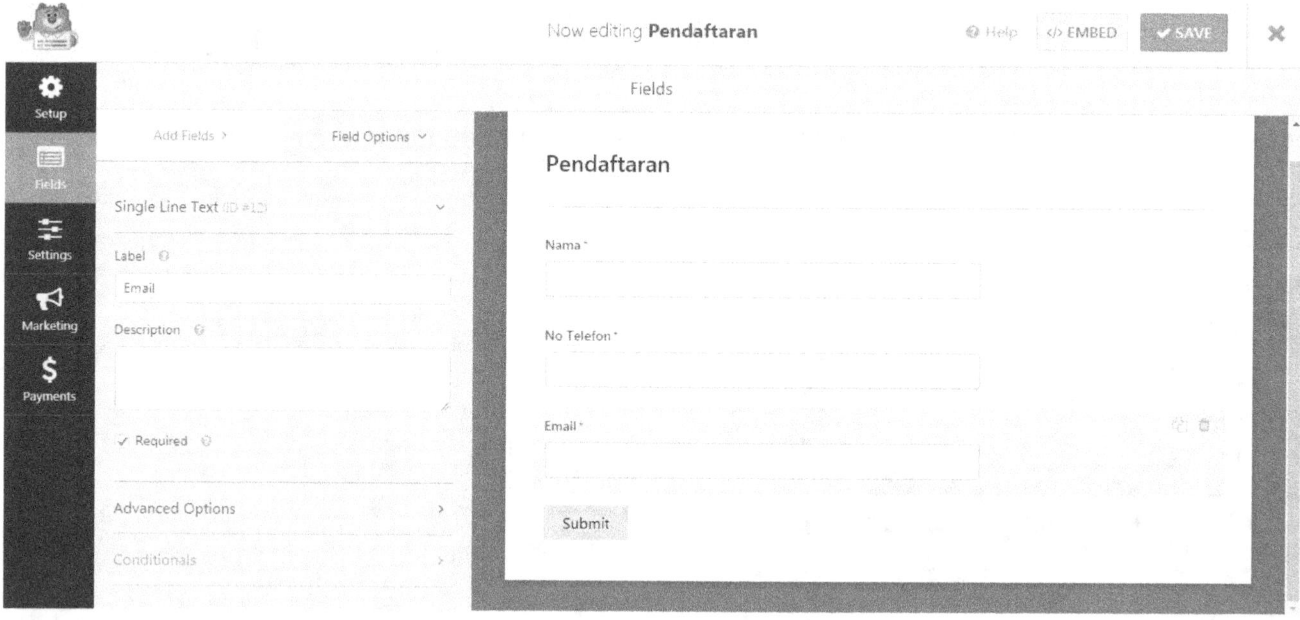

13. If you want to ask your audience's opinion or comment, you can enter the Paragraph text in the forms.

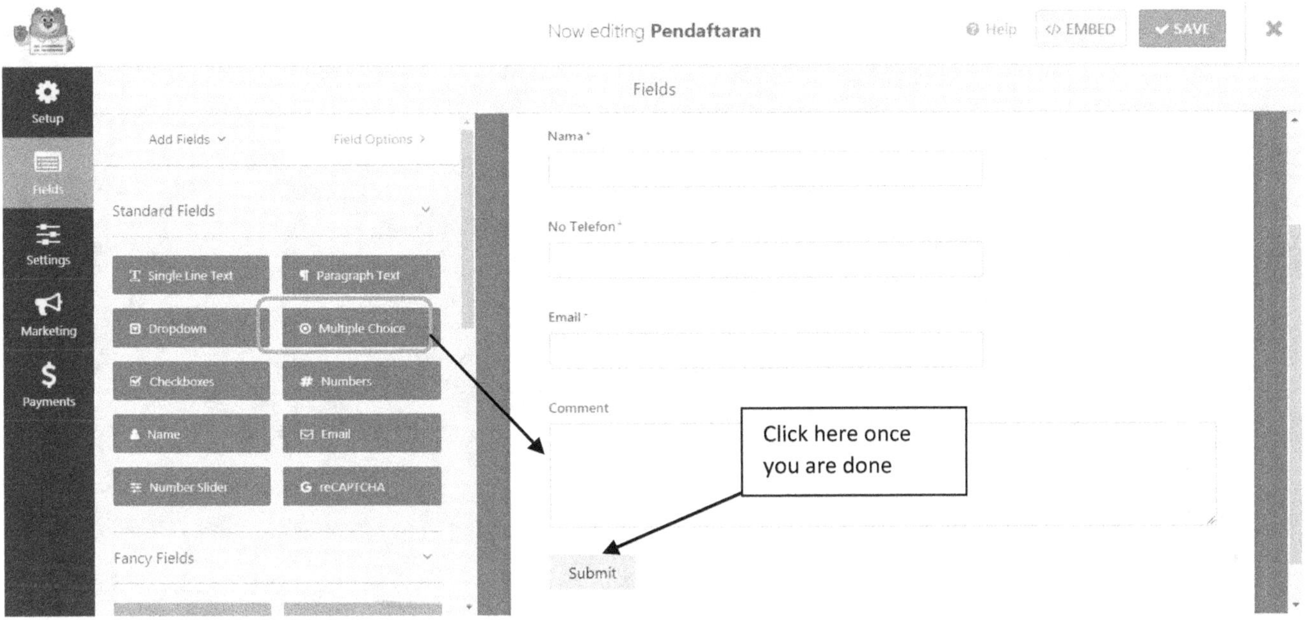

14. When done, click on the Submit button. You will be taken to the General settings, Notifications, and Confirmation settings.

15. In General Settings, you can change the Submit Button Text from Submit to Send and Submit Button Processing Text from "Sending ..." to Send ... or you can just leave it be.

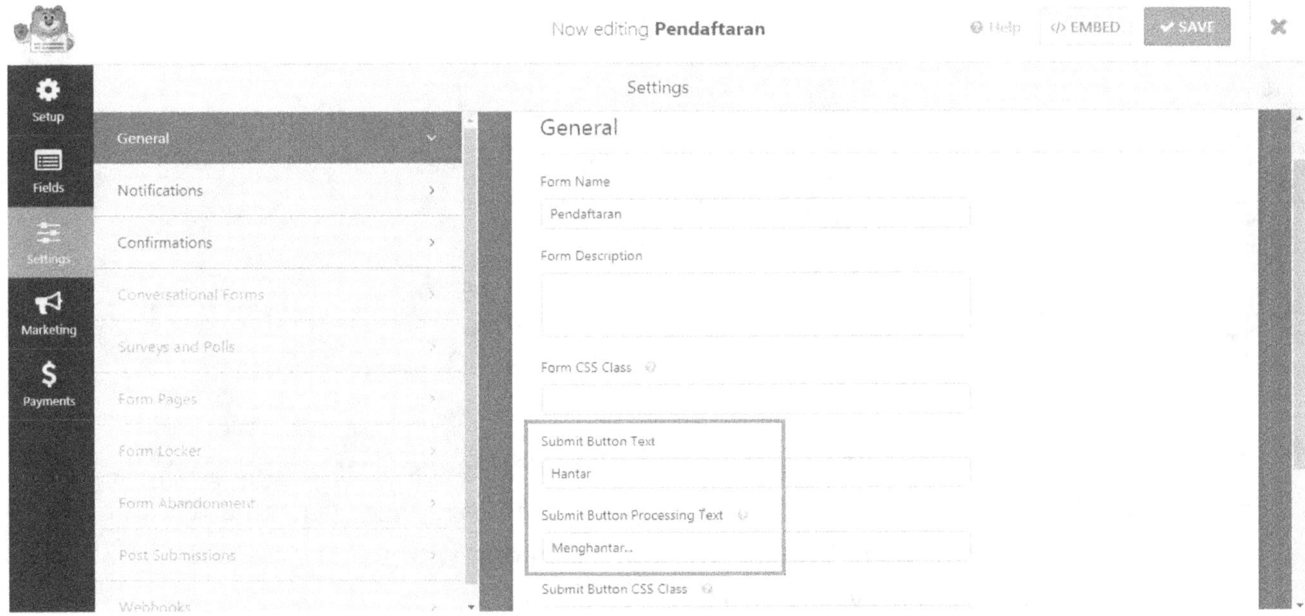

16. Scroll down and tick on Enable anti-spam protection.

17. Click on Notification settings.
18. Make sure Notifications is ON.
19. Send to Email Address > Type your email (You will receive all data here).
20. Email Subject> Type the subject or title of the email to be sent.
21. From Name> Type your name or any name you want to use. (Recommend: Enter the name of your website)
22. From Email> Type your email
23. Reply-To> Ignore this
24. Message> Ignore this

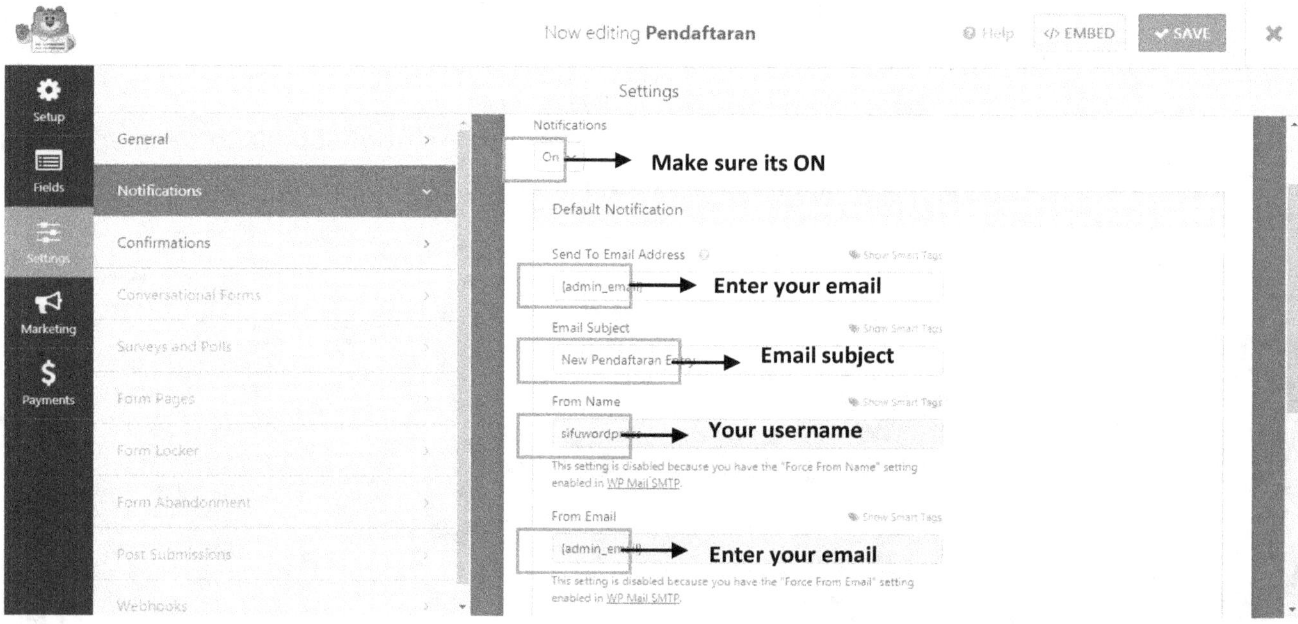

25. When done, click on Confirmation settings. You can select in the Confirmation Type box whether you want Message, Page, and URL. If you select Message, you can edit the Confirmation Message below. For example, " Thank you for registering with us! Your ebook sample will be sent to the email address provided. Please see your email. "

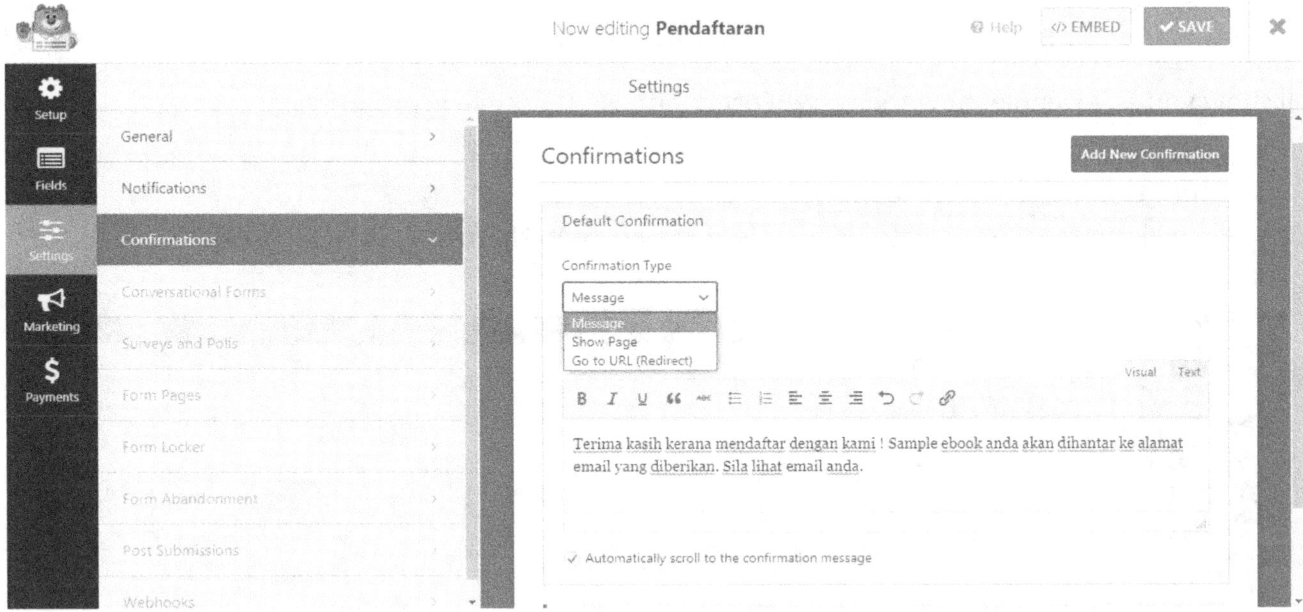

26. If you select a Page, you need to create a new page near your website using WordPress.

27. When done, click on the Save button.

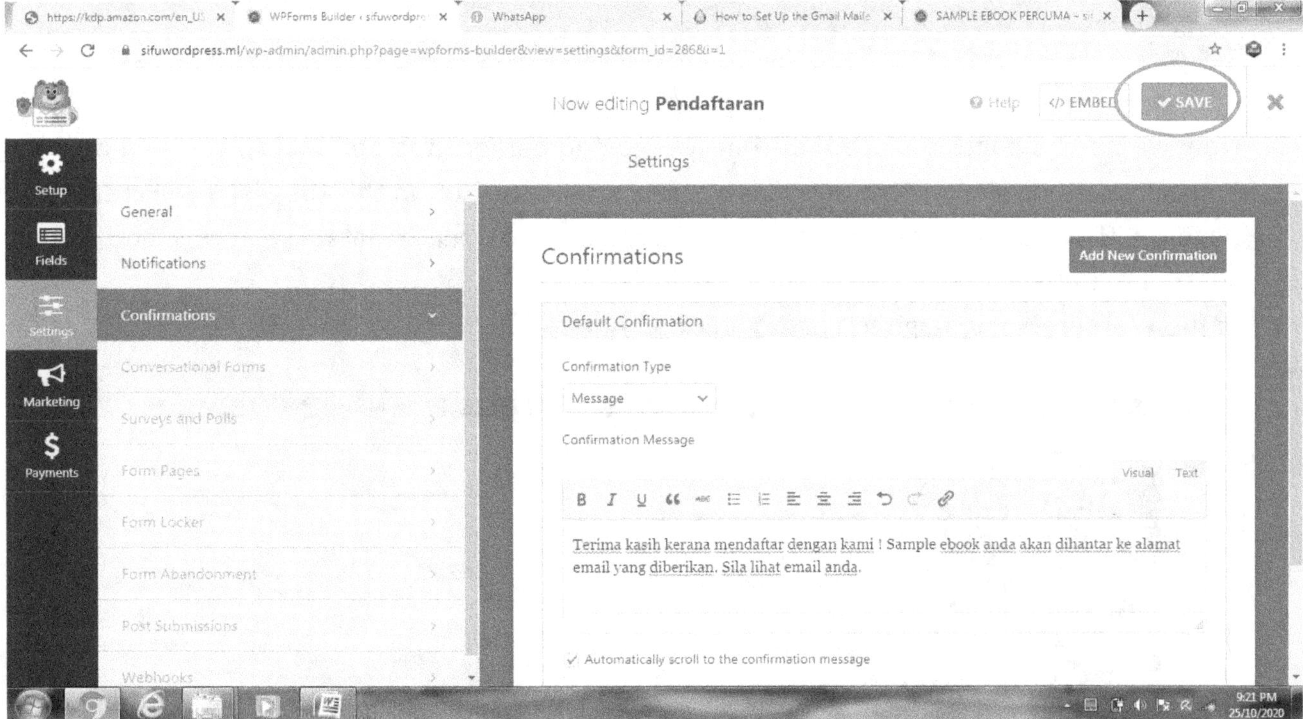

Way to use WPForms

I will show you an example, how to use WPForms with New Page in WordPress.

1. Return to the WordPress Menu.
2. You will see the Form created earlier is in the list of WPForms

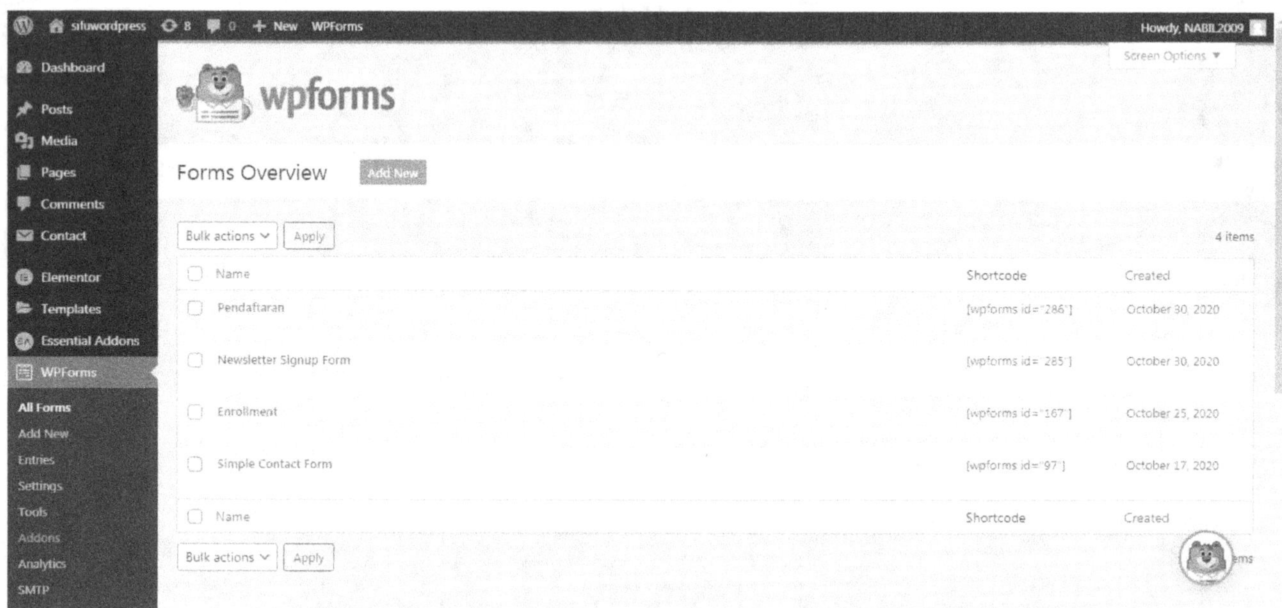

3. Now we need a page to place the form we created earlier. It is optional to create a new page. You can use the existing one, depends on your creativity. But, in this tutorial, I will create a new page so that you can get a clear picture of how to create database forms and get your subscriber's email.
4. In the WordPress menu, go to Pages > Click on Add New

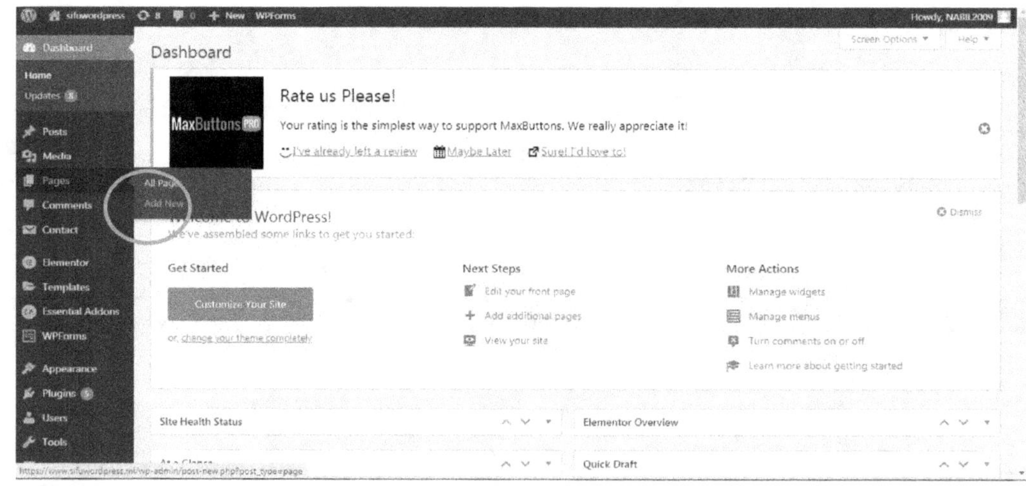

5. Click on Edit with Elementor.

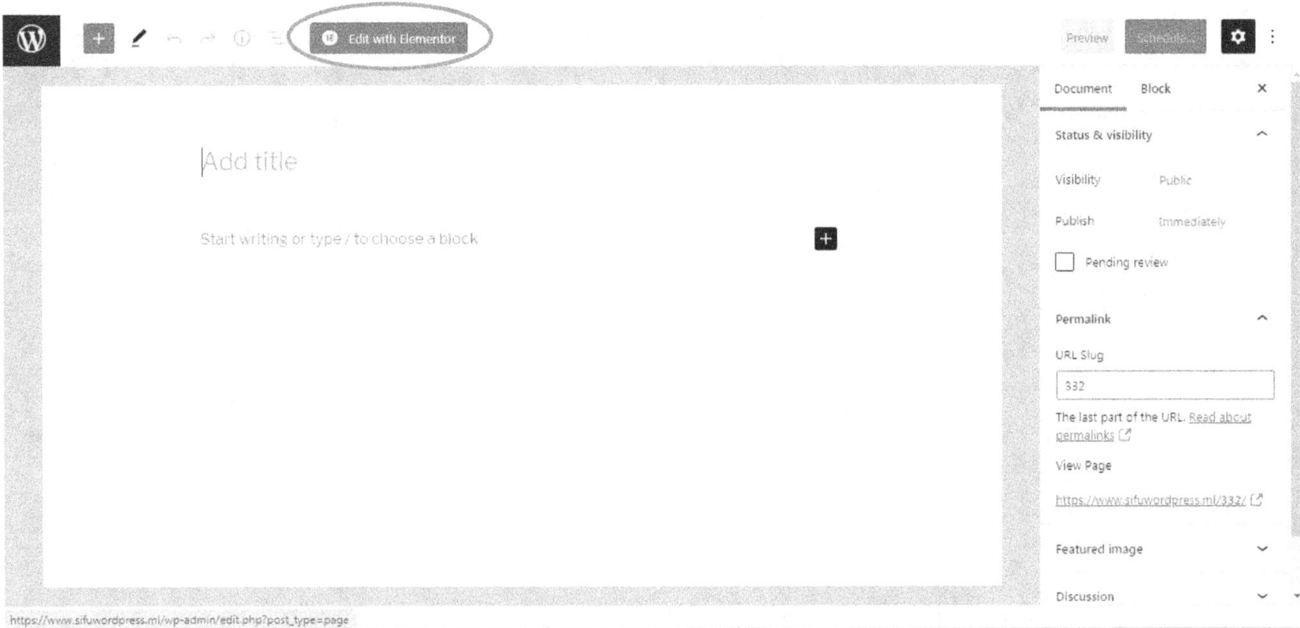

6. On the element page, click on the icon + near the drag widget section.
7. Choose the layout you like.

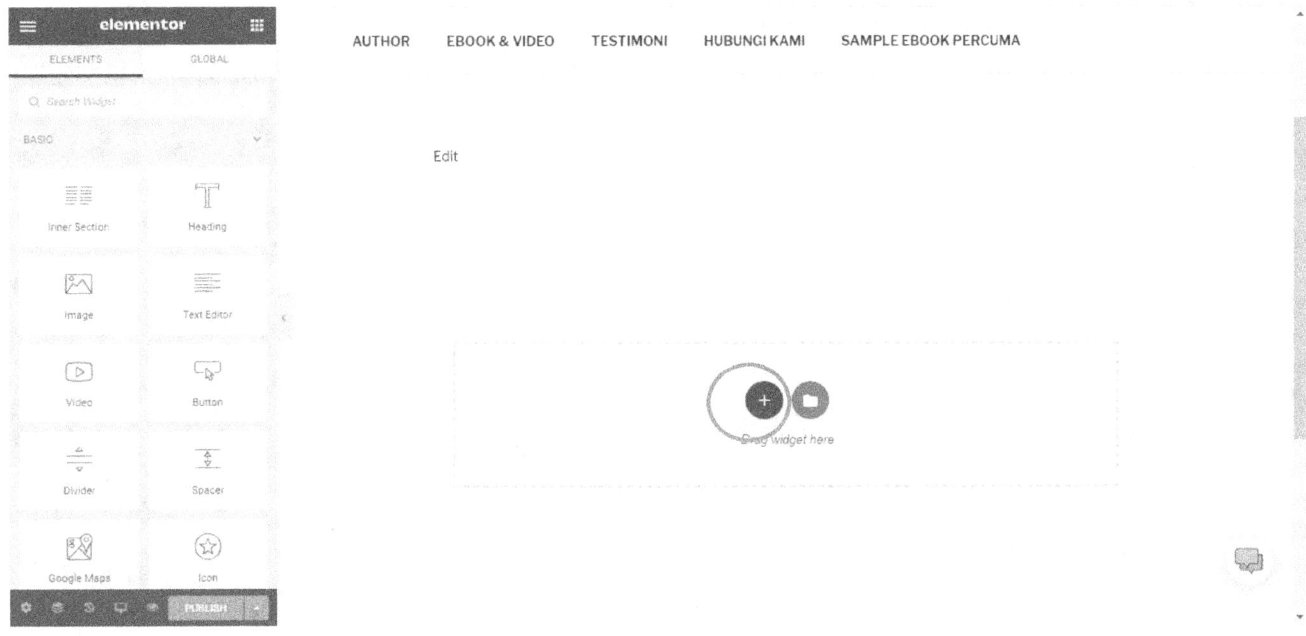

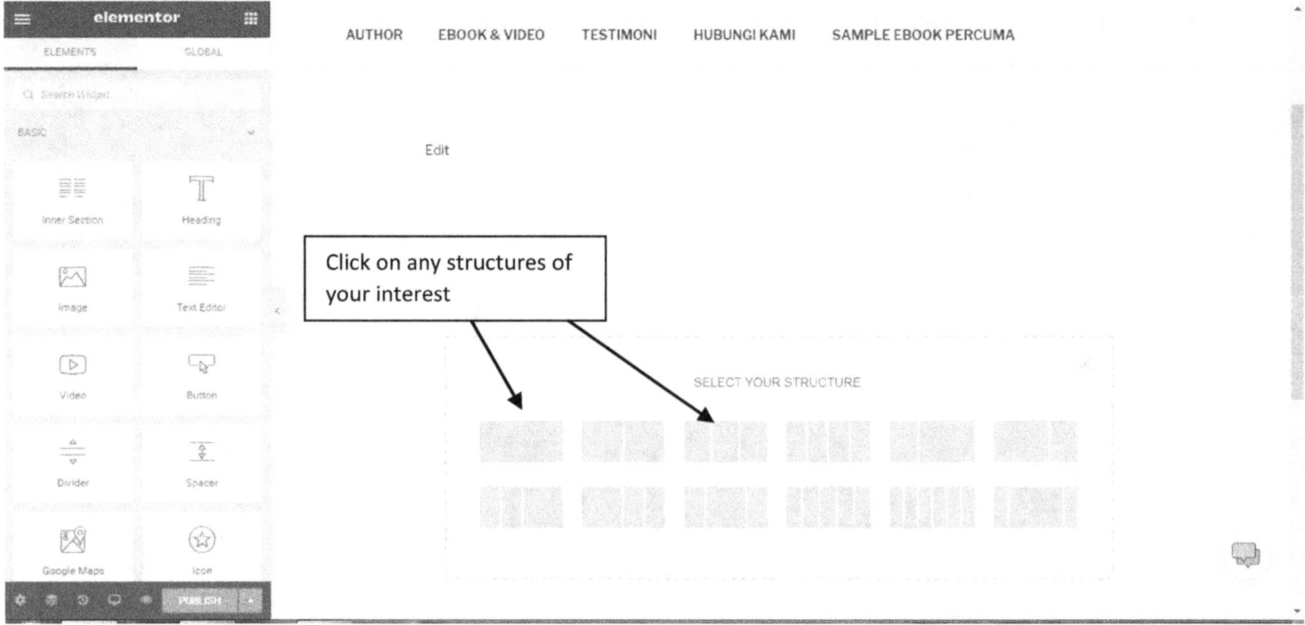

8. After that, click on the (+) button, to place the widget form.
9. Find the WPForms widget in the search bar.
10. Drag or drag the WPForms widget to the (+) icon.

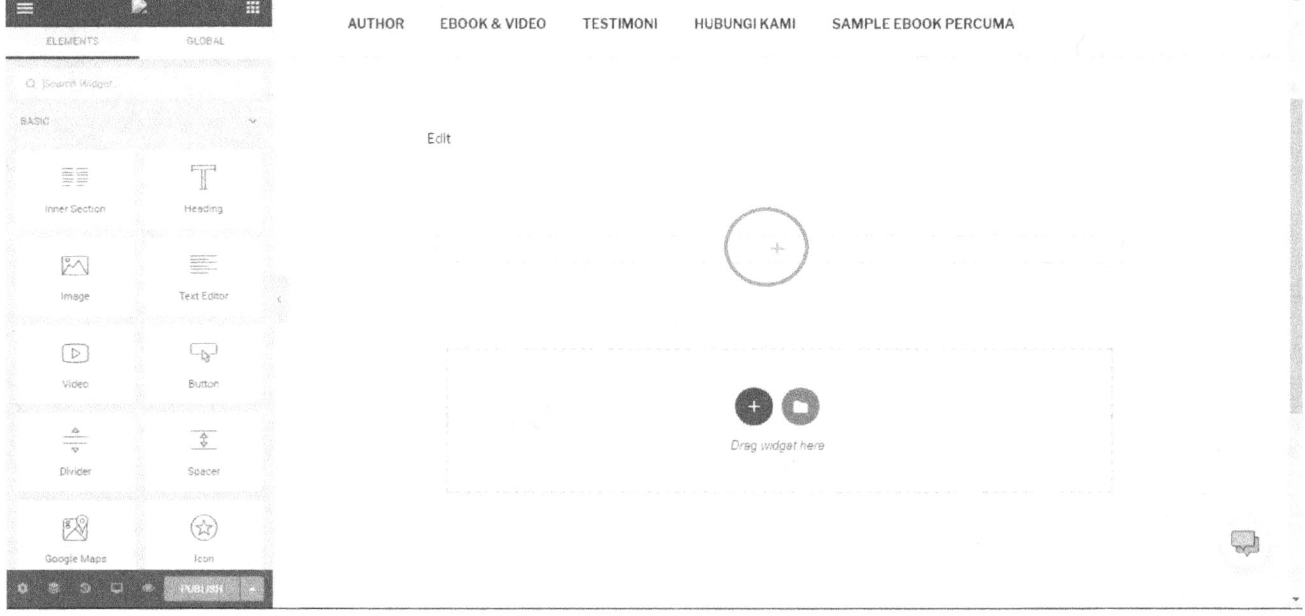

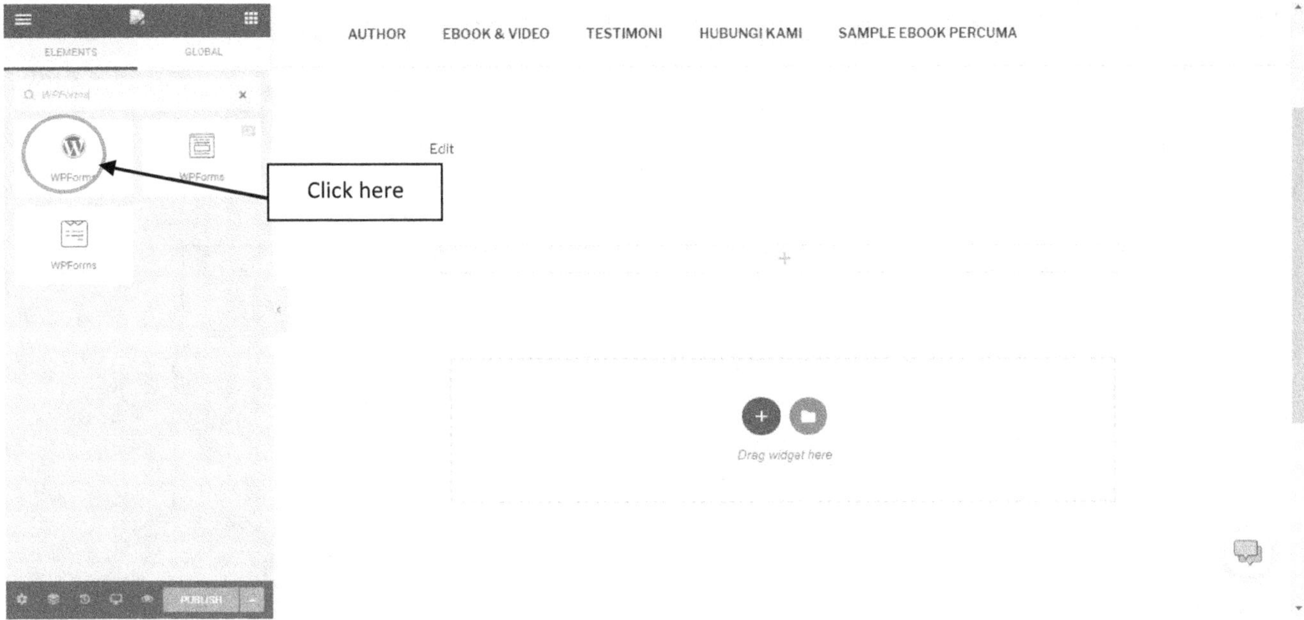

11. Select the Form you registered before.

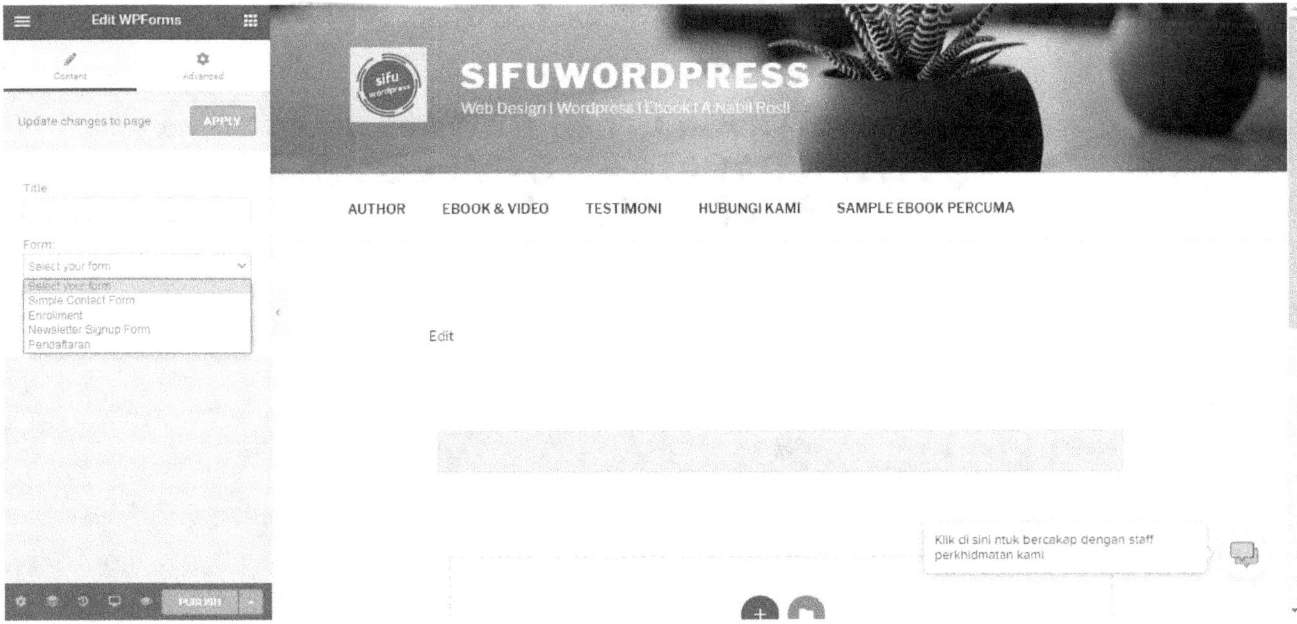

12. And, automatically, the form we created before will appear.
13. My suggestion, at the top of the form, there should be a header widget to fill in the title. You can make copywriting on promotions, gifts, or free trials so that the audience is interested in buying the form and then become our customer.
14. For more, I will show you how to create a promotional campaign in the next topic.

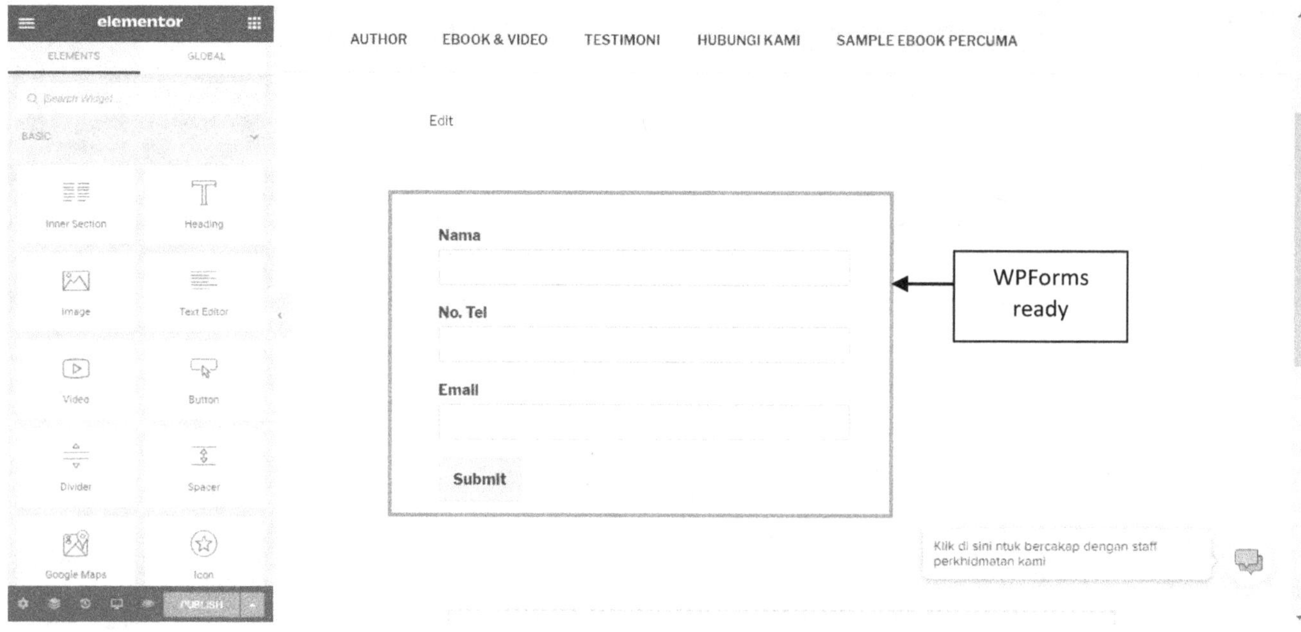

15. When done, click on the Publish buttons.

16. And look at your page. Examples are as below.

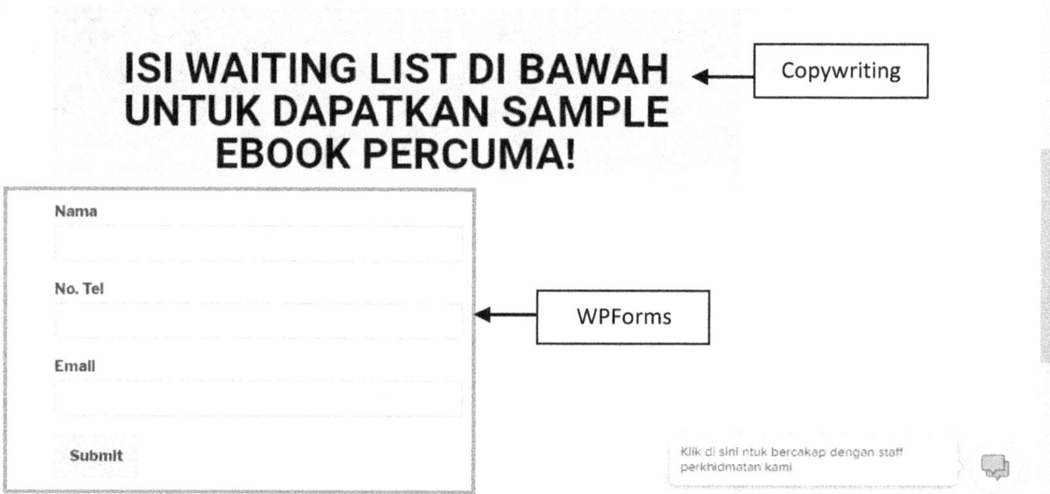

17. Try to fill in the form you created and press the submit button. What will happen?

18. Later, the message that you have written in the previous WPForms settings will come out right near the bottom of the form.

Terima kasih kerana mendaftar dengan kami ! Sample ebook anda akan dihantar ke alamat email yang diberikan. Sila lihat email anda.

19. Then, you check your email, do you find any notifications about the information you entered just now?
20. Surely, you will not find it because we need an APIs system for sending information to the email list.
21. I will show you how, please follow the steps below carefully because it is quite complex.

WP Mail SMTP

Here we will use Gmail from Google. For email users other than Gmail such as PHP, mailgun, SendGrid, or Outlook or other SMTP. You can personalize my WhatsApp to get another coach because the set up is quite different and difficult. But, I recommend we use Gmail.

If you are new user to gmail. Sign Up Now.

1. First of all, we need to go to the WordPress Menu.
2. Click on WP Mail SMTP.

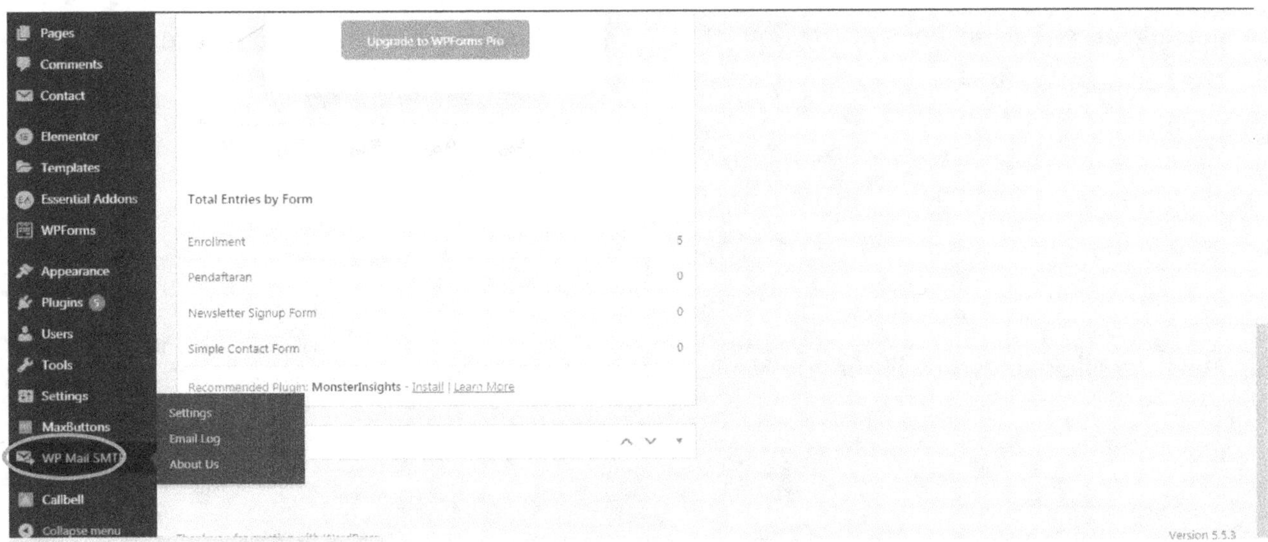

3. At the top of the Settings page, you will see the From Email option. You can just ignore it because Google will force From Email to match (matching) the email account which you will enter shortly in this tutorial (later, you will see this field will be disabled).

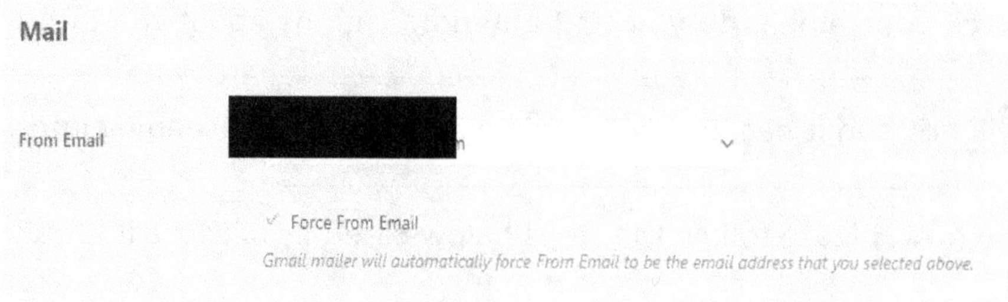

4. Under "From Email", you can fill in the "From Name". Here is the name associated with the email that will be sent, and be set to the name of your website by default. You can adjust any value you want. You can also select the Force From Email tick to activate this option throughout the website.

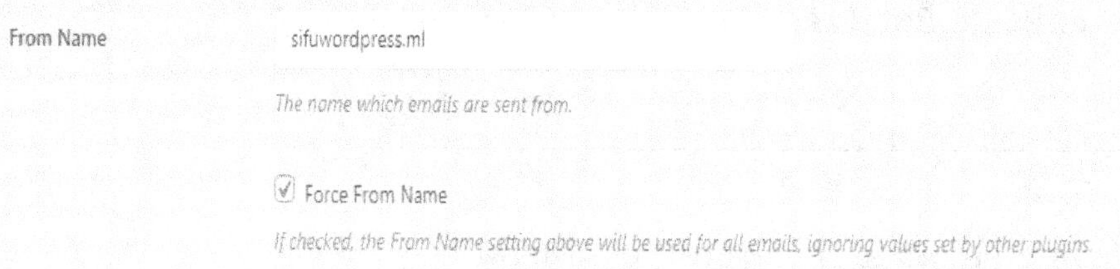

5. I recommend ticking the Return Path box to set the Return-path to match From Email. With this setting, an email will be sent to you if there is a bounce message due to a problem or error with the recipient's email.

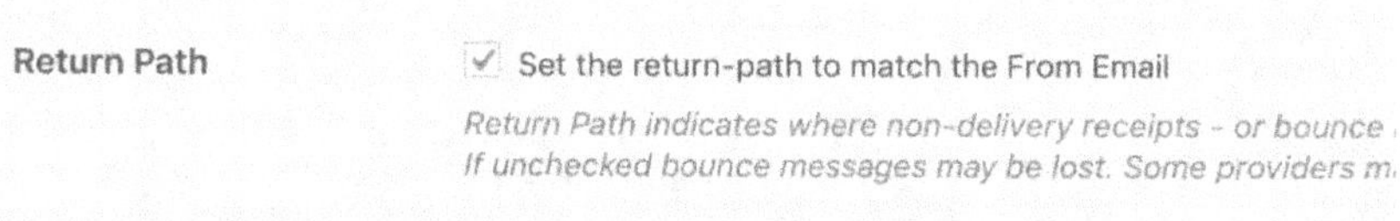

6. Next, scroll down, you will see the Mailer section. Select Gmail

7. Now that you have selected Gmail Mailer, you will see that two new sections are embedded with the Gmail headline, namely Client Secret and Client ID.

8. You need both of this information, specific to your website. To get the information needed for this section, you need to use your Google account to create a web application. This process does not require any coding. I will show you, what to do in the next step.

Gmail

Send emails using your Gmail or G Suite (formerly Google Apps) account, all while keeping you require enabling less secure apps in your account and entering your password. However, this issues while keeping your site secure.

Read our Gmail documentation to learn how to configure Gmail or G Suite.

Client ID

Client Secret

Create a Web App in Your Google Account

We will return to the SMP WP Mail settings page shortly, so for the next step, you need to open a new tab or window in the browser. In the new tab/window, log in to your Gmail account and access the Gmail application registration. Please click the link below.

Google Cloud Platform < Click here

Note: For those of you who use G Suite, make sure the Google account you are using has email access to the inbox.

9. After logging in to your Google account. Pop-ups like this will come out. Tick on Terms and Conditions. Click Agree and Continue.

10. Click on Create Project.

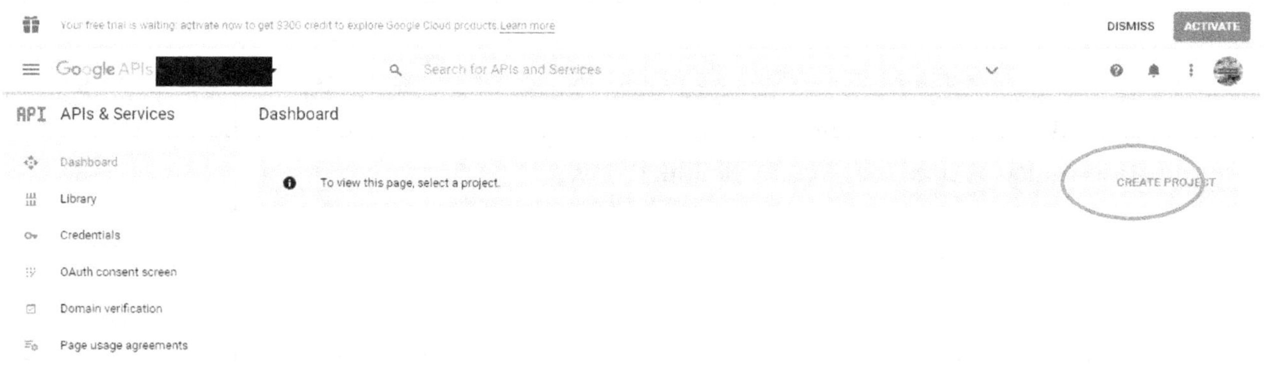

11. Enter the site name you use in Project Name. Click on Create.

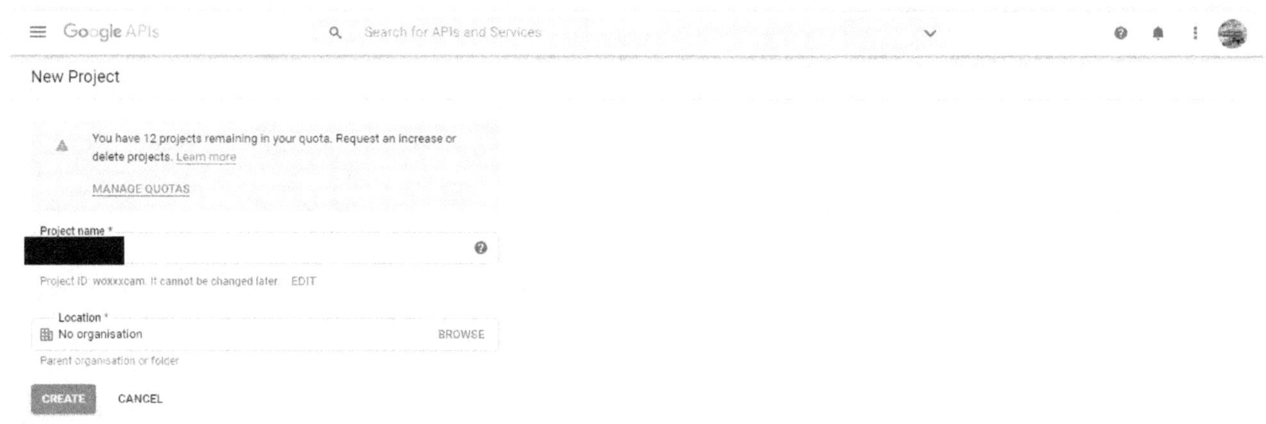

12. Click on **ENABLE APIS AND SERVICES**. You will be taken to the Library API. Search Gmail API>
click on Gmail API and Install.

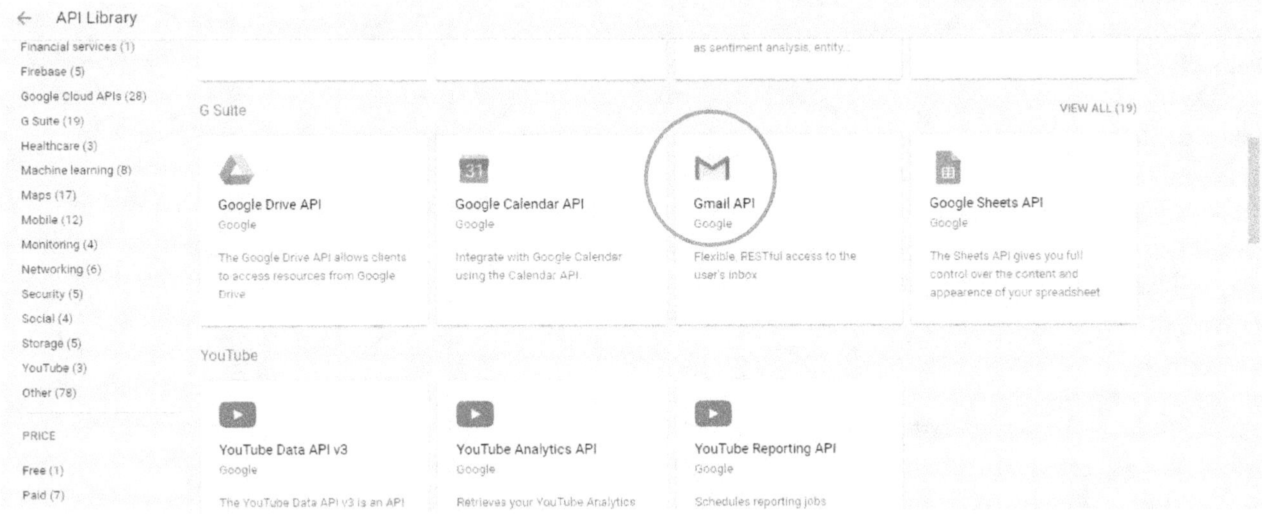

13. After completing Install > Click on **MANAGE**

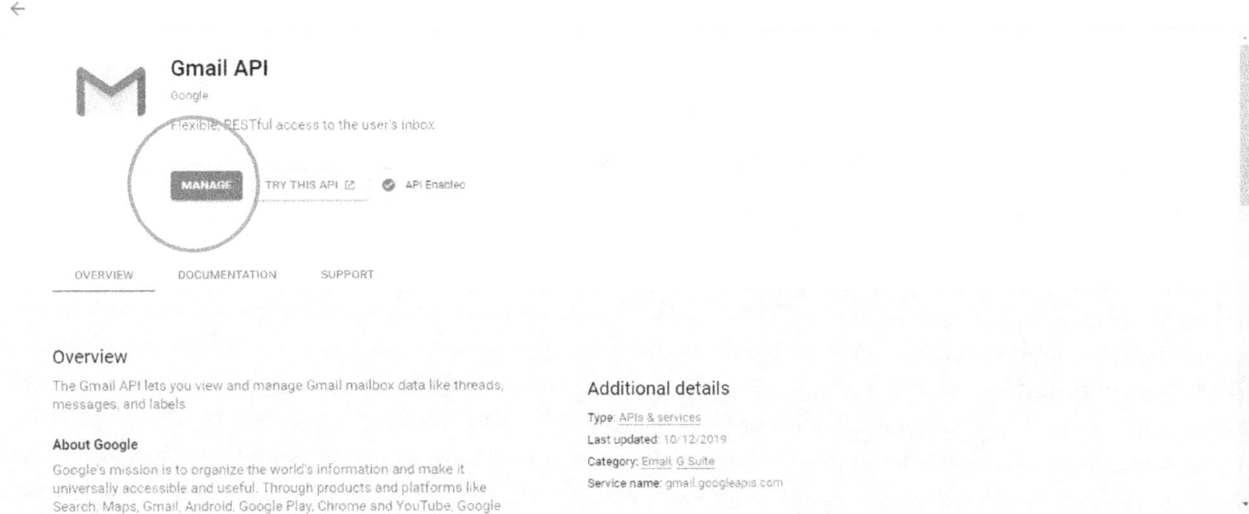

14. Click on **CREATE CREDENTIALS**

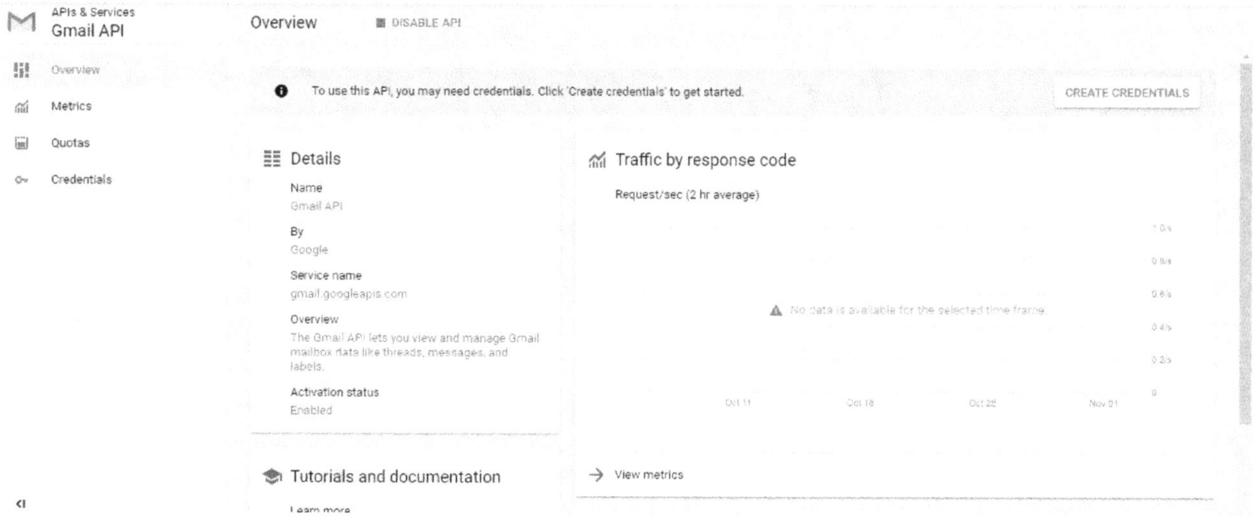

Google will ask some questions:

1) Which API are you using? > Select Gmail API
2) Where will you be calling the API from? > Select Web Server (e.g. node.js.Tomcat)
3) What data will you be accessing? > Select User data

After that, Click What Credentials do I need?

See the next page.

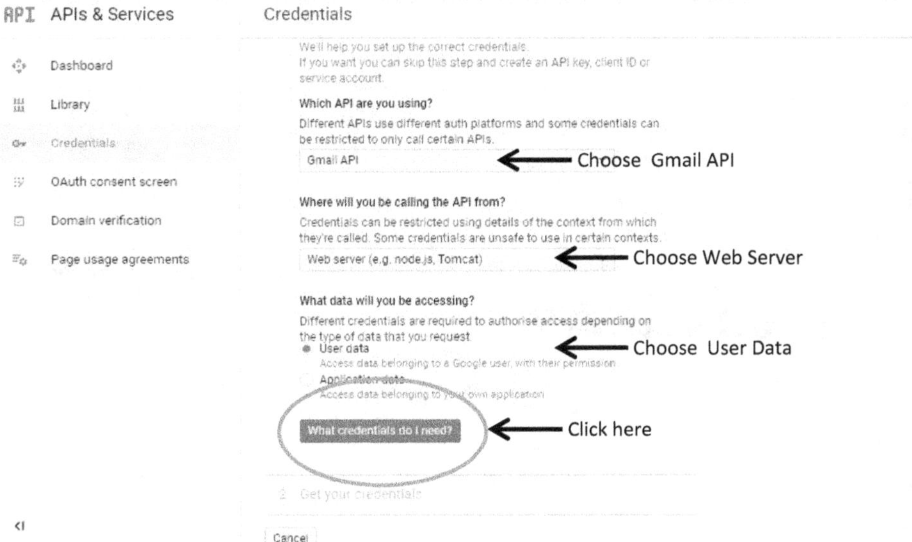

15. Under Create an OAuth 2.0 client ID, Name> Enter the name of your website
16. Authorized Javascript origins> Enter your website URL starting with https: //
17. Authorized redirect URLs> Enter URLs from SMTP Wpforms.

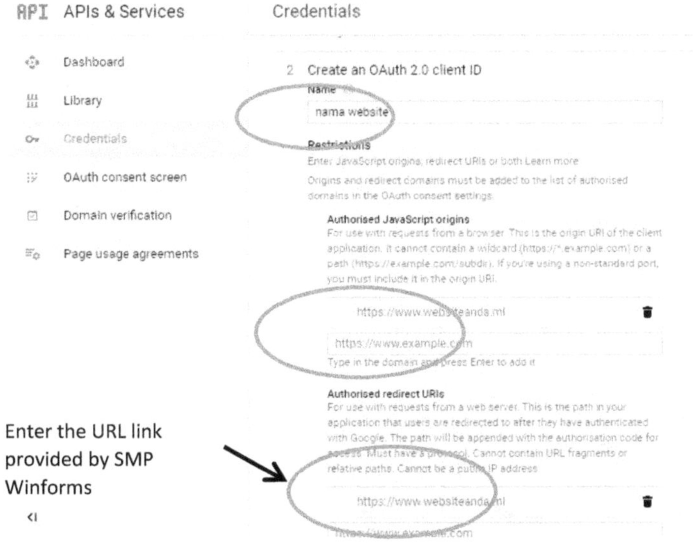

18. Go to Worpress again, Copy the URL link from WP Mail SMTP

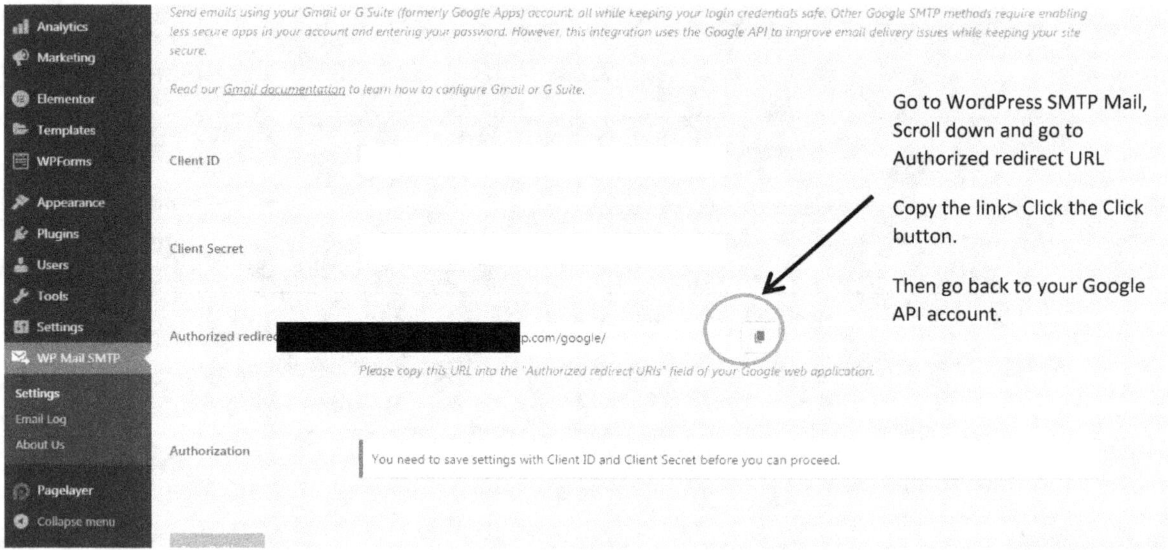

Go to WordPress SMTP Mail, Scroll down and go to Authorized redirect URL

Copy the link> Click the Click button.

Then go back to your Google API account.

19. Return to **Google API**

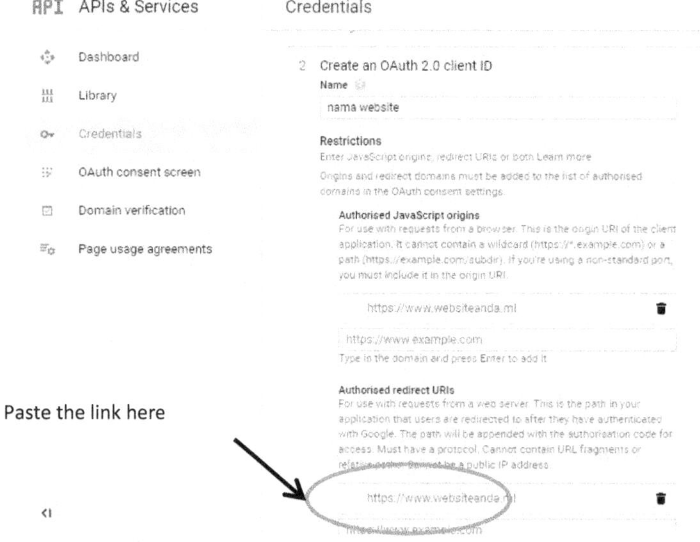

Paste the link here

20. Scroll down, and click on **Create OAuth client ID**

21. Click **I'll do this later**

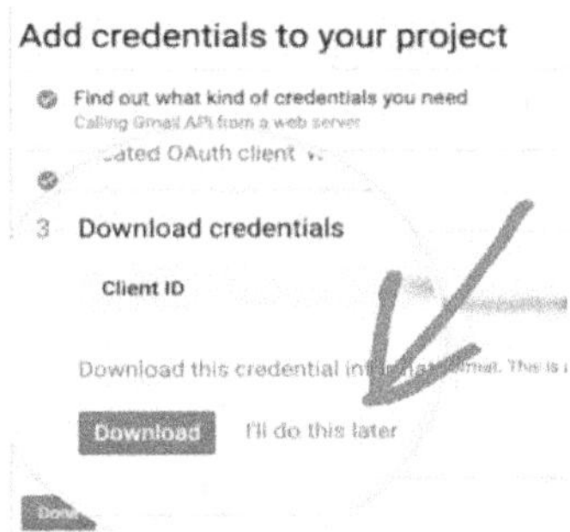

22. You go to the OAuth Consent Screen> Tick on **External**> Click **CREATE** section.

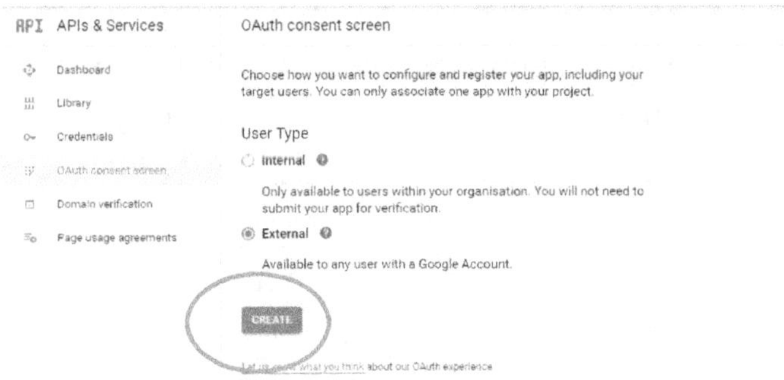

23. For those of you who use a G Suite account, you need to click on Internal.

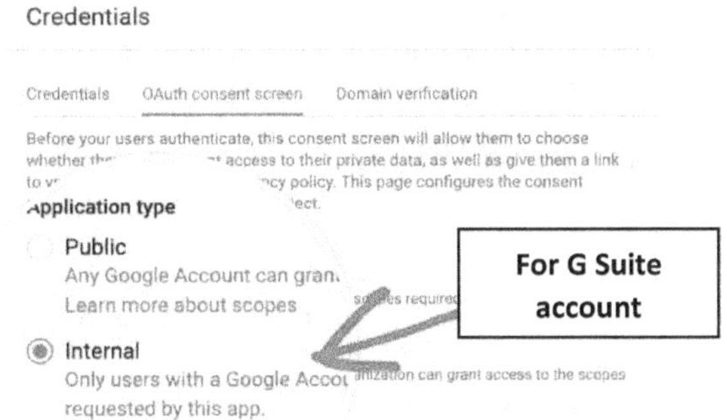

24. Near App Information, for Application name, you can enter the name of your website or any name you like.
25. For User Support email> Enter the Gmail you are using.
26. In the Logo App, you can Browse your logo. The logo verification process takes 2 days.

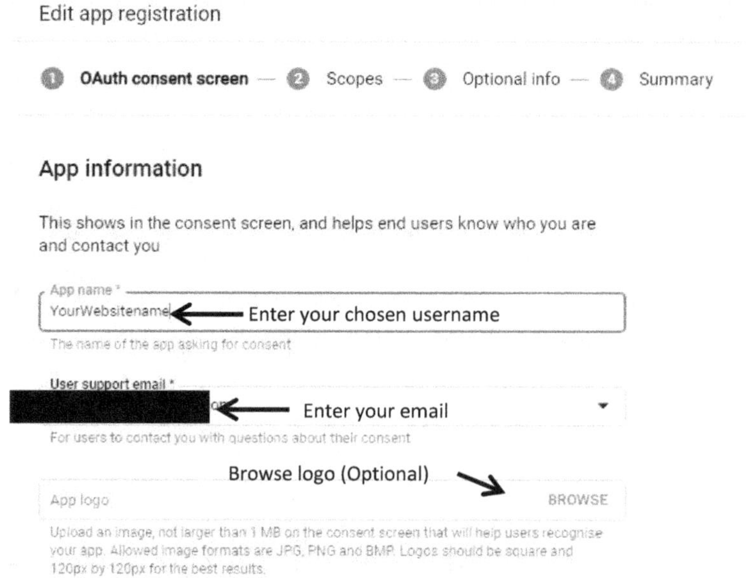

27. Scroll down to the App Domain section, for the Application Homepage link, Application Privacy Policy link, and Application Terms of Service link, you need to enter your website URL. You do not need a special privacy or terms page in this app because this consent screen only for you to see.

28. Make sure you enter your website URL starting with http:// or https://. I recommend you use https: // for a secure website. If your website is not yet secure, please follow the tutorial 4.

After that, scroll down, go to the Authorized domains section> Click ADD DOMAIN> Enter your website name (Make sure you type without http: // or https: //)

29. In the Developer Contact Information section > Enter whatever email you use.
30. After that, scroll down> Click **SAVE AND CONTINUE**

Getting Permissions and Send Test Email

1. On the Credentials page, and now you can see Client ID and Customer Secrets.
2. Click on the pencil icon

3. You will see Client ID and Client Secret in the upper right corner.

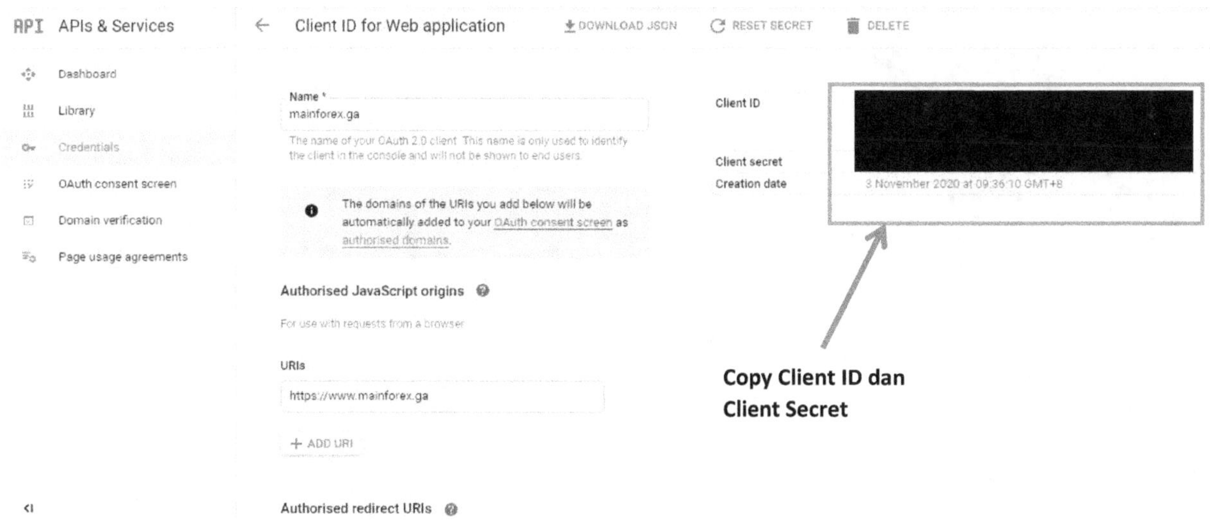

4. Both of these information is for your website only. You need to copy both in the WP Mail SMTP settings column near your WordPress.

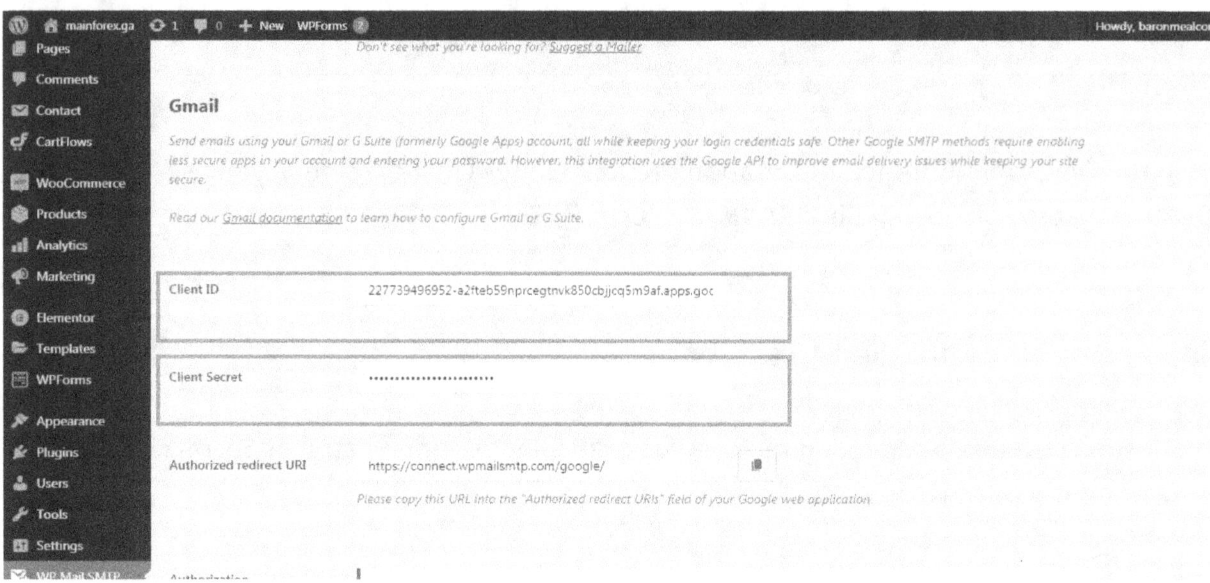

5. Scroll down > click on Save (Orange button)
6. After saving these settings, the page will auto-refresh again. Before Google allows this information to be used to connect to your account, however, you must first grant permissions (permission).
7. To do so, scroll down to this page> Click Allow plugin to send emails using your **Google account.**

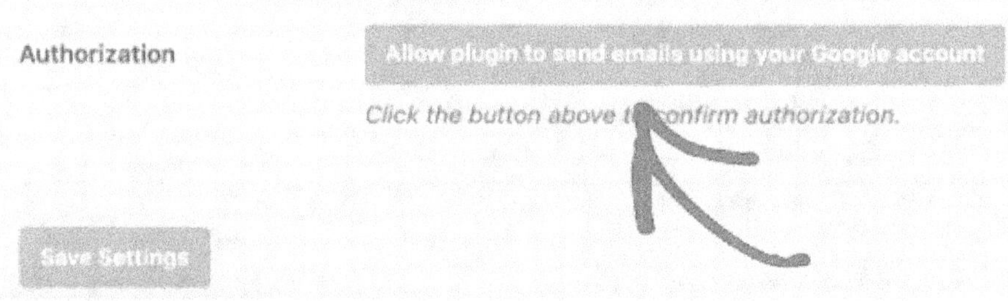

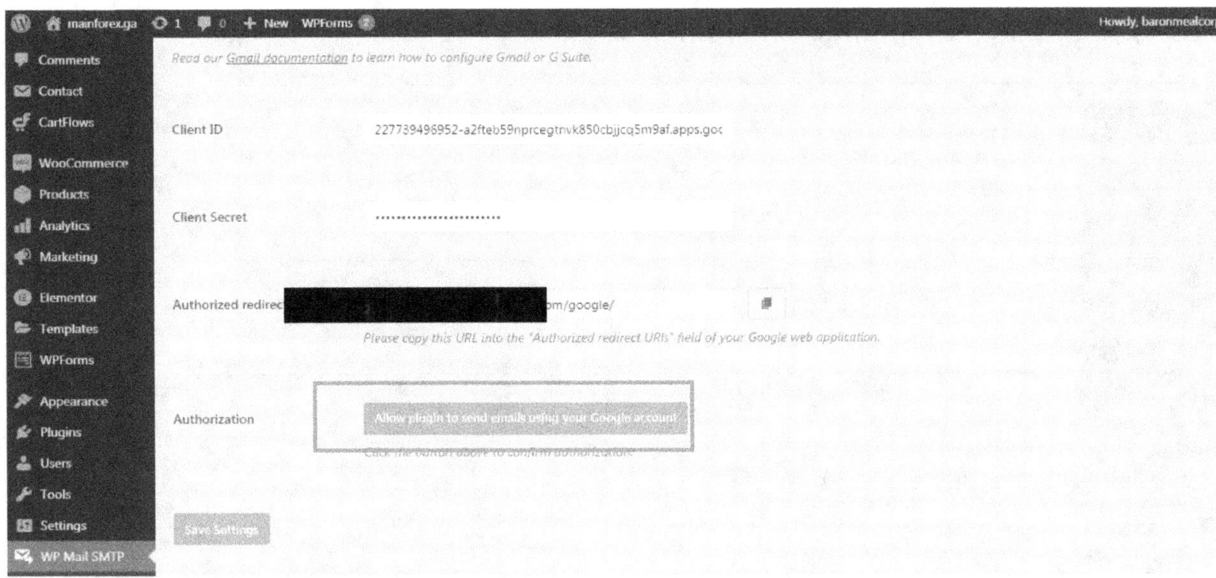

8. Google login screen will appear then. You need to log in as usual. You will see the Permissions screen for this site to send an email on your behalf.

9. Click Advanced> Click Go to wpmailsmtp.com (unsafe)

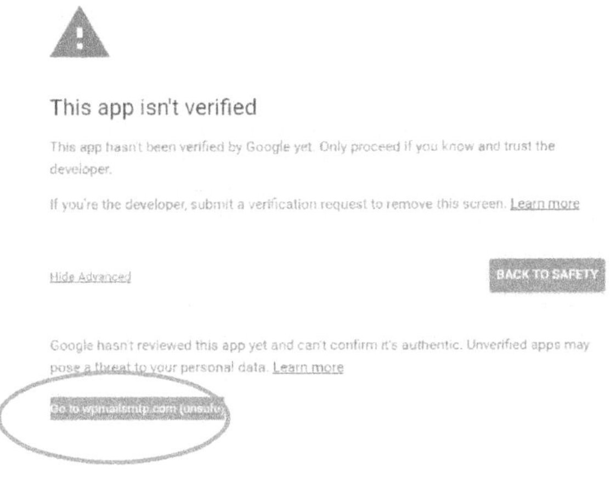

10. Click Allow

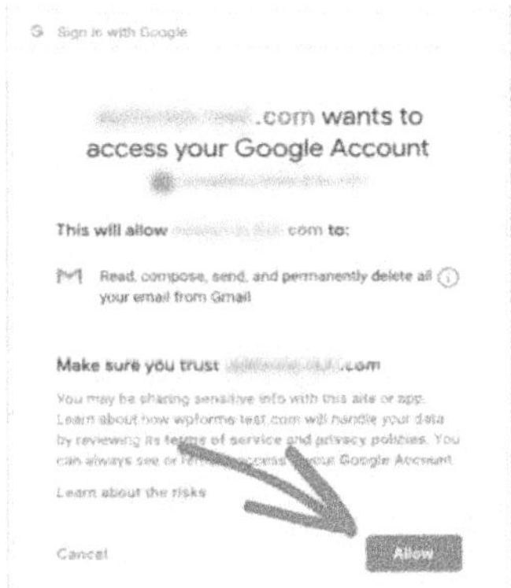

11. Next, you will see a notification in WordPress showing the success message.

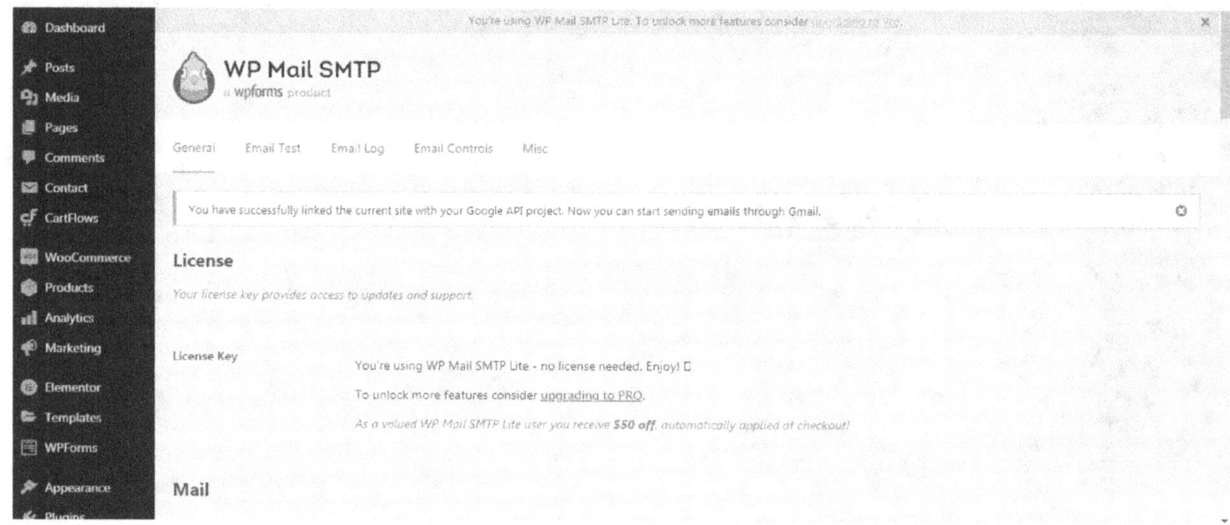

12. Now we need to test our email. Go to the WP Mail SMTP page. Click on Test Mail.

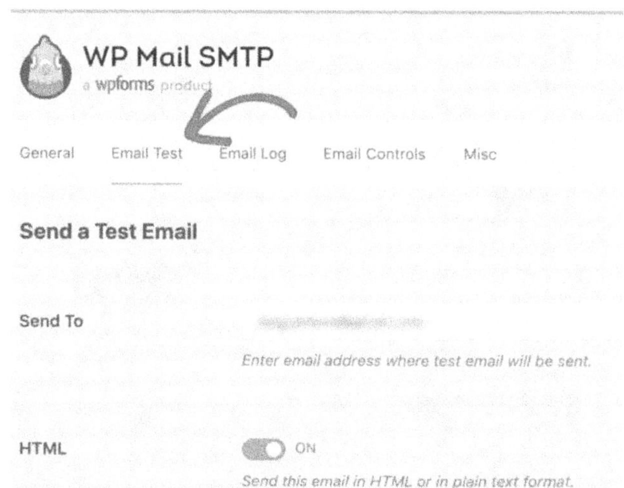

13. Make sure the email in the Send To field is your correct email.

14. Drag HTML in ON mode.

15. Click Send Email

16. A success message will appear that a test email has been sent to your email.

17. Open your email and check the email again. There is no inbox from WP Mail SMTP.

18. You will get a message like this. (See next page)

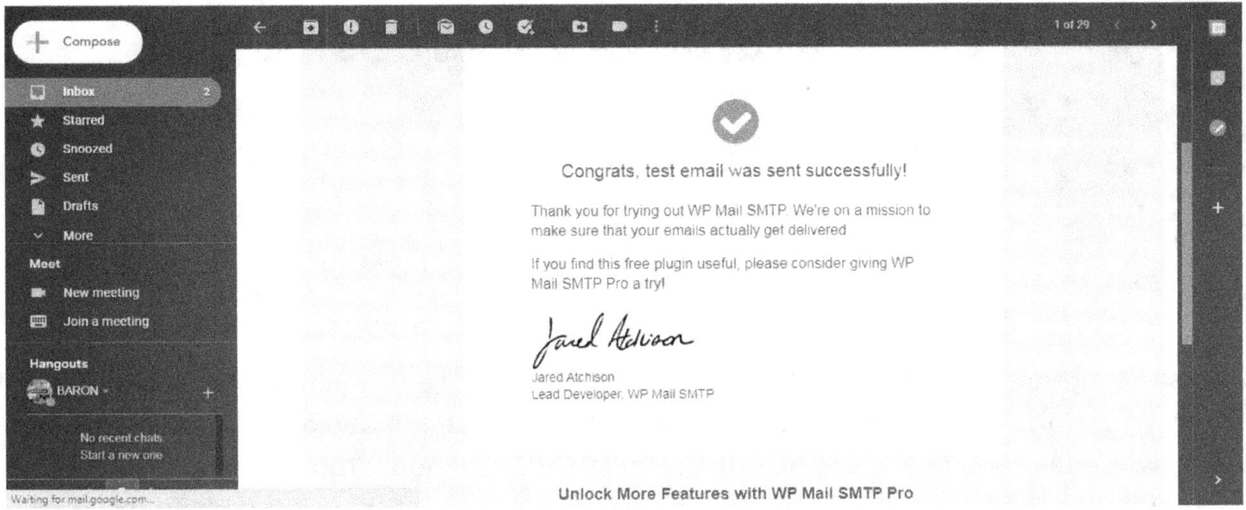

Congratulations, you already have an admin email. It means that every time your audience enters their information (etc. Name, Tel No, Email), it is automatically sent to your inbox.

For example,

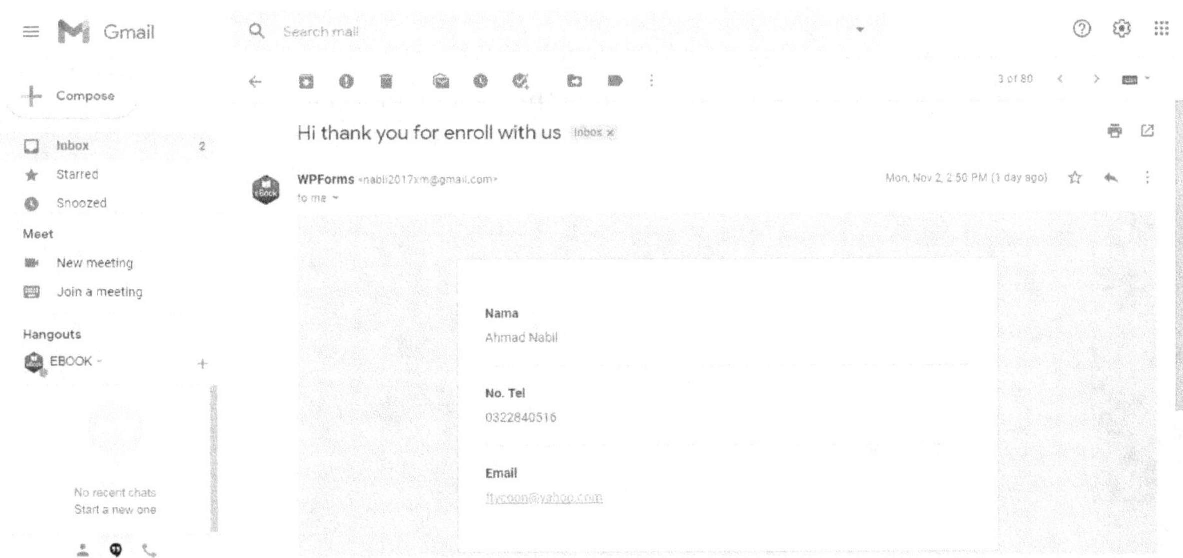

Trust me. Try to fill in WPForms near the page you created and see the results.

Multilingual Website

I will be showing you how to translate your Wordpress website in multiple languages. Apart from English, there are also many websites on the internet that serve the audience in other languages. All the steps involvedare simple and can be finished in less than an hour. You can simply edit your posts, tags,categories and themes into many languages. The most important thing is it is all for free.

In this guide, I will show you two popular WordPress plugins with steps-by steps guide how to set them up. These two plugins are:

- GTranslate
- Polylang

Create Multilingual Website using Gtranslate

It is super easy to use Gtranslate because all languages generated are automatically translated. Simply go to plugins > Add new > Search for Gtranslate. Install this plugin and make an activation.

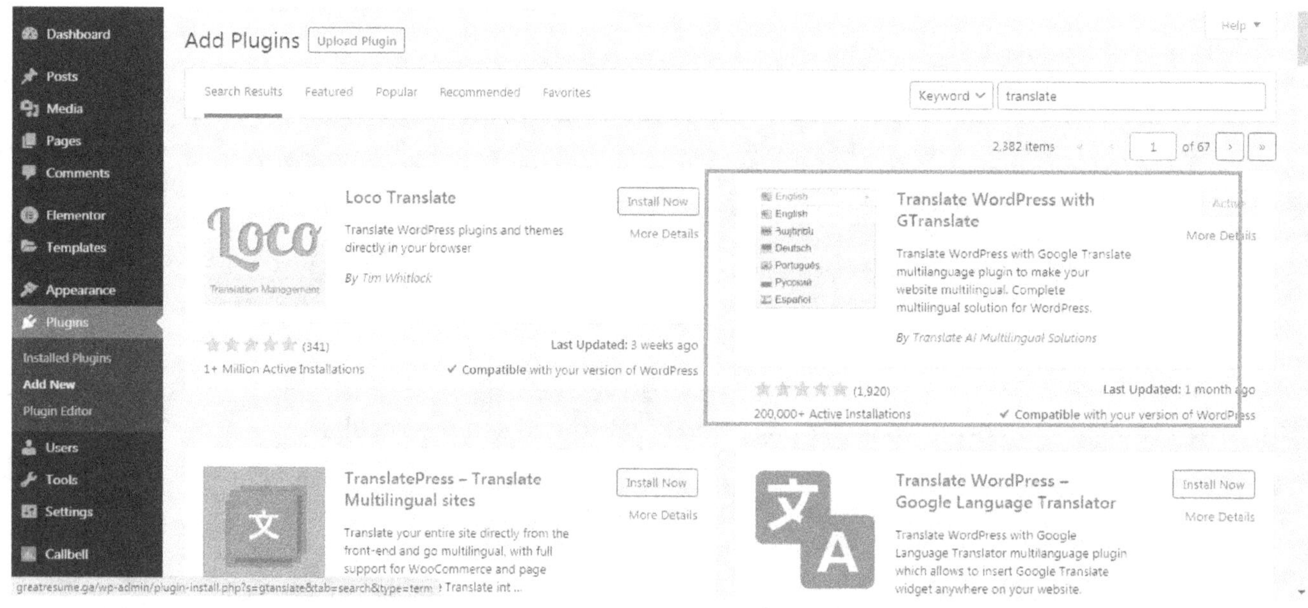

1. Upon activation, go to Settings > Click on **GTranslate**.

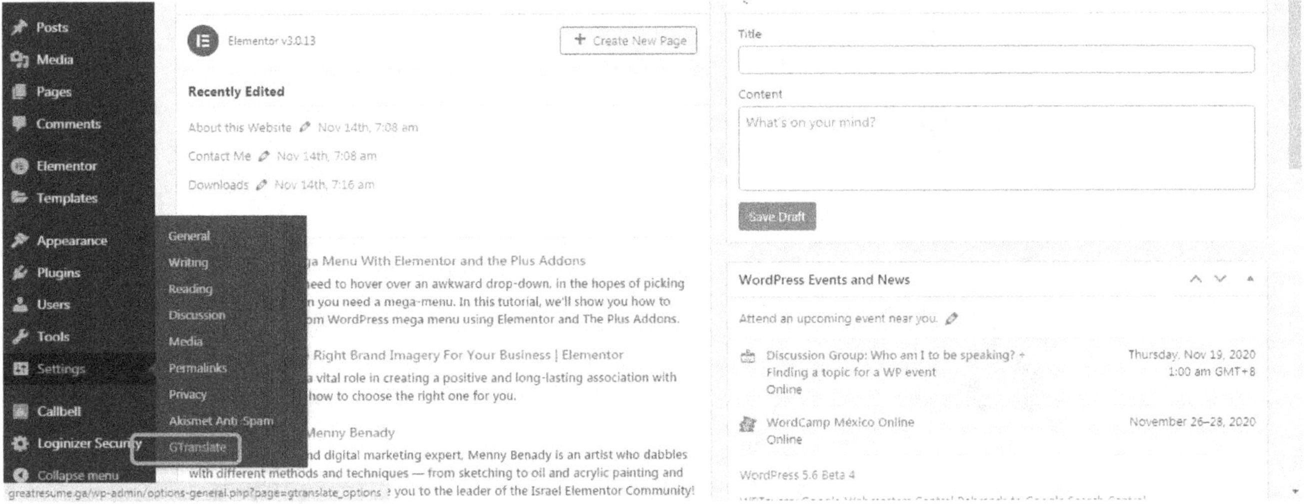

2. In GTranslate tab, you need to set up your widget options.
3. Simply choose how your widget will look like.

4. Scroll down, you will notice the Flag languages settings. Tick all languages that you wanted.

5. Upon finish, scroll down > Click Save changes

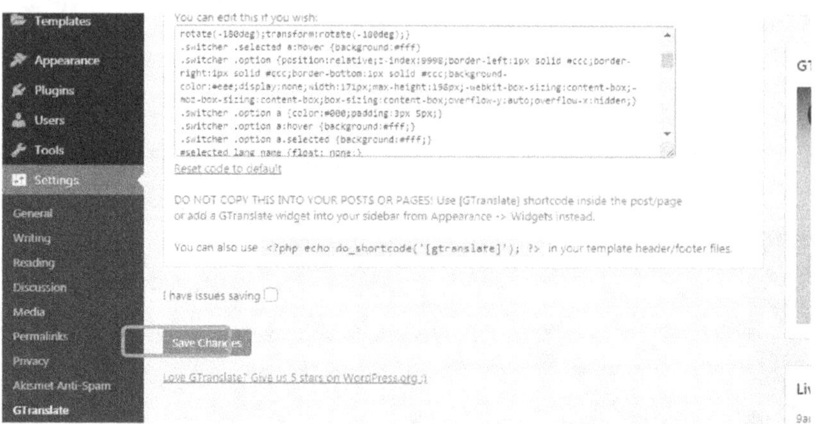

6. Go to Apperance > Click on Widgets.

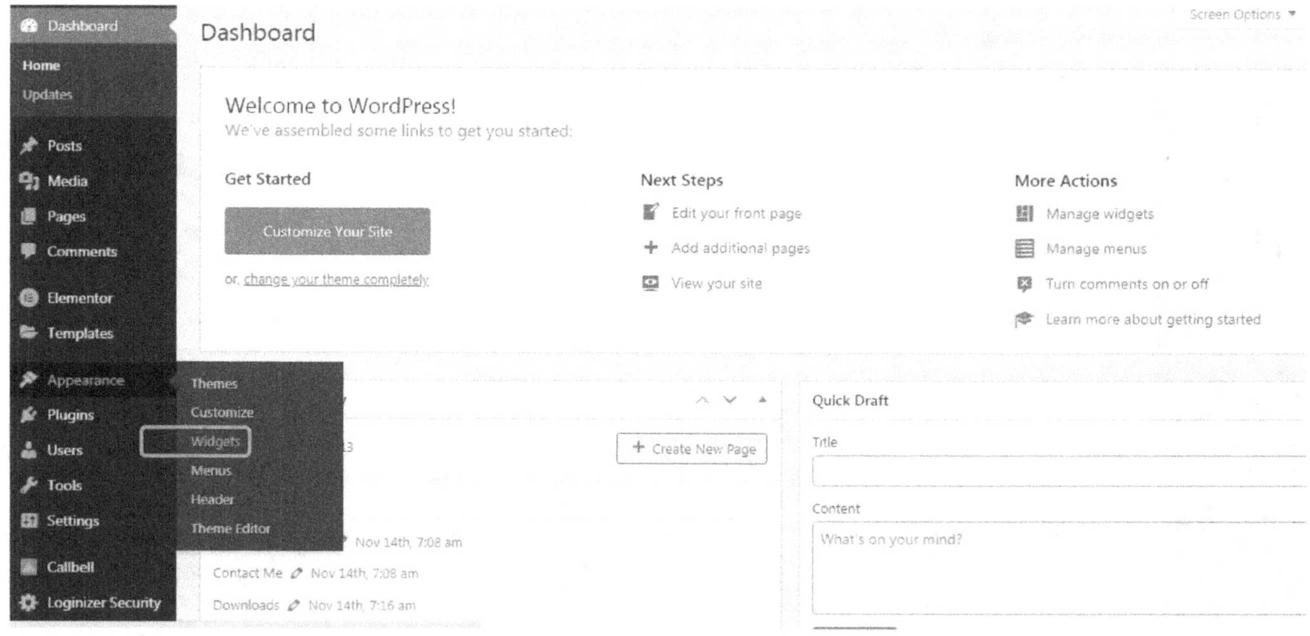

7. Look for GTranslate widgets. Add the language switcher widget to your sidebar or another widget area.

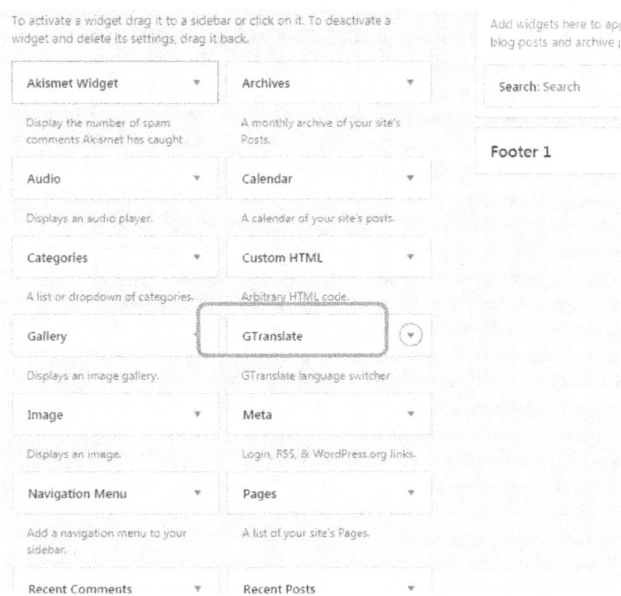

8. Then visit your website and try to check the widget.

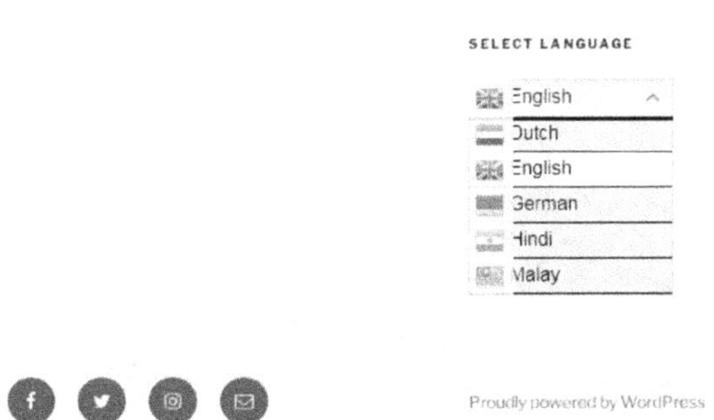

9. Simply click the language, it will automatically be translated.

Create Multilingual Website using Polylang

1. Firstly go to Plugins on your Wordpress menu > Click **Add New.**
2. Search for Polylang > Click Install Now and activate the plugin.

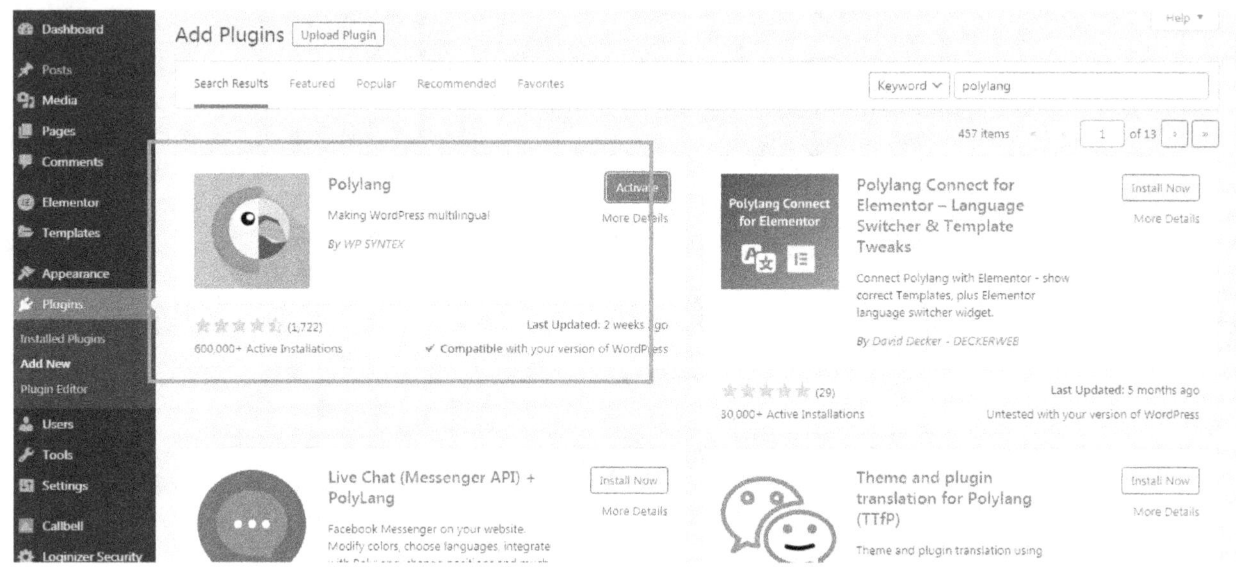

3. Upon activation, you need to run the setup wizard

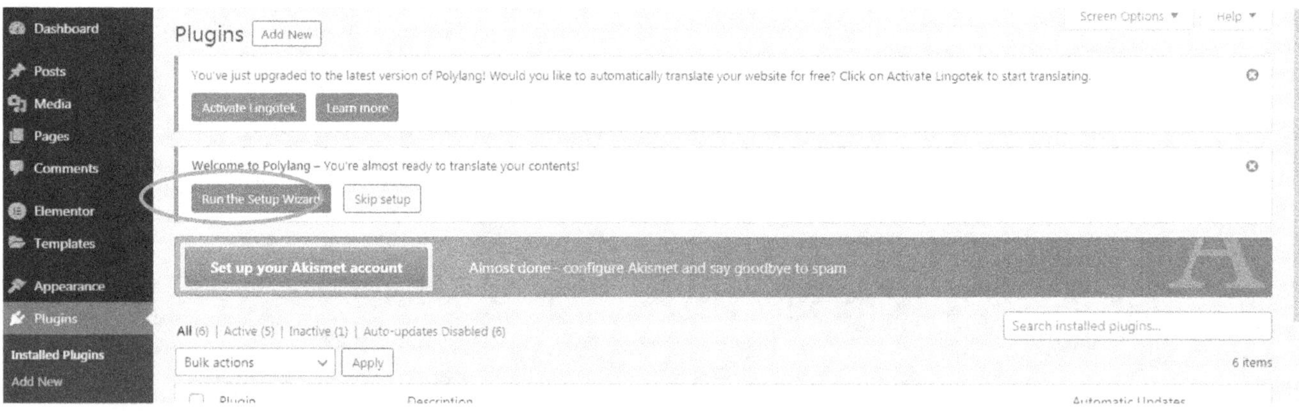

4. Select the languages you would like to be added. Click Add New Language. After that, click Continue.

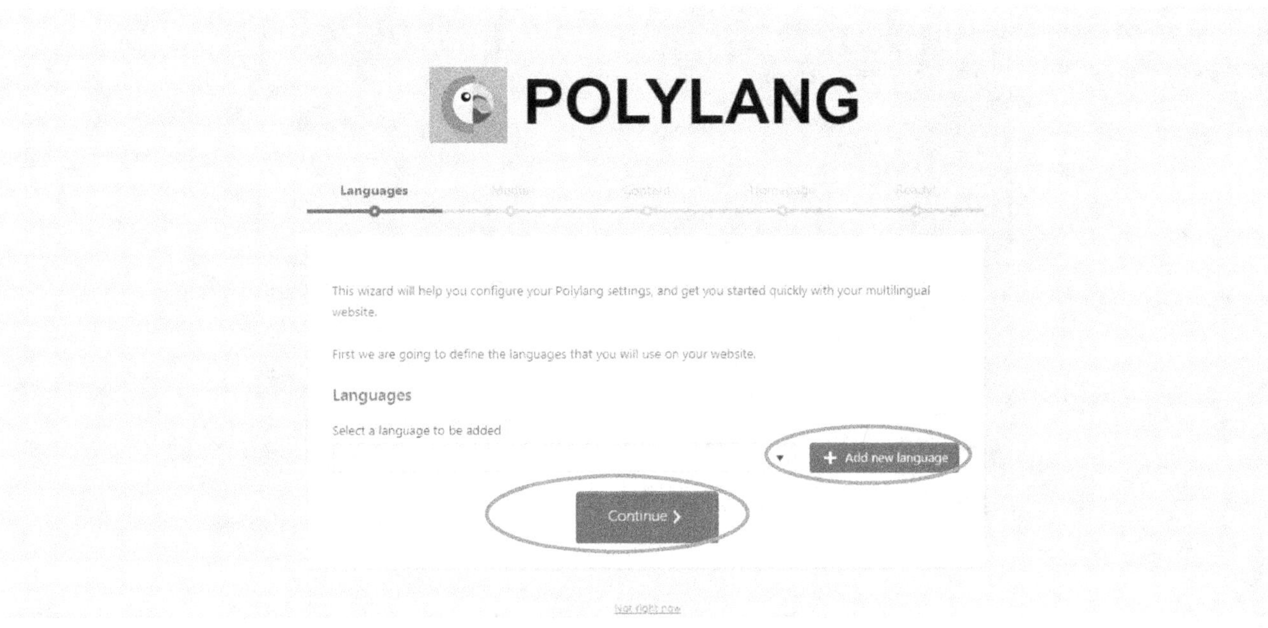

5. Click Continue and Proceed. (Allow Polylang to translate media).

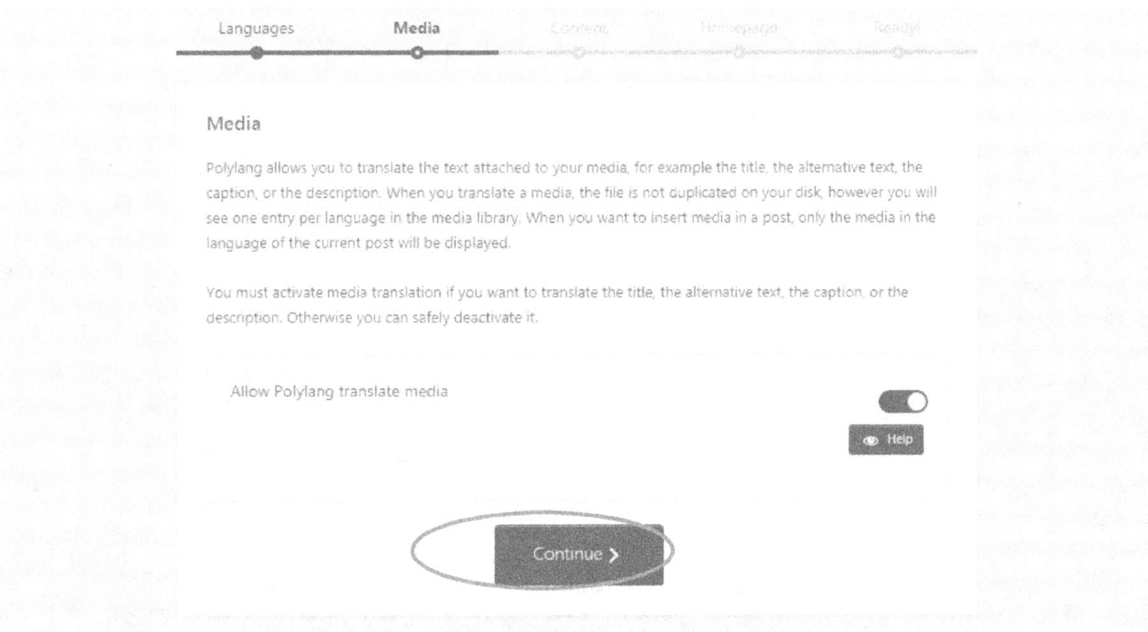

6. Keep going by clicking Continue.
7. At Ready section, Scroll down > Click Return to the Dashboard

8. Visit Languages > Language to configure the plugin

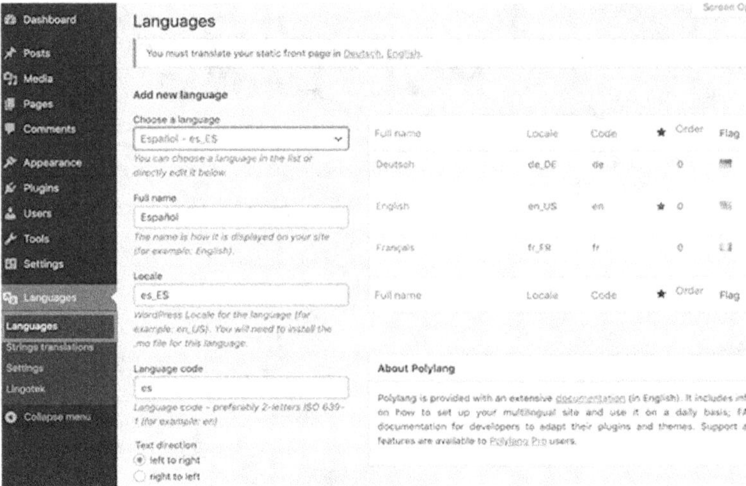

9. There are three tabs we need to fill under Language settings. Under Language tab, this where we add languages we want to use on our site.
10. We need to add the default language and all other languages that audiences can choose on our site.

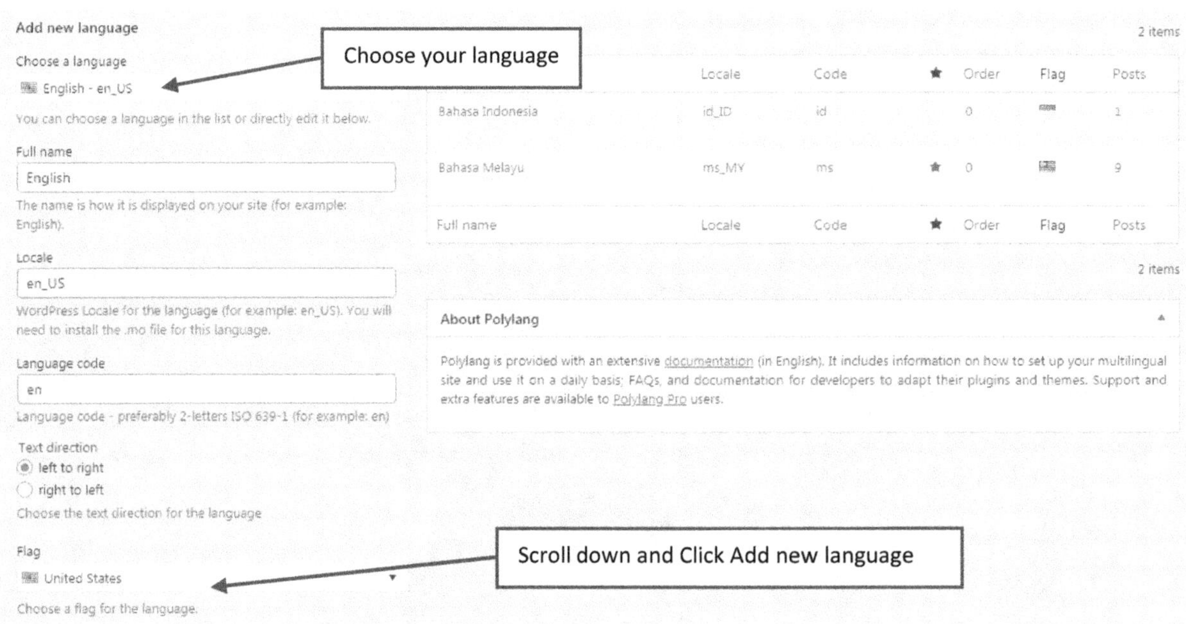

11. After finish adding the languages, go to the String Translations tab. This is where we translate site title, description and choose date and time format.

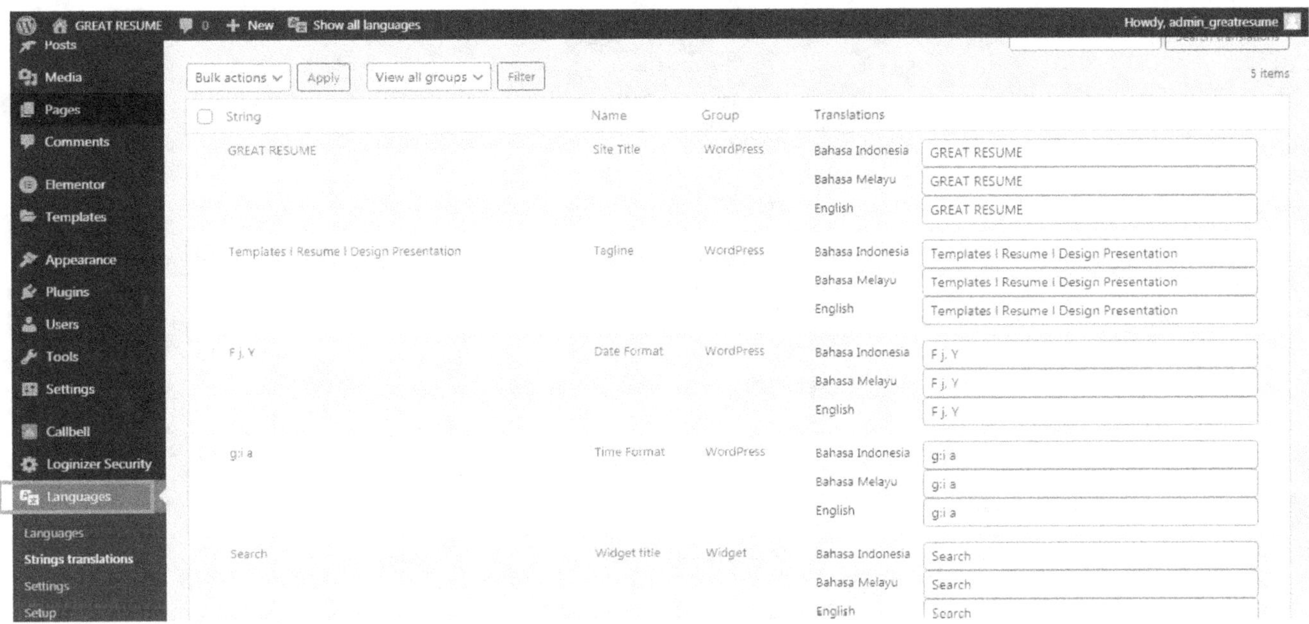

12. Next, go to Languages > Click on Setings tab. Here, you can set the URL settings, media and set up SEO friendly URLs.

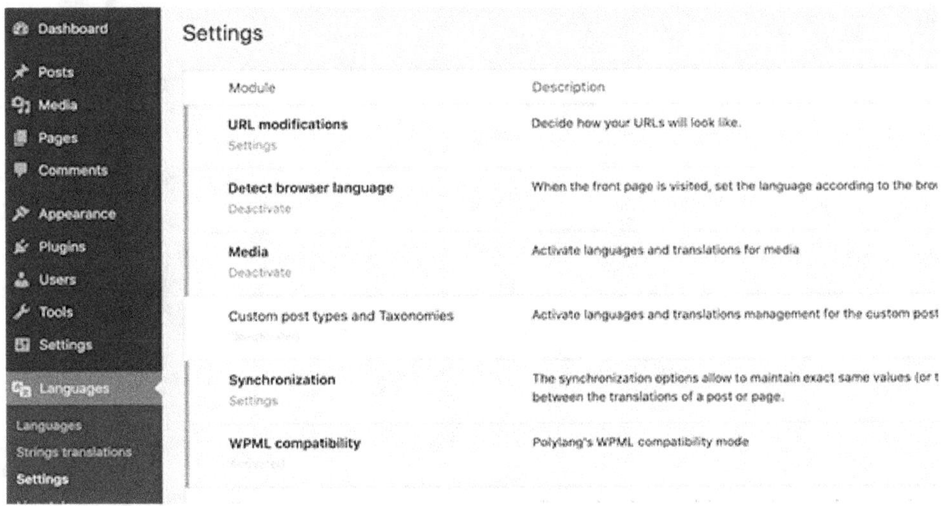

13. Once you are done, click on the save changes button to store your settings.

Polylang plugin is super easy to use. You can create a new page or edit an existing post. On the post edit page, you will see the language meta box.

Default language will atumatically be selected. For starter, add content in the default language and then translate it into other languages. In order to translate, just click on the (+) button, and enter yout text for that language.

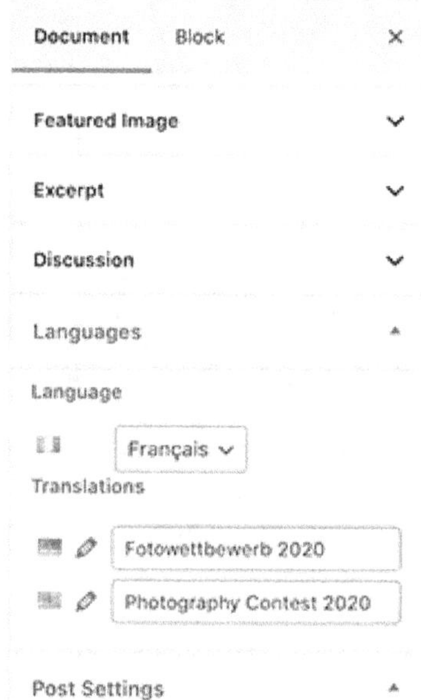

Do the same process fo all languages. After that, your post or pagescan be published. Besides that, categories and tags can also be translated. Simply go to **Posts** > **Categories.**

Displaying Language Switcher on Your Site.

It is very easy for your audience to choose what language they want to use. Go to Appearance > Widgets. Add your language switcher widgets to your footer or sidebar. Once you are done, click the save button to store settings. Now, try to preview your site to see your language switcher.

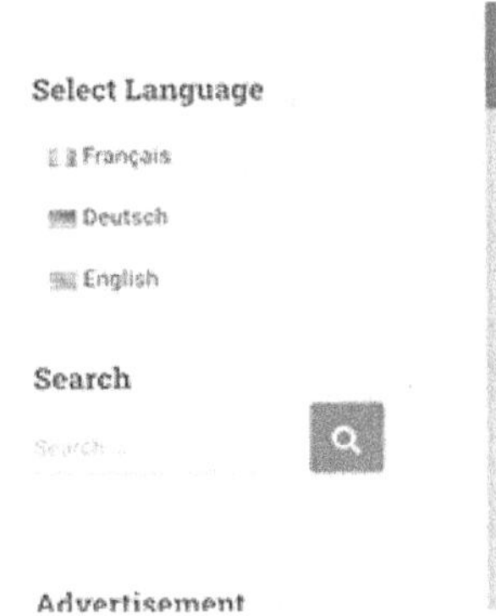

References : List of Plugins and Its Functions

bbPress

bbPress is forum software for WordPress.

By The bbPress Contributors

Install Now

More Details

★★★★☆ (315)

300,000+ Active Installations

Last Updated: 1 week ago

✓ Compatible with your version of WordPress

It is a special plugins for forum site. If you are building a forum site and require large sum of members for forum discussion, this plugins is a must.

Really Simple SSL

No setup required! You only need an SSL certificate, and this plugin will do the rest.

By Really Simple Plugins

Install Now

More Details

★★★★★ (6,043)

5+ Million Active Installations

Last Updated: 3 months ago

✓ Compatible with your version of WordPress

Setup your SSL Certificate. This plugins automatically detects your settings and configures your website to run over https.

Wordfence Security – Firewall & Malware Scan

Secure your website with the most comprehensive WordPress security plugin. Firewall, malware scan, blocking, live traffic, login security & more.

By Wordfence

Install Now

More Details

★★★★☆ (3,613)

3+ Million Active Installations

Last Updated: 3 weeks ago

✓ Compatible with your version of WordPress

Wordfence includes an endpoint firewall and malware scanner that were built from the ground up to protect WordPress. Their Threat Defense Feed arms Wordfence with the newest firewall rules, malware signatures and malicious IP addresses it needs to keep your website safe.

UpdraftPlus WordPress Backup Plugin

Backup and restoration made easy. Complete backups; manual or scheduled (backup to Dropbox, S3, Google Drive, Rackspace, FTP, SFTP, email + others).

By UpdraftPlus.Com, DavidAnderson

Install Now

More Details

★★★★☆ (3,789)

3+ Million Active Installations

Last Updated: 2 weeks ago

✓ Compatible with your version of WordPress

UpdraftPlus simplifies backups and restoration. Backup into the cloud directly to Dropbox, Google Drive, Amazon S3 (or compatible), UpdraftVault, Rackspace Cloud, FTP, DreamObjects, Openstack Swift, and email.

Classic Editor

Install Now
More Details

Enables the previous "classic" editor and the old-style Edit Post screen with TinyMCE, Meta Boxes, etc. Supports all plugins that extend thi ...

By WordPress Contributors

★★★★★ (900)   Last Updated: 3 months ago
5+ Million Active Installations   ✓ Compatible with your version of WordPress

Classic Editor is an official plugin maintained by the WordPress team that restores the previous ("classic") WordPress editor and the "Edit Post" screen. Administrators can select the default editor for all users. Administrators can allow users to change their default editor. When allowed, the users can choose which editor to use for each post.

Akismet Spam Protection

Active
More Details

The best anti-spam protection to block spam comments and spam in a contact form. The most trusted antispam solution for WordPress and WooCommerce.

By Automattic

★★★★½ (907)   Last Updated: 3 weeks ago
5+ Million Active Installations   ✓ Compatible with your version of WordPress

Akismet checks your comments and contact form submissions against our global database of spam to prevent your site from publishing malicious content. Automatically checks all comments and filters out the ones that look like spam. URLs are shown in the comment body to reveal hidden or misleading links.

Jetpack – WP Security, Backup, Speed, & Growth

Install Now
More Details

The best WP plugin for backup, anti spam, malware scan, CDN, AMP, social, search, contact form, and integrations with Woo, Facebook, Instagram, Google

By Automattic

★★★★☆ (1,557)   Last Updated: 4 days ago
5+ Million Active Installations   ✓ Compatible with your version of WordPress

Security, performance, marketing, and design tools — **Jetpack** is made by the WordPress experts to make WP sites safer and faster, and help you grow your traffic.

BuddyPress

Install Now
More Details

BuddyPress helps site builders & developers add community features to their websites. with user profiles, activity streams, and more!

By The BuddyPress Community

★★★★☆ (336)   Last Updated: 2 months ago
200,000+ Active Installations   ✓ Compatible with your version of WordPress

BuddyPress is a suite of components that are common to a typical social network, and allows for great add-on features. BuddyPress is focused on ease of integration, ease of use, and extensibility. It is deliberately powerful yet unbelievably simple social network software.

Contact Form 7

Install Now
More Details

Just another contact form plugin. Simple but flexible.

By Takayuki Miyoshi

★★★★☆ (1,821)   Last Updated: 3 weeks ago
5+ Million Active Installations   ✓ Compatible with your version of WordPress

Contact Form 7 can manage multiple contact forms, plus you can customize the form and the mail contents flexibly with simple markup.

The form supports Ajax-powered submitting, CAPTCHA, Akismet spam filtering and so on.

Yoast SEO

Install Now
More Details

Improve your WordPress SEO: Write better content and have a fully optimized WordPress site using the Yoast SEO plugin.

By Team Yoast

★★★★★ (27,274)   Last Updated: 2 weeks ago
5+ Million Active Installations   ✓ Compatible with your version of WordPress

Yoast SEO does everything in its power to please both visitors and search engine spiders. A dedicated team of developers, testers, architects and SEO experts work daily to improve the plugin with every release. Improve your WordPress SEO: Write better content and have a fully optimized WordPress site.

WordPress Importer

Import posts, pages, comments, custom fields, categories, tags and more from a WordPress export file.

By wordpressdotorg

★★★☆☆ (296)

4+ Million Active Installations

Install Now | More Details

Last Updated: 7 months ago

Untested with your version of WordPress

> Import posts, pages, comments, custom fields, categories, tags and more from a WordPress export file.

Yoast Duplicate Post

Copy posts of any type with a click!

By Enrico Battocchi & Team Yoast

★★★★★ (475)

3+ Million Active Installations

Install Now | More Details

Last Updated: 2 months ago

✓ Compatible with your version of WordPress

> This plugin allows users to clone posts of any type, or copy them to new drafts for further editing. In 'Edit Posts'/'Edit Pages', you can click on 'Clone' link below the post/page title: this will immediately create a copy and return to the list.

All-in-One WP Migration

Move, transfer, copy, migrate, and backup a site with 1-click. Quick, easy, and reliable.

By ServMask

★★★★½ (6,503)

3+ Million Active Installations

Install Now | More Details

Last Updated: 3 days ago

✓ Compatible with your version of WordPress

> This plugin exports your WordPress website including the database, media files, plugins and themes with no technical knowledge required. Upload your site to a different location with a drag and drop in to WordPress.

All in One SEO Pack

The original WordPress SEO plugin, downloaded over 65,000,000 times since 2007.

By All in One SEO Team

★★★★½ (1,151)

2+ Million Active Installations

Install Now | More Details

Last Updated: 2 months ago

✓ Compatible with your version of WordPress

> Use "**All in One SEO Pack**" to optimize your WordPress site for SEO. It's easy and works out of the box for beginners, and has advanced features and an API for developers.

Google XML Sitemaps

This plugin will improve SEO by helping search engines better index your site using sitemaps.

By Auctollo

★★★★★ (2,114)

2+ Million Active Installations

Install Now | More Details

Last Updated: 3 months ago

✓ Compatible with your version of WordPress

> Use this plugin to greatly improve SEO to create special XML sitemaps which will help search engines like Google, Bing, Yahoo and Ask.com to better index your site. It's much easier for the crawlers to see the complete structure of your site and retrieve it more efficiently.

WP Super Cache

A very fast caching engine for WordPress that produces static html files.

By Automattic

★★★★½ (1,258)

2+ Million Active Installations

Install Now | More Details

Last Updated: 2 months ago

✓ Compatible with your version of WordPress

> This plugin generates static html files from your dynamic WordPress blog. After a html file is generated your webserver will serve that file instead of processing the comparatively heavier and more expensive WordPress PHP scripts.

MC4WP: Mailchimp for WordPress

Mailchimp for WordPress, the #1 unofficial Mailchimp plugin.

By ibericode

Install Now

More Details

★★★★☆ (1,306)

2+ Million Active Installations

✓ Compatible with your version of WordPress

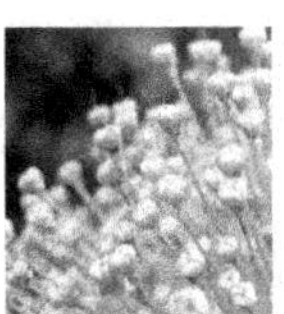

Redirection

Manage 301 redirections, keep track of 404 errors, and improve your site, with no knowledge of Apache or Nginx needed.

By John Godley

Install Now

More Details

★★★★½ (538)

1+ Million Active Installations

✓ Compatible with your version of WordPress

Smush – Lazy Load Images, Optimize & Compress Images

Compress images & optimize images with lazy load, WebP conversion, and resize detection to make...

By WPMU DEV

Install Now

More Details

★★★★☆ (5,322)

1+ Million Active Installations

✓ Compatible with your version of WordPress

Advanced Custom Fields

Customize WordPress with powerful, professional and intuitive fields.

By Elliot Condon

Install Now

More Details

★★★★★ (1,115)

1+ Million Active Installations

✓ Compatible with your version of WordPress

Duplicate Page

Duplicate Posts, Pages and Custom Posts easily using single click

By mndpsingh287

Install Now

More Details

★★★★½ (153)

1+ Million Active Installations

✓ Compatible with your version of WordPress

Regenerate Thumbnails

Install Now
More Details

Regenerate the thumbnails for one or more of your image uploads. Useful when changing their sizes or your theme.

By Alex Mills (Viper007Bond)

★★★★½ (357)

1+ Million Active Installations

Last Updated: 3 weeks ago

Untested with your version of WordPress

Regenerate Thumbnails allows you to regenerate all thumbnail sizes for one or more images that have been uploaded to your Media Library. This is useful for situations such as a new thumbnail size has been added and you want past uploads to have a thumbnail in that size. It also offers the ability to delete old, unused thumbnails in order to free up server space.

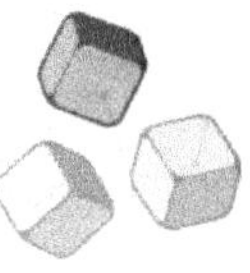

Duplicator – WordPress Migration Plugin

Install Now
More Details

WordPress migration and backups are much easier with Duplicator! Clone, backup, move and transfer an entire site from one location to another.

By Snap Creek

★★★★★ (2,923)

1+ Million Active Installations

Last Updated: 1 month ago

✓ Compatible with your version of WordPress

Duplicator successfully gives WordPress users the ability to migrate, copy, move or clone a site from one location to another and also serves as a simple backup utility.

W3 Total Cache

Install Now
More Details

Search Engine (SEO) & Performance Optimization (WPO) via caching. Integrated caching: CDN, Page, Minify, Object, Fragment, Database support.

By BoldGrid

★★★★½ (4,629)

1+ Million Active Installations

Last Updated: 3 days ago

✓ Compatible with your version of WordPress

W3 Total Cache (W3TC) improves the SEO and user experience of your site by increasing website performance and reducing load times by leveraging features like content delivery network (CDN) integration and the latest best practices.

Loco Translate

Install Now
More Details

Translate WordPress plugins and themes directly in your browser

By Tim Whitlock

★★★★★ (341)

1+ Million Active Installations

Last Updated: 3 weeks ago

✓ Compatible with your version of WordPress

Loco Translate provides in-browser editing of WordPress translation files and integration with automatic translation services. It also provides Gettext/localization tools for developers, such as extracting strings and generating templates.

Disable Comments

Install Now
More Details

Allows administrators to globally disable comments on their site. Comments can be disabled according to post type. Multisite friendly.

By WPDeveloper

★★★★★ (232)

1+ Million Active Installations

Last Updated: 3 months ago

✓ Compatible with your version of WordPress

This plugin allows administrators to globally disable comments on any post type (posts, pages, attachments, etc.) so that these settings cannot be overridden for individual posts. It also removes all comment-related fields from edit and quick-edit screens. On multisite installations, it can be used to disable comments on the entire network.

Rank Math – SEO Plugin for WordPress

Install Now

More Details

Rank Math is a revolutionary WordPress SEO plugin that combines the features of many SEO tools in a single package & helps you multiply your traff ...

By Rank Math

★ ★ ★ ★ ★ (2,022)

500,000+ Active Installations

✓ Compatible with your version of WordPress

Last Updated: 13 hours ago

Rank Math, a WordPress SEO plugin, to help every website owner get access to the SEO tools they need to improve their SEO and attract more traffic to their website.

Coming Soon Page, Maintenance Mode & Landing Pages by SeedProd

Install Now

More Details

The #1 Coming Soon Page, Maintenance Mode & Landing Page plugin for WordPress.

By SeedProd

★ ★ ★ ★ ★ (3,857)

1+ Million Active Installations

✓ Compatible with your version of WordPress

Last Updated: 1 week ago

Create a Coming Soon Page, Maintenance Mode Page, Landing Pages and Custom 404 pages. Work on your site in private while visitors see a "Coming Soon" or "Maintenance Mode" page.

File Upload Types by WPForms

Install Now

More Details

Easily allow WordPress to accept and upload any file type extension or MIME type, including custom file types.

By WPForms

★ ★ ★ ★ ★ (2)

2,000+ Active Installations

✓ Compatible with your version of WordPress

Last Updated: 2 months ago

Do you want to let your WordPress website accept uploads from your users for more file types and to freely upload files? We created the File Upload Types plugin to make it simple for anyone to easily add support for any file types with any extension or MIME type.

www.ingramcontent.com/pod-product-compliance
Lightning Source LLC
Chambersburg PA
CBHW081929120726
47997CB00010B/3086